TRANSGRESSIONS: CULTURAL STUDIES AND EDUCATION

TRANSGRESSIONS: CULTURAL STUDIES AND EDUCATION

Cultural studies provides an analytical toolbox for both making sense of educational practice and extending the insights of educational professionals into their labors. In this context *Transgressions: Cultural Studies and Education* provides a collection of books in the domain that specify this assertion. Crafted for an audience of teachers, teacher educators, scholars and students of cultural studies and others interested in cultural studies and pedagogy, the series documents both the possibilities of and the controversies surrounding the intersection of cultural studies and education. The editors and the authors of this series do not assume that the interaction of cultural studies and education devalues other types of knowledge and analytical forms. Rather the intersection of these knowledge disciplines offers a rejuvenating, optimistic, and positive perspective on education and educational institutions. Some might describe its contribution as democratic, emancipatory, and transformative. The editors and authors maintain that cultural studies helps free educators from sterile, monolithic analyses that have for too long undermined efforts to think of educational practices by providing other words, new languages, and fresh metaphors. Operating in an interdisciplinary cosmos, Transgressions: Cultural Studies and Education is dedicated to exploring the ways cultural studies enhances the study and practice of education. With this in mind the series focuses in a non-exclusive way on popular culture as well as other dimensions of cultural studies including social theory, social justice and positionality, cultural dimensions of technological innovation, new media and media literacy, new forms of oppression emerging in an electronic hyperreality, and postcolonial global concerns. With these concerns in mind cultural studies scholars often argue that the realm of popular culture is the most powerful educational force in contemporary culture. Indeed, in the twenty-first century this pedagogical dynamic is sweeping through the entire world. Educators, they believe, must understand these emerging realities in order to gain an important voice in the pedagogical conversation.

Without an understanding of cultural pedagogy's (education that takes place outside of formal schooling) role in the shaping of individual identity–youth identity in particular–the role educators play in the lives of their students will continue to fade. Why do so many of our students feel that life is incomprehensible and devoid of meaning? What does it mean, teachers wonder, when young people are unable to describe their moods, their affective affiliation to the society around them. Meanings provided young people by mainstream institutions often do little to help them deal with their affective complexity, their difficulty negotiating the rift between meaning and affect. School knowledge and educational expectations seem as anachronistic as a ditto machine, not that learning ways of rational thought and making sense of the world are unimportant.

But school knowledge and educational expectations often have little to offer students about making sense of the way they feel, the way their affective lives are shaped. In no way do we argue that analysis of the production of youth in an electronic mediated world demands some "touchy-feely" educational superficiality. What is needed in this context is a rigorous analysis of the interrelationship between pedagogy, popular culture, meaning making, and youth subjectivity. In an era marked by youth depression, violence, and suicide such insights become extremely important, even life saving. Pessimism about the future is the common sense of many contemporary youth with its concomitant feeling that no one can make a difference.

If affective production can be shaped to reflect these perspectives, then it can be reshaped to lay the groundwork for optimism, passionate commitment, and transformative educational and political activity. In these ways cultural studies adds a dimension to the work of education unfilled by any other sub-discipline. This is what Transgressions: Cultural Studies and Education seeks to produce—literature on these issues that makes a difference. It seeks to publish studies that help those who work with young people, those individuals involved in the disciplines that study children and youth, and young people themselves improve their lives in these bizarre times.

Landscapes and Learning

Place Studies for a Global World

Margaret Somerville
Kerith Power
Phoenix de Carteret

Monash University, Australia

SENSE PUBLISHERS
ROTTERDAM/BOSTON/TAIPEI

A C.I.P. record for this book is available from the Library of Congress.

ISBN: 978-94-6091-081-4 (paperback)
ISBN: 978-94-6091-082-1 (hardback)
ISBN: 978-94-6091-083-8 (e-book)

Published by: Sense Publishers,
P.O. Box 21858,
3001 AW Rotterdam,
The Netherlands
http://www.sensepublishers.com

Printed on acid-free paper

TABLE OF CONTENTS

SECTION III: THEORISING PLACE DIFFERENTLY

ACKNOWLEDGEMENTS

In addition to those acknowledged by the many authors in their individual contributions, the Editors would like to acknowledge the Australian Research Council for funding the two projects about pedagogies of place that led to the support of this collaborative activity. We also thank the Faculty of Education at Monash University for their support for this work.

We are grateful to Shirley Steinberg, Associate Professor in Education at McGill University and Director of The Paulo and Nita Freire International Project for Critical Pedagogies, for her enthusiastic response to the book proposal and her offer to include the book in her Transgressions Series. Sense Publishing were prompt in offering a contract for publication at her invitation and we appreciate their efficiency in the publishing process.

We would especially like to acknowledge the assistance of Sue Collins, who, newly appointed to her role as Research Support Officer in the Faculty of Education at Monash University, took on the management of the copy editing process and contributed a great deal to the copy editing work. Linda Mink, the Executive Officer of the Monash Institute of Regional Studies, and Miriam Potts, Research Assistant, also contributed to this essential work and we thank them for their invaluable contribution.

All figures, images and photos are provided courtesy of the respective authors unless otherwise indicated.

Finally, we would like to thank the academic scholarly community for engaging in the exciting conversations that have led to this publication.

Margaret Somerville
Kerith Power
Phoenix de Carteret

Clouds

Early morning walk with dogs down through the roundabout on the edge of town. Here the world of suburban houses opens out and there is a wonderful big puff of clouds licked pink from the sunrise against a pale blue sky. But as the street opens out the view I can see the six chimneys of the power station, two by two by two, with a thin trail of umbilical vapour connected to the big cloud. It's a power station cloud. I run back home to get my camera, worried that by the time I get back to this spot, it will have gone. Dogs running, camera slung around my neck, only a few minutes - and yes, it has changed. Pink tinge gone, it is lit bright in the early morning light, more normalised, a bright daytime cloud in a bright blue day. I have to take a photo so you will understand. Space, place and time, weather, climate change, culture and nature, the significance of that moment of representation?

(Somerville 2008, p. 1)

MARGARET SOMERVILLE, KERITH POWER,
AND PHOENIX DE CARTERET

INTRODUCTION

Place Studies for a Global World

This book began with a provocation to think 'place' differently. The aim was to create conversations – multiple, contingent, divergent, and situated conversations – to move us beyond the limits of our current thinking. This introduction includes the ideas from the paper that was circulated to leading researchers in the newly emerging field of place studies to stimulate these conversations (Somerville, 2008). The paper proposed a new post-poststructural and postcolonial understanding of place, and place learning. The researchers responded with their latest work-in-progress, leading edge place research. As editors, we set out in this introduction to map the ideas in the provocation, and the chapters that have come to form this book.

Our provocation was this: Around the globe intransigent problems confront us. Every day we are presented with news about the effects of climate change, the rapid loss of endangered species, and the impact of extreme weather events. Postcolonial issues of displacement and migration, the widening gap between rich and poor, and people living in degraded environments, are experienced in many local sites. These can be understood as geo-political issues of space and place. And yet the response to these problems has largely been framed in terms of the techno-scientific solutions of modernity – developing 'clean' coal, moving water, building de-salination plants – combined with a neoliberal economic approach such as water and carbon trading. While research in the physical sciences has typically been seen as the solution for such complex socio-environmental problems, emerging research in eco-humanities suggests that changing our relationship to our places is as important as techno-scientific solutions. Education, and educational research, seems to have vacated the field. We ask then, beyond discourses of crisis, what might be an adequate educational response? How might we educate a generation of children and adults who live in a global cyberworld to be attached to their local places, to inhabit, and to know place differently?

As children we all have places that we are attached to, places that we care about. We grow up attached to the places of our earliest memories. At an international education conference in Brisbane we asked participants in a collective biography workshop to recall their earliest memory of a water place (Devos, de Carteret & Somerville 2008). Was it a place where you played or swam? A beach, a storm water drain, or a puddle, a public or a lurky place?

M. Somerville, K. Power and P. de Carteret (eds.),
Landscapes and Learning: Place Studies for a Global World, 03–20

My earliest memories of water are growing up by the side of Belfast Lough in Ireland. Here, I skimmed stones across the Lough with my brothers, shivered as I learned to swim, chased gulls and watched the big ships glide down from the harbour, on their way to other places. On the surface the water seemed safe and inviting. It sparkled on summer days. As children we splashed through the waves, the water raced over our toes, washing stones as shiny as a seal's back. I remember the sea at night with lights in the distance; the other side, across the water. As a child, I dreamed of rowing to the other side to see what was there. But on dull, winter days when the mist settled over the Lough we imagined the water as deep, mysterious and frightening. Ships were shadows in the fog, and their foghorns were familiar sounds of winter. They were going somewhere into the world beyond (Collective biography participant, AARE, 2008).

Much of our learning about space and place as young children is through our immediate sensory experiences. This exercise, in which adults recalled the places of childhood through memory work, evoked strong embodied memories. Their memories had an intensity as if the experiences were still present; often positive, sometimes frightening or overwhelming: "Some memories I associate with childhood playfulness and wonder. But other memories are dark and painful." Participants were able to recreate detailed childhood landscapes, highlighting "the primacy of place in human experience" (Schroder, 2006, p. 312). And yet, the aim of the educational processes of modernity is to achieve placelessness, and the highest form of knowledge is seen as the most abstract, the most universal. We wondered if as a society we erase a sense of place in our schools rather than teaching with it.

One of our first conversations was about science education. Somerville engaged in conversation with Gough's work published in a special edition of *Educational Philosophy and Theory* (2006). Authors in this special edition critiqued the philosophical bases of science education from several different perspectives. The relationship of science education to non-Western knowledges, for example, was characterised as Eurocentric and androcentric. In response to the Eurocentric nature of western scientific knowledge, Lyn Carter proposed "a postcolonial border epistemology" to open up spaces to "other thinking" (Carter, 2006, p. 683). Science education was also criticised as ignorant of popular media culture, contributing to what Sandra Harding calls "an increasingly visible form of scientific illiteracy" (Gough, 2006, p. 626). Fendler and Tuckey suggested unsettling the certainties of scientific knowledge by combining literacy and science in a deconstructive textual practice to undo the binary assumptions of western science: "life versus non-life, objective versus subjective, and scientific versus cultural" (Fendler & Tuckey, 2006, p. 602). These propositions had strong resonances with our original context of global postcolonial uncertainties and the question of how to educate a generation of children and adults who live in a global cyberworld to learn place differently.

It was the reconstructive potential of Gough's "nomadic geophilosophy of science education", however, that connected most strongly with our intentions:

Peter Gabriel and Youssou N'Dour's song, 'Shaking the Tree', is in several ways emblematic of my project. It is a call to change and enhance lives composed in a spirit which complements Deleuze and Guattari's (1994) practical 'geophilosophy' (p. 95), which seeks to describe the relations between particular spatial configurations and locations and the philosophical formations that arise therein. Both Gabriel and N'Dour compose and perform songs about taking action to solve particular problems in the world, and Deleuze (1994) believes that concepts should intervene to resolve local situations' (p. xx) (Gough, 2006, p. 625).

For us this passage represented a move to a different sort of thinking and writing. Introducing the metaphor of singing, of sound and the human voice, and of creative expression in song, is a move between a metaphysics of logics ('concepts') and a metaphysics of poetics ('song'). The subject of the song, 'shaking the tree', is an image of nature being shaken, a vigorous physical action related to radical social critique that has both practical and symbolic implications. The image of 'shaking the tree' is connected with Deleuzian notions about the problem of the tree as a metaphor of knowledge. Deleuze and Guattari offer the rhizome as an alternative, a pattern of root growth that makes multiple random connections. The tree, in this paper, stands for the certainties and hierarchies of western scientific knowledge. The paper is Gough's rhizomatic thinking, his song, a song that is both practical and located, metaphysical and transformational. In his paper he names the variety of assemblages available to shake the tree of modern Western science: "arts, artefacts, disciplines, technologies, projects, practices, theories and social strategies" (Gough, 2006, p. 626). Disrupting taken for granted knowledges, then, is a multidisciplinary activity akin to Steinberg's 'bricolage' (Steinberg, 2006), requiring diverse theoretical strategies and practical technologies. To enable us to further develop conversations across different knowledge systems, however, we need to develop some elements of a common language. For this purpose we propose the concept of 'place'.

PLACE

We are arguing for a newly conceptualised understanding of place. The fate of the local in the age of the global has emerged as a key theme in contemporary social science research. Academic assertions are plentiful about both the 'unbounded' nature of the locality or region and about hybridised global networks in the formation of identities and communities (Amin, 2004). Yet many anthropologists, sociologists, historians and geographers have questioned such claims about the "discursive erasure of place" (Escobar, 2001, p. 141). They have instead suggested that (shifting) geographies, boundaries and multiple scales continue to matter "as expressions of social practice, discourse and power" (Paasi, 2003, p. 541). We agree with these assertions, because we believe that without an intimate knowledge of, and attachment to, local places there is no beginning point. One is always situated in a local place, and without a concept of the local, change is not possible. Through place it is possible to understand the embodied effects of the global at a local level. For us, this is fundamental to taking action about global problems. Place has the potential to offer alternative storylines about who we are in the places where we live and work in an increasingly globalised world.

Our question here is, not what place is, but rather what does place as a concept do. As we have maintained above, place functions as a bridge between the local and the global, allowing us to comprehend the ways that global processes, such as climate change, affect local places in particular ways. Scientific research tells us about the enormity of the problems caused by global warming but "scientific research has traditionally offered only a partial vision of the reality it seeks to explore, pedagogical bricoleurs attempt to widen their perspectives through methodological diversity" (Steinberg, 2006, p. 120). For the pedagogical bricoleur, place is productive as a framework because it allows ordinary people to express their concerns about their local places, and to be involved in 'shaking the tree' of established knowledges. The language of place enables a conversation between the grounded physical reality of positivist scientific research and the metaphysical space of representation, the realm of the arts and storytelling. It is through place making and storytelling that place and identities are known and transformed. This bridging of scientific realism and the representational practices of the arts and social sciences comes together in the emerging field of 'ecological humanities' (Rose, 2004). Conversations between different paradigms, and disciplinary and subject areas, are imperative if we are to begin to address the intransigent problems of space and place that we have alluded to earlier. Place can offer an important framework for an integrated educational curriculum which seeks to address environmental issues from a range of perspectives across traditional subject boundaries of science, history, geography, creative arts and English.

PLACE STUDIES

'Place studies' is a new interdisciplinary formation that takes as its focus these new understandings of place. A recent website, *Research on Space and Place*, for example, offers bibliographies in twenty disciplinary areas ranging from archaeology/anthropology to sociology and social sciences, with a key interest in place studies (Janz, 2004). This new interdisciplinary field significantly reconceptualises the work of early place theorists (eg. Bachelard, 1958; Relph, 1976; and Tuan, 1977). It draws on contemporary cultural theorists such as Soja (2000, xx), who focus on "the recently reinvigorated and transdisciplinary interest and emphasis on all aspects of the spatiality of human life". Just as cultural studies provides insights to educational theorising for cultural transformations, place studies, a subset of cultural studies, offers insights about the relationship between cultures and environments. Place studies emphasises the more-than-human aspects of our places as active participants in our knowledge making, and explores alternative understandings of our relationship to place. Rose (1996, p. 7) for example, reports, that for Australian Indigenous peoples, "Country is a place that gives and receives life. Not just imagined or represented, it is lived in and lived with. ... People talk about country in the same way they would talk about a person: they speak to country, sing to country, visit country, worry about country, feel for country, and long for country". In *Landscapes and Learning* we map the possibilities for cultural transformations through place studies. Through its focus on the mutual constitution of bodies, identities, histories, spaces and places, place studies offers a conceptual tool for important cultural transformations.

Place studies in Australia has the potential to make a distinctive contribution to inform global scholarship. Research in place studies in Australia is characterised by a necessary engagement with the relationship between Indigenous and non-Indigenous peoples and knowledges. During the last wave of global colonisation, in which almost all of the major lands of the world were colonised, the great European migrations met with the world's oldest surviving culture in Australia's Indigenous inhabitants. Rather than fade away, as has been imagined of Australian Indigenous cultures, they have survived as dynamic living cultures with an internationally recognised unique relationship to land: "Aboriginal Australians regard the land as a totality, connection to country being the very essence of their belief structure and subsequent social organisation" (Ward, Reys, Davies & Roots, 2003). This remains true despite dispossession, displacement, and genocide of Australian Aboriginal cultures since colonisation (Langton in Behrendt & Thompson, 2003) and has profound implications for an Australian understanding of relationship to place (Somerville, 1999). Australian scholars and researchers cannot begin to articulate a position about place without confronting the complex political realities of the relationship between Indigenous and non-Indigenous relationships in place. They are in a unique position to articulate what it means to learn about place in the newly emerging global context, "a postcolonial and reflexive contemporaneity" (Carter, 2006, p. 684).

Education generally, and schooling in particular, is potentially an important site for learning about place. Modernity, according to Green (2007), is about placelessness, and schooling is the quintessential project of modernity in which we unlearn our earliest sense of attachment to places. Postmodernity requires us to recognise the multiplicity of places. How, then, do we begin to address the question of teaching and learning place differently? David Gruenewald's (2003a, 2003b) articles radically transformed place studies because of the explicit linking of place and pedagogy. 'Place', according to Gruenewald, is "profoundly pedagogical": "as centers of experience, places teach us about how the world works, and how our lives fit into the spaces we occupy. Further, places make us: As occupants of particular places with particular attributes, our identity and our possibilities are shaped" (Gruenewald, 2003b, p. 647). Although identifying himself as a critical theorist, Gruenewald described 'decolonisation' and 're-inhabitation' as the two broad and interrelated objectives of a critical place pedagogy (2003a). These parallel processes of decolonisation and reinhabitation are profoundly postmodern and postcolonial in their intention. Decolonisation involves developing the ability to recognise ways of thinking "that injure and exploit other people and place". Reinhabitation involves "identifying, affirming, conserving, and creating those forms of cultural knowledge that nurture and protect people and ecosystems" (Gruenewald, 2003a, p. 9).

In our provocation paper, Somerville engaged in conversation with David Gruenewald's call for a critical place-based pedagogy. Earlier theorists, exemplified by Wendell Berry (eg Berry, 1977; 1993), had linked place and learning, foregrounding the significance of local places in educational processes. This "ecologised humanist tradition" (Ball & Lai, 2006, p. 262) was underpinned by a romantic view of nature and the autonomous, rational, patriarchal subject of liberal humanism (Weedon, 1997). Gruenewald's critical place-conscious education was a response to "the romantic excesses of ecohumanists" (Ball & Lai, 2006, p. 270). Somerville responded to Gruenewald's critical pedagogy of place with a poststructural and postcolonial framework for a new pedagogy of place evolved from fifteen years of collaborative place research with Australian Indigenous people.

Somerville's (2008) proposal for a new pedagogy of place takes up the ideas of decolonisation and reinhabition but differs philosophically, methodologically and practically from Gruenewald's critical framework. A crucial feature of a postcolonial pedagogy of place is the necessity to move beyond binary constructions of thought. This characteristic of Australian place studies was articulated in a call for papers in the new ecological humanities section of *Australian Humanities Review*: "The ecological humanities works across the great binaries of western thought" (Rose, 2004). A postcolonial pedagogy of place moves beyond deconstruction in an attempt to articulate how to create something new from the space between binary oppositions. Within this reconceptualised concept of place are three key elements or principles: our relationship to place is constituted in stories and other representations; place learning is local and embodied; and deep place learning occurs in a contact zone of contestation.

Our Relationship to Places is Constituted in Stories (and Other Representations)

This element recognises story as the primary unit of meaning, the means through which we make sense of the world. The concept of story is enlarged here to embrace the representations of visual artists, sculptors, and poets, as well as scientists, policy makers and agriculturalists. Each discipline and artistic modality has its own forms and genres of place stories. The analytical strategy of storylines, developed in feminist poststructuralism (Davies, 2000; Søndergaard, 2002), can be used deconstructively to analyse how stories function to shape our relationship to places. Dominant colonial storylines of place "deny our connection to earthly phenomena [and] construct places as objects or sites on a map to be economically exploited" (Gruenewald, 2003b, p. 624). Deconstructing such storylines is therefore part of the process of 'decolonisation'. These dominant storylines depend for their justification and legitimation on the suppression of alternative stories that already exist, often as the shadow side of dominant stories. The concept of story and storylines can be used reconstructively to seek out previously invisible place stories, or to generate new stories about place. Changing our relationship to places means changing the stories we tell about places. According to Rose (2004) the major shift in 'ecological humanities' has been to introduce new storylines of embodied connection.

Place Learning is Necessarily Embodied and Local

If the objectifying strategies of science distance us from recognising our connection to place, this element emphasises the mutual constitution of places and bodies. Because of the fundamental difference between this idea and the practices of western science, it is the most radical, transformative, and challenging of the three elements of a new place pedagogy. In *Volatile Bodies*, feminist philosopher Liz Grosz proposed to interrogate philosophy by "putting the body at the centre of our notion of subjectivity" (Grosz, 1994, p. 5). This strategy can be applied to place, inviting a rethinking of place projects and experiences to put the body, our bodies, at the centre (Somerville, 1999). Soja (2000, p. 361), for example, suggests that "the space of the human body is perhaps the most critical site to watch the production and reproduction of power". Even more radically, however, this principle opens us to the materiality of places. As a non-Aboriginal Australian, working with Aboriginal people and their places required Somerville to be open to the materiality of places as well as their stories. Experiences of body/place connection led her to see the landscape itself as the third subject, present in all of her research (Somerville, 1999). Place learning that derives from a deep, embodied sense of connection gives rise to a different ontology, an ontology of self becoming-other in the space between self and a natural world, composed of humans and non-human others, animate and inanimate; animals and plants, weather, rocks, trees.

Place is a Contact Zone of Cultural Contestation

Specific local places offer a material and metaphysical in-between space for the intersection of multiple and contested stories. This is especially significant in the relationship between indigenous and other subjugated knowledges, and Western academic thought. It is equally important when considering the multiplicity of different stories about the same place, such as scientific stories, oral histories of place, media representations of places, immigrant experiences of place and so on. This aspect of place has been characterised as a 'contact zone' (Pratt, 1992). The contact zone has been theorised in different ways, depending on whether the focus is on hybrid productions from 'the third space' (eg Bhabba, 1994) or on difference. Paul Carter, the lead author in this book, has offered a unique contribution to thinking about the contact zone. Based on records of first contact between the colonising cultures of Europe, and Australian Indigenous peoples as the oldest continuing culture in the world, Carter theorises the incommensurability of the contact zone. In his perspective, it is important to hold the different stories in productive tension, and the main function of the contact zone is to preserve difference, even to the point of suspending meaning (Carter, 1992).

These principles give rise to new emergent arts-based methodologies for developing and practising place-responsive pedagogies.

EMERGENT ARTS BASED METHODOLOGIES

Our provocation proposed that a methodology for a place pedagogy needs to encompass the multiple forms in which alternative representations of place are expressed; the embodiment of experiences in place; and the multiple alternative voices and stories about any particular place. The methodology is emergent, because the emphasis is on undoing dominant stories of place (decolonisation) and the collective and relational making of new place stories (re-inhabitation). These stories are local and responsive. They cannot be pre-empted prior to creating the conditions for their telling, their emergence must be facilitated in the process. The methodology is arts-based in order to encompass the multiple forms in which alternative representations of place are made possible. It requires bodily engagement with the materiality of specific local places and the conscious facilitation of the representation of alternative and invisible stories. It also requires the development of a new ontology, or way of being-in-the-world, and a new epistemology, or way of knowing-the-world.

AN ONTOLOGY OF EMERGENCE

In order to engage with a new postcolonial pedagogy of place we need to become other-to-ourselves. The notion of the becoming self is well developed in feminist poststructural theory. The subject is reconceived from the fixed liberal humanist self to one that is in process, coming into being each time he or she is spoken into existence (Davies, 2004). To take up this self that is in a process of becoming, and extend it into an ontology of emergence as becoming-other, is far more radical. Such an ontology needs to incorporate elements of our past self history (ontogeny), who we imagine ourselves to be, and our embodied relationship with others. It also includes our participation as bodies in the 'flesh of the world' (Merleau-Ponty, 1962), a reciprocal relationship with objects and landscapes, weather, rocks and trees, sand, mud and water, animals and plants, an ontology founded in the bodies of things.

Within this ontology of becoming-other, there is an epistemological relationship with the objects and technologies that we, in the process of becoming-other, can intentionally manipulate. These include the tools of artists and writers, academics, and artisans, who choose to be engaged in processes of becoming-other:–stone, wood, and clay, pencils, crayons, brushes and paints, computers, words and paper, cloth, thread and scissors – among the myriad other things that we humans have chosen to use to create. Through these processes of creation we can begin to know the world anew, and each expression is part of a larger ongoing process. Every time we make a single individual representation of our places, it exists beside a proliferation of other representations, a pause in an iterative process of representation and reflection through which we can come to know differently (Somerville, 2007).

The place studies researchers in this book entered these conversations through their own processes of becoming-other. We invited them to respond to the paper that was circulated as a provocation and to develop a paper for presentation at a symposium in which we would begin a collective conversation. The idea for a symposium, *Landscapes and Learning*, was itself a mode of public pedagogy, positioning academics, theorists and researchers as bricoleurs in a contact zone of disciplinary diversity. We sought rhizomatic connections and divergent desires (Deleuze and Guattari, 1987, p. 18) to map the pedagogical potential of place studies for a global world. The symposium offered a methodology of collaborative bricolage, exploring ideas from a number of sometimes contradictory research paradigms with the aim of producing a conversation that offered "expanded insight via historical contextualisation, multiple theoretical groundings, and a diversity of knowledge" (Kincheloe 2005 in Steinberg, 2006, p. 120).

The symposium was held, aptly, amidst the vapour clouds of the coal-fired generators of Latrobe Valley, but when traditional Gunnai/Kurnai Elder, Doris Paton welcomed us to her country, she looked out of the window and saw something different:

Firstly I want to acknowledge my Ancestors of my country and I want to acknowledge where I come from. Where I come from I owe to my parents who are both Elders who have passed their knowledge on to me. My way of knowing comes from them. Looking out of the window now I can see the tarook on the lake. My Indigenous knowledge tells me that in the spring, it comes back green, and that's when you can pick the *tarook*. When I look out the other window, I can see the wattles are in bloom and I know through my Indigenous knowledge from my parents and Ancestors that when the wattle is out, it's time to gather the eggs. That kind of knowledge wasn't privileged through my education process. My schooling experiences were non-Indigenous and I really only learned one way of thinking, doing and being.

BECOMING-OTHER

Many of the authors in this book address their position in relation to two major waves of globalisation - the colonisation of the world that created the nation of Australia in the eighteenth century, and the current wave of economic, cyber, and environmental globalisation. Paul Carter's chapter, 'Care at a distance', leads the book with his proposition that the purpose of postcolonial place-making is to create "a fabric of passages, or exchange-ways, held together by the prospect of meeting". Paul Carter is an interdisciplinary scholar whose books *The Road to Botany Bay* (1987) and *The Lie of the Land* (1996) established his reputation as a pioneer of 'spatial history' and place-making. His arts-based approach to place studies has led to prestigious public space design/public art commissions and he is internationally-recognised for his contribution to the methodology of public space design in a number of papers and in his book, *Material Thinking* (2004). In his chapter, Carter begins with the idea that we all come from another place. He uses examples from museum practice, urban design and innovative community arts projects to show how the new places where we are now located can be connected to those places where we come from.

Carter proposes an ethic of 'care at a distance' as a way of acknowledging what we bring with us from the places we have left behind. He offers the idea of 'an educative doubling', a learning that allows for a movement towards processes of place-making that are open to influence and participation by Indigenous, 'settler', and successive 'migrant' cultures. In a critique of the Eurocentricity of some postcolonial theorists, Carter draws on traditional and postmodern Indigenous narratives of place and belonging. He proposes countering imperial myths built on conquest and erasure with place stories that create a discursive environment in which all the participants are players. 'Care at a distance' opens up the possibility for multiple and mobile identities of selves in relation to places. Its doubling of poetic and linear logics allows for a nuanced account of historical, environmental and spiritual realities moving with the changing character of specific places.

CREATIVE PLACE MAKING

Each of the writers in the book moves between the ways that local places and global concerns are mutually entangled. In the first section we explore the possibilities for making different places through the use of arts based or creative methodologies. These include specifically using arts practices such as quilt making and performance, but also include different ways of writing and thinking about place.

In 'Co-creating a place that lies between' Aunty Doris[1] Paton, a local Indigenous Elder of the Gunnai/Kurnai language group, begins with her location in the country of her ancestors. The *tarook* on the lake is ready for picking, and the wattle is in bloom outside the window where we are sitting. She invites the audience to her country through these signs of the cycles of seasons in the here and now. She is present to her landscape and draws us into it with her.

Aunty Doris and Laura Brearley then go on to explore learning between Indigenous and non-Indigenous knowledge systems through the methodology of 'deep listening'. A number of Indigenous research students from different Indigenous language groups in Australia developed the methodology of deep listening in collaboration with Brearley for researching aspects of Indigenous cultural knowledge and community leadership. Deep listening is enunciated as a concept in many Australian Indigenous languages and embodies a profound and deep respect for others through processes of mutual storytelling. Five principles are further developed as extensions of the deep listening methodology in this chapter: cultural ways of knowing, reciprocal and respectful relationships, talking circles, stories in conversation, and community protocols.

Aunty Doris describes her project about the hopes and dreams for a community school where Indigenous children can learn the cultures from which they have become alienated. With Laura Brearley she explores the place making practices of Peruvian indigenous quilt-makers where the quilts become narrative forms that allow for multiple meanings to emerge. Aunty Doris' findings are offered in the form of three quilts described in the chapter. Together the authors conclude by proposing that re-ordering our understanding of relationships is the key to co-creating a place where Indigenous and non-Indigenous people can work together.

Katrina Schlunke explores the pedagogical possibilities of place in 'Possession Island: Pedagogies of "possessed" place' through a form of body/place writing. She takes a literal journey to the remote island in the Pacific Ocean where the European explorer Captain Cook is said to have taken possession of the island continent that became the Australian nation. This journey of becoming-other-to-herself is "intensely, sensorally concrete". The sensory quality of the experience is expressed in the alternative writing style through which Schlunke explores the tension between Indigenous oral stories and the foundational myths of nation building. It is here that 'Australia' falls into place for her.

On Possession Island Schlunke draws out the ideological, discursive and material effects of Cook's specific act of colonial possession in that place. She contrasts these effects with the continuity of presence of a mangrove tree that grows there. The act of possession is realised as "A force that maps and names but also shoots and legalises ... the east coast of New Holland into Australia, a silencing into a discovery, the presence of people into an absence". Alternatively, the mangrove tree bears its rhizomatic roots horizontally to shed salt and breathe, to stabilise sediments and nurture crabs and molluscs, not really in opposition to anything. Here national possession seems not merely incommensurate with lived Indigenous sovereignty but seems an impossibility, because to be white on Possession Island would be to starve. Through this chapter she explores the way such foundational stories of nationhood structure a national unconscious that "both names and forgets" the places where they reside.

In 'Footprints in the Mallee' Emily Potter takes up a Foucauldian deconstructive critique to draw parallels between settler discourses of clearing the land and climate change discourses of the carbon footprint. Potter suggests that "The making of colonial places thus depended upon a profound historical repression–the erasure of prior human and non-human ecologies. This was a poetic as well as a practical project." In poetic writing that draws on metaphor as much as logics, she draws parallels with contemporary neoliberal discourses of sustainability, "the calculative frames of governmentality" such as the carbon emissions trading scheme and its co-inhabitant, the carbon footprint.

The notion of 'hybrid geographies' offers Potter a way out of these techno-scientific storylines. Hybrid geographies, she claims, "give voice to alternate histories of encounters, entanglements, and unresolved arrangements of 'words and worlds'". Within a logic of narration, or storytelling, hybrid geographies trace out a pattern that is both water's history and its possible future, linking to Somerville's final chapter about water in the Murray-Darling Basin.

In a doubling between research sites in Great Britain and Australia, Anna Hickey-Moody investigates creative place-making activities for young people. In the Stratford Circus in East London and the Youth Theatre in Geelong, arts based projects are used as 'public pedagogies', creating a way for young people in these places to actively engage in place making. While typical arts projects may enable the creative labour of young people, they do not necessarily facilitate their social inclusion. In the projects described, social inclusion is made possible through an unlikely arts scene that is "resilient, interesting and often low budget". Creativity here is seen to offer a mode of resistance to the present and to an obsession with 'the way things are'.

Creative place-making is suggested as a way to imagine what might be possible, 'resisting the inertia of the present'. For example, through drama, circus skills and dance, creativity can push the bounds of the familiar in the direction of change. In both places, the arts based methods are place responsive and driven by the needs and desires of ethnically and socially diverse communities in the local areas. The youth theatre includes and speaks to marginalised communities "promoting diverse conceptions of place and community" that unsettle dominant discourses and brings different communities together. As responses to local places, youth arts projects are shown to open up possibilities for becoming, and for mobility beyond the constraint of present circumstances, to those young people who might otherwise be imprisoned within them.

LANDSCAPES OF LEARNING

In the second section the authors focus on ideas of place as applied specifically in educational settings. The four chapters are characterised by engaging with 'difference', ranging from difference constituted through socio-economic disadvantage to difference in ethnicity and knowledge systems.

In her chapter, 'If you see a bubble coming up', Jennifer Rennie draws on her research in the Tiwi Islands to challenge hegemonic notions of literacy that privilege western knowledge. Rennie highlights a lack of understanding, valuing, and acknowledging of Indigenous community literacy and numeracy practices, by western schooling systems. Because of the lack of understanding of the multiple, complex and creative place literacies that students from the Tiwi Islands bring to the classroom, they are deemed illiterate when making the transition from primary to secondary schooling. Through complex place literacies Tiwi children move between the places and practices of traditional culture and art, personal story and contemporary spaces of the Internet. School, in contrast, is a place of limitation that fails to acknowledge the literacies demonstrated by these students in reading and writing the landscape. Through stories from the Tiwi children, the multiple and creative place knowledges are made visible.

The chapter introduces the story of one Year 8 student, 'Darcy', who takes Rennie and her readers on a guided journey of his place. He teaches us about two kinds of edible shellfish that are represented in traditional ochre colours in his grandmother's current painting. He explains the historical records, cultural traditions, and identity in country, of his people, through the skin group and dreaming of his late father, 'the last potter'. Darcy tells Rennie that he will become 'the next pot man', inheriting these traditions. He explains the contemporary micro-politics of the community art centre and the meaning of its website. Rennie concludes that understanding literacy as occurring through a range of different modalities, which include visual, oral, kinaesthetic, digital and written forms, requires a new approach to literacy. Teachers who do not recognise the opportunities of tapping into children's rich existing knowledge risk perpetuating their exclusion. The alternative is to take a different approach and welcome the place literacies these children bring to the classroom to open up social futures for them and expand the knowledge of their classmates.

In 'Pedagogies of place and possibility' Debra Hayes addresses issues of disadvantaged schools, many with a high Indigenous population. She conceives of place as a metaphor for structurally inequitable social positioning in her work with schools in challenging circumstances. If you are disadvantaged in Australia, Hayes claims, the education system does not serve you as well as systems in other comparable countries. Parents who can afford to choose, send their children elsewhere, leaving behind in public schools a larger proportion of students who lack the social capital to take up the opportunities school offers. These students are often poor, immigrant and/or Aboriginal children. Moreover, these schools, which are identified as disadvantaged, are often 'equipped with less to deal with more'. Hayes' research team used narrative methodologies to seek a complex hope in which schools may become places of possibility.

Using 'day diaries' the researchers facilitated conversations with school leaders and classroom teachers to identify default scripts characterised by low learning expectations and outcomes. They then identified classroom practices, which differed from the default script, where some teachers expressed a different logic of practice from the majority of their colleagues. These particular teachers believed in their students' abilities to learn, and in their capacity to teach them. One of the teachers was found to employ specifically spatial strategies by constructing an inviting, relaxing and stimulating music space where he would move around as a facilitator rather than a teacher. The chapter contests deficit narratives of social positioning, and identifies possibilities for teachers to exert agency. Alternative spatial practices can transform the possibilities of the classroom as learning space.

In Nixon and Comber's chapter 'Literacy, landscapes and learning in a primary classroom', primary school children become designers of place. They learned to constitute themselves as powerful place-makers in a school whose surrounding area is undergoing 'urban renewal'. Some children and adults in such communities are characterised in deficit terms and constituted as passive in the gentrification of the places where they live. The children involved in the place-making project worked across architecture, communication and education to create new learning spaces. They engaged in consultative processes of design and place-making to shape a garden in their school grounds. The researchers and teachers together designed pedagogical practices attending to space and place, by focusing on what changing a place might mean in the lives of the people who inhabit and use that place. The children translated their ideas from talk into writing, drawing, and model-making, moving between one semiotic medium and another. Through this experience the children developed new literacies of place and they learned to become social actors and agents in their own lives, active members and participants in their societies.

Roslyn Appleby's travel tale of English teaching in East Timor takes us into the relationship between English language teaching and the imperialism of western development. Travellers' tales are one storyline through which 'the other' becomes an exotic subject in the traveller's story. This is, however, a travel tale with a difference that explores the processes of self reflexivity through which self and other are re-conceived with place as a conceptual frame. It tells of one teacher's mission, and how that mission was translated into a spatial practice through experiences of embodied engagement in the contact zone. The tale critiques the temporal male logic of Development discourses that privilege western time over the female specificities of space and place. Appleby deconstructs the effects of this logic as they are applied to English language teaching, where education presumes to equip teachers from English speaking countries of the global centre with universally relevant skills that are applied in language teaching programs throughout the global periphery. In this Australian teacher's experience, the scripts and representations of English language textbooks were divorced from the places of East Timor that existed outside of the classroom. They functioned to produce an 'English bubble', a disciplinary schema, that floated detached from the unfamiliar social and historical context of the periphery.

As a teacher, Jane became aware that her own deficiencies in understanding East Timor left her 'out of place'. On her second teaching expedition to East Timor Jane "slipped the temporal bonds to engage with an embodied sense of place". She defied warnings about her physical safety by walking home rather than being chauffeured, in a metaphor for her move from the inside space of the classroom to the outside place of East Timor. Jane visited a Timorese beach with her students and on the beach together, other stories surfaced, fragments and memories of other times in this place. The students told her that going down to the water and swimming is not something that they do, because when the Indonesians were there that was part of the torture. In this new spatial practice the talk between teacher and students turned from the routine functions set out in the Australian textbook to talk emerging from the contingencies of place, not only alluding to past trauma, but also discussing the construction of a new nation. Jane entered the uncertainty of a contact zone which opened up new spatial and temporal possibilities to enable a different connection between teacher, student and the production of spatial history.

THEORISING PLACE DIFFERENTLY

In the final section of the book we have grouped the chapters that fundamentally question current conceptions of place and offer an approach to developing new alternatives. These include Noel Gough who questions the idea from the provocation paper that places are pedagogical and explores the precise processes through which place can become pedagogical. Alan Mayne questions an epistemology of place as a passive stage or backdrop for the dramas of social life through considering such contemporary places as Dharavi in Mumbai, London's

East End, Melbourne's Little Lon, and New York's Five Points. Place, he maintains, is distinguished as delineated and enduring by human association. Jane Kenway problematises conventional conceptions of place as the blank space to be coloured in by teachers with local colour and the current privileging in top-down curriculum discourse of spatial relationships of the nation. She seeks to elucidate what globalisation looks like from below, in young people's social practices at the local/global nexus in remote Coober Pedy, coastal Eden, agricultural Renmark, and deindustrialised Morwell. Finally, Margaret Somerville completes the circle with a return to the provocation paper as it is applied in re-shaping the Murray-Darling Basin, a region that has recently entered both Australian and the global imaginary as a system in distress.

In 'How do places *become* pedagogical?' Noel Gough examines the ways that nature is envisioned, named, traversed and transformed. Through a method he calls 'rhizosemiotic play' he evokes some of his own travels and transformations from a "travelling text worker" to a more sedentary eco-critical stance on outdoor and environmental education. Gough suggests that acts of creative un-naming and un-counting nature are productive approaches to the problems caused by the scientific practices of naming, classification and enumeration.

Two specifically pedagogical projects illustrate the importance of situating learning in sites that are culturally significant for young people. One example, 'Making video games in the woods', taps into the new literacies and learning styles that today's screen focussed adolescents develop through playing video games. The second project enacts a pedagogy designed to develop deep consciousness of particular places through a learning activity that involves the interweaving of knowledge about wildlife with personal stories and social relationships. The qualities of this as a pedagogical activity makes the experience more like an Indigenous way of knowing place, and less like a field trip for science or walking for sport. Eco-critical projects such as these take account of the broader ramifications of understanding environmental education as a textual practice which necessarily includes language arts, semiotics, literary criticism and cultural studies.

Traditional concepts from history are challenged and extended by Alan Mayne's advocacy for a historical ethnography of place. In 'Strange Entanglements: Landscapes and historical imagination', Mayne questions a discipline where people are analysed at a remove from the places they shaped, and which shaped their lives and identities. He observes that while historians have physical access to and contact with the land, its fields, houses, and buried broken crockery, only the written word is regarded as meaningful and useful historical data. He explores city slums and frontier landscapes as examples of sites in which the ethnographic interpretation of the material culture of obscure, mundane, and seemingly insignificant things and places has become a means of glimpsing the homeliness and social identity of subaltern performances.

One example is Dharavi in Mumbai, India, one of the world's largest slums, but by far its most prosperous. It has a thriving business centre propelled by thousands of micro-entrepreneurs who have created an invaluable industry turning around the discarded waste of Mumbai's nineteen million citizens. For a growing number of environmental campaigners, Dharavi is becoming the green lung stopping the huge urban conglomeration of Mumbai choking on its own waste. Stereotyping such communities as slums hinders appreciation of the actual social dynamics of contemporary places such as Dharavi, and past places such as London's East End, Melbourne's Little Lon, and New York's Five Points. Slum stereotypes also obscure and contradict the subaltern performances that are played out in such spaces as elements in grassroots place making, neighbourliness, and community building. Mayne argues the best way to learn about the past is not by superimposing present-day roadmaps upon its unfamiliar landscapes, but by attempting to translate and comprehend the idiomatic content of past places.

Jane Kenway's chapter, 'Beyond conventional curriculum cartography via a global sense of place', proposes to move beyond conventional curriculum cartographies and address the educational being and becoming of young people in a global world. The four local Australian sites are already interpenetrated by global phenomena. In Coober Pedy the Aboriginal 'homeboys', in Eden the 'surf chicks', in Renmark the 'Greek boys' doing laps in their cars, and the 'not-really-local welfare poor' in Morwell, all take up their identities through a global sense of place.

Kenway explores three alternative angles on globalisation's spatial geometry: 'Complex connectivity', 'Global scapes' and 'Geographies of centrality and marginality' arising in her study. Collectively these angles intersect and point to the necessity of a place-based global curriculum. Characterising 'parables of place' as global, temporal, spatial, ecological, political, imaginary and personal, Kenway argues that teachers need to be provided with opportunities to develop a nuanced understanding of place and thus of the places that they are teaching in. It is vital that they are able to rise above place prejudice and to move beyond simplistic and romantic views of place. The curriculum that guides teaching and learning needs to attend to this spatial paradox, to have an intimate global sense of place.

In the final chapter, 'Transforming pedagogies of water', Margaret Somerville moves beyond the classroom to alternative learning spaces and art as a public pedagogy. The chapter addresses the international crisis of water, particularly in the global south, where the differential impact of climate change is predicted to cause continuing drought. In an application of the postcolonial place pedagogies framework outlined in this Introduction, Indigenous artist/researchers are engaged in partnership research to ask how we can change our approach to water in the Murray-Darling Basin. Somerville outlines some of the key storylines that have emerged from this research in terms of intimate attachments, flows and connections, and deep mapping. The chapter finishes with the art exhibition as public pedagogy, circulating artworks and stories from the particular local space of the exhibition to other continents and worlds of meaning.

Reading through each of these papers is itself a movement through the diversity of new empirical and theoretical work that is currently being undertaken in place studies. We hope that this leading edge research expands our readers' ideas about the possibilities of place studies and the particular contribution that Australian place studies researchers can make in an increasingly globalised world.

NOTES

[1] The English language kinship term 'Aunty' is used as a sign of respect for female Indigenous holders of significant cultural knowledge and kinship responsibilities in many Australian Indigenous cultures.

REFERENCES

Amin, A. (2004). Regions unbound: towards a new politics of place. *Geografiska Annaler, 86B*(1), 33–34.

Bachelard, G. (1958). *The poetics of space*. Boston: Beacon Press.

Ball, E. L., & Lai, A. (2006). Place-based pedagogy for the arts and humanities. *Pedagogy: Critical Approaches to Teaching Literature, Language, Composition, and Culture, 6*(2), 261–287.

Behrendt, J., & Thompson, P. (2003). *The recognition and protection of Aboriginal interests in NSW Rivers*. Sydney, NSW: Healthy Rivers Commission.

Berry, W. (1993). *Sex, economy, freedom and community*. New York: Pantheon.

Berry, W. (1977). *The unsettling of America: Culture and agriculture*. San Francisco: Sierra Club Books.

Bhabba, H. (1994). *The location of culture*. London: Routledge.

Carter, L. (2006). Postcolonial interventions within science education: Using postcolonial ideas to reconsider cultural diversity scholarship. *Educational Philosophy and Theory, 38*(5), 677–691.

Carter, P. (1987). *The road to Botany Bay: An essay in spatial history*. London and Boston: Faber and Faber.

Carter, P. (1992) *The sound in-between: Voice, space, performance*. Sydney, NSW: University of New South Wales Press and New Endeavour Press.

Carter, P. (1996). *The lie of the land*. London: Faber and Faber.

Carter, P. (2004). *Material thinking: The theory and practice of creative research*. Carlton: Melbourne University Press.

Davies, B. (2000). *A body of writing, 1990-1999*. Walnut Creek, CA: Altamira Press.

Davies, B. (2004). Poststructuralism and lines of flight in Australia. *International Journal of Qualitative Studies in Education, 17*(1), 3–11.

Deleuze, G., & Guattari, F. (1987). *A thousand plateaus: Capitalism and schizophrenia* (B. Massumi, Trans.). Minneapolis, MN: University of Minnesota Press.

Devos, A., de Carteret, P., & Somerville, M. (2008, November 30th–December 4th). *Collective biography workshop*. AARE International Education Conference, Brisbane.

Escobar, A. (2001). Culture sits in places: Reflections on globalism and subaltern strategies of localization. *Political Geography, 20*(1), 139–174.

Fendler, L., & Tuckey, S. F. (2006). Whose literacy? *Educational Philosophy and Theory, 38*(5), 677–691.

Gough, N. (2006). Shaking the tree, making a rhizome: Towards a nomadic geophilosophy of science education. *Educational Philosophy and Theory, 38*(5), 625–645.

Green, B. (2007). *Teacher education for rural and regional sustainability*. Gippsland: Seminar presentation, Faculty of Education, Monash University.

Grosz, E. (1994). *Volatile bodies: Towards a corporeal feminism*. Sydney, NSW: Allen and Unwin.

Gruenewald, D. A. (2003a). The best of both worlds: A critical pedagogy of place. *Educational Researcher, 32*(4), 3–12.

Gruenewald, D. A. (2003b). Foundations of place: A multidisciplinary framework for place-conscious education. *American Educational Research Journal, 40*(3), 619–654.

Janz, B. B. (2004). Research on space and place. Retrieved September 18, 2009, from http://pegasus.cc.ucf.edu/~janzb/place/

Merleau-Ponty, M. (1962). *Phenomenology of perception.* New York: Humanities Press.

Paasi, A. (2003). Region and place: Regional identity in question. *Progress in Human Geography, 27*(4).

Pratt, G. (1992). *Imperial writing and transculturalism.* London and New York: Routledge.

Relph, E. C. (1976). *Place and placelessness.* London: Pion.

Rose, D. B. (2004). The ecological humanities in action: An invitation. *Australian Humanities Review.* Retrieved September 18, 2009, from http://www.lib.latrobe.edu.au/AHR/archive/Issue-April-2004?rose.html

Rose, D. B. (1996). *Nourishing terrains: Australian Aboriginal views of landscape and wilderness.* Canberra, ACT: Australian Heritage Commission.

Schroder, B. (2006). Native science, intercultural education and place-conscious education: An Ecuadorian example. *Educational Studies, 32*(3), 307–317.

Soja, E. W. (2000). *Postmetropolis: Critical studies of cities and regions.* Oxford, UK: Blackwell.

Somerville, M. (1999). *Body/landscape journals.* Melbourne, VIC: Spinifex Press.

Somerville, M. (2007). Postmodern emergence. *Qualitative Studies in Education, 20*(2), 225–243.

Somerville, M. (2008). A place pedagogy for global contemporaneity. *Educational Philosophy and Theory.* doi: 10.1111/j.1469-5812.2008.00423.x.

Søndergaard, D. M. (2002). Poststructural approaches to empirical analysis. *International Journal of Qualitative Studies in Education, 15*(2), 187–204.

Steinberg, S. (2006). Critical cultural studies research: Bricolage in action. In K. Tobin & J. Kincheloe (Eds.), *Doing educational research – a handbook* (pp. 117-137). Rotterdam, The Netherlands: Sense Publishers.

Tuan, Yi-Fu. (1977). *Space and place: The perspective of experience.* Minnesota: University of Minnesota Press.

Ward, N., Reys, S., Davies, J., & Roots, J. (2003). *Scoping study on Aboriginal involvement in natural resource management decision making and the integration of Aboriginal cultural heritage considerations into relevant Murray-Darling Commission programs.* Murray-Darling Basin Commission.

Weedon, C. (1997). *Feminist practice and poststructural theory.* Oxford, UK: Blackwell Publishers.

Margaret Somerville
Kerith Power
Phoenix de Carteret
Monash University

PAUL CARTER

1. CARE AT A DISTANCE

Affiliations to Country in a Global Context

A tension exists between discourses of place-making and the theoretical paradigms of well-being that inform them. While places are conceived as localised, the systems theory (whether it is derived from philosophical anthropology, social ecology, or geographically-based concepts of region) that accounts for their distinctiveness is generalist (placeless). The same tension is played out at a community level, where insiders are distinguished from outsiders, notably in the conflict-riven interventions that Green Movement activists organise. These conflicts in place-making theory and praxis can easily be multiplied. In this context, a concept of 'care at a distance' is canvassed. Originally formulated as a response to the conundrums collecting institutions find themselves in when pressured to repatriate culturally-sensitive materials, it has since been adapted and extended to offer a different approach to place-making in Alice Springs, a locus of intense social suffering. In this chapter, the notion of 'care at a distance' is further extended to incorporate the subject-position of the outsider into the place-making process. In affiliating to others' country, it seems essential to declare where one comes from – even if, in the rhetoric of nation building, the past life of migrants must be annulled. The implication of this declaration is that creativity exercised at this place will stage a conversation with those who have departed; just as the outsider artist is, from the perspective of the environment whence they came, classified as departed and ghostlike. There emerges from this dialectic the recognition of the doubled or multiple identities of selves and places. To endow this ambiguity with epistemological significance, to appreciate it as a technique for letting back into the design of the future a complex emotional domain whose elements always come from somewhere else (even when that 'somewhere else' is here) seems to me to give a better account of historical, environmental and spiritual realities in a global context. Because of this, it suggests new ways of thinking the boundaries of places and the communities who produce and enjoy them.

Last year in Brisbane Christine Peacock, a Torres Strait Islander woman with affiliations through marriage to the Turrbal people, whose country includes Brighton and Margate, invited me to be involved in a project called 'Margate to Margate'. Under the rubric supplied by T.S. Eliot in 'Little Gidding' (*Four Quartets*), that 'We shall not cease from exploration/ And the end of all our exploring/ Will be to arrive where we started/ And know the place for the first time...', she was proposing a creative research project involving, among others, the

M. Somerville, K. Power and P. de Carteret (eds.),
Landscapes and Learning: Place Studies for a Global World, 21–33
© *2009 Sense Publishers. All rights reserved.*

London Print Studio, the artist Leah King-Smith and artists in the immigrant communities of Margate (England). I have written about the poetic colonisation of countries through names. Transposed to new places, place names like Margate embody, articulate and indeed promote complex and troubled senses of belonging that are characteristic of white settler cultures throughout their colonised world. They allude to a desire to connect but also recognition of disconnection. They ironise a sense of not belonging; they also repress the local genealogies of place and ownership that resist their usurpation. Applied to Christine's proposal, these reflections indicate that her proposed project is not a variation on the officially-sanctioned sentimental journeys through which the descendants of immigrants reconnect to the homelands of their ancestors. Refracted through the lens of its colonial history, 'Margate' returns to Margate with interest, opening it towards another identity. But perhaps this was always implicit in the name as Margate, or 'sea gate', was always a hinge place, located between land and sea, a focal point of immigration and, as the recent epic art event Exodus Day, staged by Artangel and Channel 4 on 30 September 2006, suggests, a site of departure.

Christine's recognition of doubling, not only as a mechanism of colonisation but as an emancipatory characteristic of postcolonial geography, provides an introduction to my theme. A tension exists between theories of place and practices of place-making. However much they are grounded, explicitly or tacitly, in the study of particular places and their communities, theories of place are, in principle, generalisable. Like the maps of geography, they may describe localities, but only in terms of a universal projection. Bachelard, Casey, Lefebvre, and other historians of place may extol and defend the aesthetic, ethical and affective values of places, but they write from somewhere else. Because of this, they invite us to behave like colonisers, taking the lessons of their examples and transporting them to other places. Thus, in the first abstraction, Pierre Bourdieu might use the Kabyle people of northern Africa to show that the physical design of a place instantiates the polarities of their worldview (Bourdieu, 1977, pp. 72-95). In a second abstraction, his notion of *habitus* may then be applied to 'our' world, helping N. Katherine Hayles explain how a "technological nonconscious" structures every aspect of cultural production (Hayles, 2006, p. 7). These examples could be multiplied endlessly: and they operate, of course, in the other direction, as we bring to bear on the characterisation and sustaining of places, perspectives derived from ecology, sociology, regional economics and planning. And the point I want to make is that these theoretical and practical antinomies may be avoided if we understand the constitution of places, and the discourse about them, as doubled.

The other context for making this claim is the persistence in place studies of what I would characterise as a kind of eco-fundamentalism, by which I mean a tendency to regard places, regions and even zones of bio-diversity as closed systems. This may be ideologically-driven, and represent the survival of a nature religion attachment to the notion of sacred places, but it also reflects the bias of systems theory itself, which is towards the characterisation of the world in terms of homeostatic complexes governed by feedback mechanisms that underpin their stability, and are internal to the system's organisation. Transposed to the historical environment, these theories of the inter-relatedness of parts can have the paradoxical effect of rendering other relationships, notably those with the outside world, superfluous and by definition destabilising. There is no easy place within these theories for the imagined community that T.S. Eliot invokes, those constitutionally extraterritorial heirs to modernity who, if they retain a nostalgia for home, recognising that its discovery is essential to understanding where they came from, must approach it from another place; or, more likely, from many places, all of which are part places, half open, half closed, Margates that were marred. Yet, we all come from somewhere else. Even if we stay at home this is true: not merely because, as our place names tell us, our homes have multiple provenances, but because, as many contributions in this collection foreground, place-making is a discursive activity, and discourse – the place of discourse – is at a minimum in-between two people. The unit of place is always a relation across difference, an educative doubling in which insides and outsides produce a new locus of movement, at once psychological, spiritual and physical.

In Australia's remaining old growth forests, the construction of places around a distinction between belonging and not-belonging assumes a particularly destructive form. It is obvious that wilderness is a cultural construct, the projection of an outside point of view. It is also obvious that its semiotic reduction in this form cuts both ways: if it enables courageous forest activists to focus media attention on their cause – as well as allowing tracts of land to be considered eligible for World Heritage status – it also encourages companies like Amcor and North Ltd to think of the forest purely as an image to be manipulated; hence their notorious preservation of roadside forest corridors, masking the clear felled slopes beyond. It is always easy in work-forces brought up on Anglo-Saxon classicism to stir up a working class resentment against the (in this case native forest activist) elites, but it is striking how this utterly mischievous social divisionism is orchestrated around the notions of insider (represented here by the sacrosanct local community) and outsider (here invariably anyone whose address is elsewhere). The actual interrelatedness of these parties is the stuff of social history, environmental science and regional planning policy, but it holds little sway in a debate that tacitly invokes the immaculate conception of the nation state, polarising the fate of places, and the rights to occupy and use them, around a distinction between residency and non-residency. They do not intend it but when Friends of the Earth speak of 'untouched wilderness', they pave the way for exploitation: for what has not been touched is *terra nullius*, that is, land that can be claimed simply by virtue of occupying it first.

The notion of 'care at a distance', which I want to introduce as a way of reconciling what I have identified as contradictions in the dominant discourses of place-making, originated in a reflection on the postcolonial responsibilities of museums. The remarks that follow derive from a presentation I gave at a U.S. symposium on memory, art museums and globalisation in late 2005. The pressure to repatriate materials that hold important personal and cultural meanings in the communities from which they are taken is often seen purely as an act of historical repair. In reality, though, it is not only the past of the museum that is in question but its presence and future. No longer a site of collection, it has yet to become another place – to find an identity, if you like, not predicated on its physical holdings of objects *belonging to other places*. The move to repatriate objects also stems from a sense that museums are dead places, not really places at all. That is, they no longer accommodate our collective memories as they used to. 'The Museum kills the vehemence of painting just as the library, as Sartre says, transforms writings which were once a man's gestures into messages. It is, Maurice Merleau-Ponty goes on, 'the historicity of death' (Merleau-Ponty, 1993, pp. 99, 100). In this context, the new mission of museums might be to *recollect* rather than to collect: not simply to recollect what has been repatriated (after all still a tiny proportion of its holdings) but to recollect the places from which the collections have come. While it is no longer ethically or politically feasible to add to anthropological and natural historical collections, these collections provide a unique introduction to the parts of the world from which they come. Therefore, they could be thought of as passages, symbolically mediating connections to, and between, other places. The role of the museum in fostering 'care at a distance' would seem to follow.

At the same time, museums and art galleries do not have a brief to engage in international environmental and social activism. Their role is to mediate the public circulation of symbolic forms. How might they marry this goal to the acquisition of a place-making conscience exercised 'at a distance'? The experience of *Nearamnew* at Federation Square suggests one possible answer. After the opening of Federation Square in late 2002, the National Gallery of Victoria decided to mount an exhibition about the making of the plaza artwork. This was a notable initiative because it showed an art museum prepared to extend its curatorial brief to the care of an art that could not be collected. The NGV not only wanted to recollect a work outside its doors but to soften the identification of the institution with a distinct territory. The significance of this, though, was that *Nearamnew* itself was a symbolic form shaped by the desire to recollect another place, Lake Tyrrell in the Mallee (itself invoked as a doubled place in which heaven and earth were mirrored). In other words, it would take only one further step and the NGV's commitment to curating *Nearamnew* would prove to be an act of symbolic environmental recollection – and this would, of course, be an act of place-making at Federation Square, one in which, in keeping with its new role, the museum recollected the culture of another place through an act of 'care at a distance'.

I hope this story of the provenance of the term 'care at a distance' is recognised as having an immediate relevance to our discussion. It places the problem of symbolic mediation at the forefront of our activities. How, that is, are places doubly constituted, both as sites of gathering and as places generating dissipation or movement outwards (towards, these days, circulation in the global imaginary)? It places this question here because it asserts the logical contradiction of any place-making discourse operating as if it did not itself take place. The places where it takes place are always the constructions – the recollections and projections – of other places. Margate is not simply a place-name, as the name of a kind of place that is constitutionally open to other places, it is the name of the principle of care at a distance. This principle can be characterised as ethical because it articulates the need for representations not predicated on conjuring up presences – whose illusionary plenitude masks, as we know, the actual disappearance of the world at large. It counters the push to enlighten the world with a recognition that its integrity depends on the management of degrees of withdrawal. Of course, the local is always spreading outwards, intermittently scintillating to the earth's furthest reaches, but it does so under the protection of distance – which, as Giacometti showed us, is the precondition of meeting, and therefore of place-making (Carter, 2002, p. 195).

The exercise of care at a distance changes the definition of places and the emphasis in place-making. It locates the beginning of places in the shuttle of movements towards and away, in a collectivity of comings and goings, and in the accumulating trace produced by these. Place-making comes to be understood in terms of creating the conditions of meeting, rather than as the provision of a theatrical backdrop to prescribed social activity. In this context care at a distance not only suggests new directions for our collecting institutions. It has applications in urban design. A recent invitation to become involved in the creation of a meeting place in Alice Springs illustrates this. The key supposition of my contribution was the point made earlier – that places are made after their stories. Just as place names describe complex, and conflicted, place-making aspirations, so with all marks associated with the marking of places: tracks, the symbolic representation of these in song, dance and poetic speech, indeed all the technologies that join up distances into narratives – they all inscribe the earth's surface with the forms of stories. Of course, these are not the same as the foundational myths of imperial cultures, whose aim is to displace any prior discourse of place-making. They are stories of, and as, journeys: passages in a double sense, constitutionally incomplete because they always await their completion in the act of crossing-over, or meeting, which, of course, is endless.

At a workshop in Alice, involving people representing black and white communities, and a range of interest groups, I tried to convey these notions in a simple form using a diagram, explaining:

> The upper ribbon represents Alice Springs' connection to the world. At the top the stars symbolise Alice's place in 'the global imaginary'. Alice has a unique iconic place in the collective Western imagination: it is the ideal 'centre' of Australia and a kind of Mecca for tourists in search of adventure. Many people who have never been to Alice 'visit' it via the internet. Underneath this global turn is the national and regional connection contemporary Alice makes to Australia through tourism; underneath this is the road system, an older communications initiative. And below and inside that is an image of camels. In this way the ribbon both spirals inwards towards Alice and backwards in time until, with an image of the telegraph wire, it plunges into the world of Alice Springs. The global ribbon shows us that Alice was, is and will be a place where the local, the regional and the global are connected. Further, they are uniquely connected by a story about communication, by a desire to connect at a distance.

The ground ribbon is also formed of five turns. It visualises the understandings of the Arrernte, and other central Australian Indigenous peoples, of place and place-making. It also spirals inwards towards the world of Alice. Creation stories are not only about the making of this visible landscape but about the universe; they generate the patterns that spiral inwards to enclose and shape us, and which have to be recreated in our own everyday rituals if a sustainable relationship between human and non-human worlds is to survive. These creative and recreative patterns take the forms of journeys: the Indigenous landscape is a network of tracks and meeting places. The communities that converge on Alice Springs come from many parts of the network. It is their place in that network that underpins their place in Alice Springs as guests of the traditional owners. At the same time, the community made in Alice Springs ultimately draws its meaning and authority from following the ground ribbon back to its ever-present origins in the spirit landscape. It is this landscape that grounds all communication and connects the local to the cosmic (Carter, 2007a).

I called the place-making proposal emerging from this summary of the discussions we had held 'Care at a Distance', again explaining: "'Care at a Distance' shows that the great stories of Indigenous and non-Indigenous culture uniquely meet in Alice Springs. This is because both are uniquely about the relationship between traveling and place-making, between communication and community. It is this relationship that the phrase 'care at a distance' tries to capture: *distance* is the precondition of communication, but communication is driven by a desire to *care* for what is far away. This reality shapes every facet of life in Alice today, a town, a place and a community that is constitutionally double, 'Care at a distance' expresses the double constitution of Alice Springs' unique and vibrant identity, and, as indicated earlier, the phrase not only applies generally but captures the genius of specific episodes in Alice's history" (Carter, 2007b). Obviously, the passages quoted are not couched in the language of cultural theory. Nor should they be. Their address is public, and responds to an occasion. They reflect the place occupied by the writer-consultant, invited into a discursive circle in the expectation that he has something to put on the table. The offering in this case takes the form of retelling a story, of transporting different threads of the collective discourse to a different place, one that is, it is hoped, interesting exactly because it emerges *inter esse*, in-between what already exist as well-marked tracks in the physical and psychic character of the place. The outsider is, in this special circumstance, a tracker who, in following the tracks of those who have gone before, allows himself to be tracked. In this way, through an act of recreative affiliation, the idea of care at a distance is to some degree embedded in the response.

These thoughts naturally lead to a reflection on the subject position of the one who comes from another place (as we all do). In my scenario, the museum is able to exercise care at a distance because it develops the capacity for recollection. Like T.S. Eliot's traveler, it learns that the 'end of all our exploring' is not the conquest of the known world but an education in self-knowledge, which takes the form of a kind of cultural homing in which we know the place where we started from for the first time. Recollection, unlike collection, is the pre-condition of invention, indeed it underpins innovations that are ethically-grounded. Again, the extension of the idea of care at a distance to Alice Springs presupposes a capacity in all the place-makers to see their stories in relation to one another, and to understand the differences between them poetically – as the ground that can be drawn together without destroying its distances *metaphorically* – figuratively, using symbolic narratives that keep in play structural and thematic analogies. In the play of these the outsider-insider dialectic is dissolved and replaced with a discursive environment in which all the participants are players, whose goal is to create and maintain a fabric of passages, or exchange-ways, held together by the prospect of meeting. What, though, in the individual can correspond to the new self definition of the museum or the amplified polyvocal discourse of a creative community? While the desire to affiliate is clear, what is the filiation that legitimates that desire? What is recollected on arrival? When the creative outsider sets about inserting themselves into the stories after which their adopted places are made, what criteria guide their advocacy of one set of symbolic correspondences over another? These are questions for place-makers of all kinds.

   To sketch a response to these issues, let me go back to my conversations with Christine Peacock. Here I should also mention Mary Graham, who discussed with me her community-based research program with the Aboriginal community organisation called Kummara – which emphasises, on the one hand, "the moral nature of physicality (especially land) and the need for relationality and interconnectedness with all life forces" and, on the other, the "dissension" usually caused "between community, clients, practitioners and experts" when "experts from outside the community [seek to] provide the theoretical understanding to solve social problems" (Graham, 2006, pp. 1–2). In the course of a conversation about parallels that can be traced between English Common Law and Indigenous understandings of land and land tenure, Christine asked me where I came from. Thinking about the pre-modern history of the countryside where I grew up in England, I referred to the Uffington White Horse, a possibly Bronze Age figure carved into a chalk escarpment, and connected in revivalist folklore with a nearby Neolithic long barrow known by its Danish name, Waylands Smithy. When Christine and Mary immediately identified the white horse with my 'dreaming', I was disconcerted. I feared I had misrepresented myself to them – these archaeological monuments were a corner of my childhood environment, but, in view of the apparent ease with which I – and our culture in general - had shrugged off any influence they might have had over our lives, it seemed like a parody of indigenous readings of country to invoke them, let alone to compare the lately revived folk tales associated with them with Indigenous creation stories underwriting the constitution of entire societies.

   It is this reaction I want to question. The first point to make is that their question has, of course, a particular inflection in modernity. Coming from somewhere else is perhaps the defining human experience as a result of the systemic disruption of pre-industrial societies due successively to the human transformations wrought by the rise of capitalism, the normalisation of imperialism, the technological triumph of quantification, and the annihilation of distance that these separately and in combination facilitate. The well-adjusted product of these processes is self-reliant, mobile and rootless. Internalising the notion that attachments of any kind represent a form of weakness or vulnerability, and that the ideal unit of production is one emancipated from all traditional obligations, heirs to modernity's dispensation seek to conceal their origins. The important thing is not to come from somewhere but to have successfully left it behind. In this powerful context of subjection to the poetics of living in the present, to be asked the question Where do you come from, or, more confrontingly, to be the victim of its corollary, Go back where you come from, is to be understood as a criticism of mal-adaptation. The one thus addressed has been caught out, their cosmopolitan pretence of belonging anywhere (and therefore here) unmasked. In any case, the point is that a culture like ours, illusorily globalising and in thrall to the notion of independence, can, when it comes to the question of origins, bear very little reality. Its particular aggression is reserved for those who insist on the ontological meaning of being migrant, who, like Ingeborg Bachmann's character, lives 'in flight' (Carter, 2008, pp. 276-277).

I am sure most here can transpose these remarks to their own lives. Spatial anomie of the kind described here is the other aspect of the objectification of places: if, as Bachmann's character does, we "lived amongst it all", we would not have to find out places where we can become ourselves. In any case, reflecting on the question addressed to me, it was evident from the context in which it was asked – and from the way in which my reply was interpreted – that the constructions I was placing on it were misplaced. The question bore a different inflection. When Christine asked me where I 'came from', she did not seek information about a place I had left behind. She wanted to know the place I had brought with me. Implicit in the question was a non-modern understanding of identity. Her question presupposed a relationship between motivation and country, and could have been recast as: what country propelled you here, allowed you to carry it everywhere you go, impressing itself on every life decision? Such a country is not a geographical unit but a kind of characterological *gestalt*, a psychic impression stamped in the mould of consciousness. Offering a perspective on the world, the experience of this spatio-temporal environment does not impose itself, but it provides the ground of every subsequent encounter. It softens, or comes between, the harsh opposition implied by the figure of 'doubling', with its threat of imminent collapse as copy and original struggle for pre-eminence. It allows for a dappled co-existence of levels and degrees of belonging, in which nearness and distance are both operative.

Writing about the processes through which Tjungkaya Napaltjarri (Linda Syddick) has gone in acquiring the right to tell her father's dreaming stories, anthropologist Fred Myers explains, "Persons literally come 'from' The Dreaming, from named places of ancestral potency; the relationship to these places is understood as central to a person's identity." (Myers, 2005, p. 172) Such places acquire their meaning through ritual and mythological practice – or active recollection. As Francesca Merlan puts it, "However absolute the 'dreaming' significance of places may seem, they were also always constituted ... within and through the range of practices which linked people with places." (cited in Myers, 2005, p. 172).

Merlan's observation is perhaps a familiar one – it can be legitimately extended to our everyday practices through which a phenomenological apprehension of the environment in which we live translates into a set of practices designed to secure and sustain it – thus improvising a *habitus* in Bourdieu's sense. But Myers is, I think, gesturing towards something more radical. Some foundational structuring of the world is taught us: it is not mystically bequeathed us by the accident of birth. It is not a Wordsworthian intuition of God in nature uniquely apprehended in childhood. We grow into it, are initiated into it. In principle, if not in cultural tradition, this place of ancestral potency could, for an explorer freed of T.S. Eliot's nostalgia for home, be the world at large. That is, the preposition *from* – which is cognate with the word *forward* – evokes a to-and-fro, a process of education, or leading out. The power of 'The Dreaming' is not that it constantly draws you back to a place but that it gives you a place from which you can go out. You come " 'from' The Dreaming", but the emphasis is on the origin of movement.

These reflections have interesting consequences for the way in which notions of place, identity and belonging are construed in Australia. The white myth of nation-making, for example, symbolically excludes anyone who arrived too late to be part of the foundations. In a sense, authority is possessed in direct proportion to the nearness of one's family to the legitimate members of the First Fleet. Despite the embrace of multiculturalism in the 1980s, the recrudescent nationalism of the present period underlines the accuracy of Adorno's dictum, that the émigré is acceptable on condition his past life is annulled (Hohendahl, 1995, p. iii). The inability of our culture to imagine, let alone commemorate, the presence here of other landscapes, communities and cultures, is not due to a lack of imagination, or the effect of a collective memory lapse: it is due to a discursive inadequacy, an incapacity to articulate the doubled identity that is inhabited by any (and perhaps all) of us who are conscious of coming from somewhere. Be that as it may, by putting this unspeakable other place firmly in the realm of discourse about the shared public space occupied here, some interesting inversions occur. For example, the definition of those who can claim to 'belong' here suddenly changes. It is no longer the imagined community of white Anglo-Celts that can lay claim to 'Australia'. As we, and they, know: because of the refusal to acknowledge the act of dispossession on which their ancestors' settlement was based, they remain uneasy and tentative in their behaviour towards the country. They cannot 'come from' here – at least from an Indigenous point of view – because they choose to be ignorant of this country's history.

On the other hand, though, they do not come from somewhere else, for they have made it an item of communal faith that, as an independent nation state, they are autochthonous. Logically, then, lacking spiritual authority here, they come from nowhere, and therefore can belong nowhere. In this situation, where 'coming from' has this positive sense of providing the psychological motivation of movement and therefore the precondition of arrival, it is the formerly marginalised migrant who suddenly possesses exceptional qualifications for belonging in Australia – precisely because they *do* come from somewhere else. Of course, Australia's white settlers did come from somewhere else (and continue to, culturally). I don't mean simply that they are descended from families many of which continue to have branches in Great Britain. I mean that ancestrally Australia's white settlers did, once upon a time, occupy named places of ancestral potency. Before the Enclosure Acts of the late 17th to mid-19th century alienated the great part of England's common land, ordinary folk in England held the land where they lived in common. Then, as Marcia Langton has pointed out, the conditions of land tenure structurally paralleled those under which Aboriginal people continue to lay claim to country. The cultural parallels between an agrarian society in the past and a hunter-gatherer one in the recent past should not be overstated. What is compelling, though, is a shared historical fate: it is the same capitalistically-fuelled alienation of common land that excluded the English peasantry that provided the ideological *raison d'etre* of Australian colonisation and rationalised the ruthless driving of Aboriginal people from *their* lands. Clinging to country, Indigenous people remind us of a fight for land rights we gave up generations ago.

Mary Graham addresses her discourse on a proposed Aboriginal Research methodology to the challenge of gaining acknowledgement within the Western legal system of Indigenous, place-based understandings of rights and obligations. I should insert here that 'place' in Graham's proposal is not our unstoried, nakedly surveyed geographical datum, but a *habitus* woven of stories, a discursive locus where belonging is figuratively defined and renewed. In any case, there is no reason why Graham's paradigm should not be extended to describe the conditions of belonging more generally. As she writes, "People flee from and flee to Place both physically and psychologically. Place is a reference point to guide to and from. Place is a physical point in the landscape, but also a point in time, an event, an imagining or even a landscape itself". But essential to places, to their constitution and maintenance is the movement they engender: as she says, "Multiple Places = Multiple Dreamings" (Graham, Mary, 2006, pp. 1–2) – and, it follows, multiple guides. In this case the experience of coming from another place – the acknowledgement of this – is a critical precondition of gaining lawful access to country here. Filiation and affiliation do not need to be opposed modes of belonging: understood as providing the ethical ground of passage – of life's journey as a whole – they serve to individualise one's location in the world, to generate places of strength when the forces of globalisation – which by the way now as in the colonial period feed on the commodification of places – do all in their power to eliminate such places.

Graham's remark that places are also 'points in time' – which is another way of talking about the character of meeting places – illuminates another aspect of my argument. Not only does a positive interpretation of coming from another place give migrants their place in the place-making, the spatial history, of Australia. It emancipates it from the modern myth of immortality, cognate with the notion of living in the eternal present. Migration, for example, is symbolically and emotionally associated with dying. It is classified in fiction and also in biography with mythological explanations of the cycle of the seasons, of which it can be considered a secular counterpart. But, if migration represents a voluntary or involuntary descent into the underworld, it also implies access to a special kind of knowledge. This is, in part, the knowledge of parting itself, the initiation into a doubled consciousness - the sense of being both here and there (and in-between). Generally, in Australian migrant narratives, the narrator adopts an abject speaking position, evoking passage in terms of irremediable loss and a more or less immaculate rebirth, but what happens when, taking heart from an Indigenous understanding of coming from, we see migrancy in terms of doubling rather than in terms of separating and dying, with their attendant senses of abjection, enslavement and withdrawal?

We speak of 'doubles' in relation to the departed. We make the dead present to ourselves by imagining them on a journey. In this sense, haven't migrants a privileged understanding of processes of departing? Do they not in a certain way stage the journeys of the ancestors, all of whom have departed only in order to stay where they belonged? Migrants will also possess this sense of a privileged access to the history of places and their making because they remember what later-comers have forgotten. Just as Italian TV comes to Brunswick in Melbourne to study regional dialects lost in Italy, so, for example, in going back to the country of my upbringing I can contribute to a process of recollection sharpened rather than weakened by many years of living in a new country. I am in touch with the dead there in a way that the living cannot be. This limitation on my capacity to affiliate to a country here is also my qualification for understanding what belonging here entails: bringing this knowledge of mortality, this impulse to recollect not only where I have come from but where my family, my ancestors have gone, I can perhaps understand better what Graham refers to as "the whole repertoire of what is possible continually present or ( ) expressed as an infinite range of Dreamings ... the *transformative dynamic of growth*" (Graham, Mary, 2006, p. 1–2). The logic of the Margate project becomes, in this light, all the more compelling: it is not about the repatriation of memory but about diplomacy, about finding the protocols for living in another's country and learning to belong there.

Wouldn't it be astonishing if we incorporated this strong sense of 'coming from' into the discourse of environmental caring? In our culture this means taking care of the places where one finds oneself. The entire drama of conservation therefore occurs at the termini of the life routes of the participants. But suppose that instead they were called upon to take care of the places from which they had travelled, migrated or fled. A post-national cosmopolitan regime of care at a distance would be installed, one rooting present decisions in the accumulated memories of past generations. You could imagine a lightly touched environment of shared memories and life paths, which claimed connection to places, without predicating this on property rights. It would be a genuinely postcolonial experience, one that transformed the meaning of 'globalisation' to comprehend the repatriation of identities in so far as they come from certain places: of course, it is the experience of the places to which one has come that influence the character of the spiritual return, and ensure that it is not a kind of earth fundamentalism or anti-modernism. But the result would be to give a serious, and constructive, ring to the jibe: 'Go back where you belong'. The extra-territorial citizenship engendered in this way, in which people (including those who stayed where they were born) enjoyed a double identity – with physical home and spiritual home, with a local community and a global community would be a bulwark against nationalism and its geographical isolationism.

From the point of view of the later comers, this exercise of care at a distance would provide a different perspective on the character of the place where they now live: coming into contact with the stories of the departed, they would be made aware not only of a past imagined in terms of generations of stably-located folk, but in terms of a history of comings and goings. They would be able to see in what is present the passages of those who left, and understand what is left not as a swarm of positivities but as a legacy of unsustainable practices, broken-off relations, failed enterprises and the inequitable distribution of resources. The prejudices against admitting these environmental revenants are deep-seated. After thirty years in the Mallee, the poet John Shaw Neilson left the area and worked for the remainder of his life in Footscray. But the biographers, critics and local historical societies pay no attention to this departure, instead treating him purely as a poet rooted in place. As a consequence the entire human achievement of recollection, the synthesis of experience and the discovery of its significance at another place is blotted out. I like to imagine Neilson as a man who imagined coming back – and when if ever he made that journey finding a land not as he saw it once but as he imagined it might be. These are also legitimate dimensions of place-making, and they stem from the concept of 'care at a distance'. Without the intrusion of the outsider, it is hard to see how the tight economy of functional relations promoted by the ecological sciences and by human sciences deriving from anthropology can place to hand a collective human mechanism for the management of change.

It occurs to me that these reflections are another form of the 'care at a distance' thesis. The sense of coming from not only locates you where you are and in relation to another place brought with you: the same propulsive logic explains why you might, in the future, find yourself in another place with a reason to be there. This argument obviously applies to the mobile history of Alice Springs. The newcomers do not come from nowhere, although this is the convention of anthropology, tourism and government. Nor do they come from anywhere: they are drawn to this place (let's say). In this are the beginnings of a basis for differentiating significant forms of arrival that are likely to reinforce a sense of local identity – because these encounters also link those who live at AS with places round the globe. (This is truly a cyber-geography and is a way to transpose that sense of culture shock suffered in flying from one country and culture to another into an ethically-responsible zone.) An example in my own experience: my attraction to the Mallee is almost coeval with my arrival in Australia. I do not have this sense of connection with mountainous or wooded places, but have felt that the combination of clarity and veiling which characterises the Mallee embodied a kind of destination for me, a site philosophically suited to resolving profound questions of dryness – in poetic language, in philosophical argumentation. In any case, an emotional projection has slowly condensed into journeys, writings and a network of associations: I have affiliated to that country though I neither originate there nor reside there. I exercise care at a distance, as I might for a place from which I have come; and if this exercise is possible it is not because I come from outside (as anyone might visit the region because of their technical expertise) but because I come from somewhere else.

REFERENCES

Artangel and Channel 4. (2006, September 30). *Exodus Day* (performance). Kent, UK: Margate.

Bourdieu, P. (1977). *Outline of a theory of practice* (R. Nice, Trans.). Cambridge, UK: Cambridge University Press.

Carter, P. (2008). *Dark writing: Geography, performance, design.* Honolulu, HI: University of Hawai'i Press.

Carter, P. (2007a, February). *Community consultation: Moving Alice ahead – Lifestyle.* Alice Springs, NT: CBD Revitalisation Project.

Carter, P. (2007b, March 15). *Care at a distance.* Material Thinking.

Carter, P. (2005, November). *The place of memory: Art museums, globalisation and cultural difference.* Paper delivered at the 'After Critique' symposium, Clark Art Institute, Williamstown, Mass.

Carter, P. (2002). *Repressed spaces: The poetics of agoraphobia.* London: Reaktion Books.

Graham, M., & Peacock, C. (2006). *Introduction to Kummara conceptual framework: A discourse on a proposed Aboriginal research methodology.* Stronger Indigenous Families Project, West End, QLD: Kummara Association. .

Hayles, N. K. (2006). Revealing and transforming: How literature revalues computational practice. *Performance Research, 11*(4), 5–16.

Hohendahl, P. U. (1995). *Theodor Adorno: Prismatic thought.* Lincoln & London: University of Nebraska Press.

Merleau-Ponty, M. (1993). Indirect language and the voices of silence (R. C. McCleary, Trans.). In G. A. Johnson (Ed.), *The Merleau-Ponty aesthetics reader* (pp. 76–120). Evanston, IL: Northwestern University Press.

Myers, F. (2005). Linda Syddick on longing. In M. J. Charlesworth, F. Dussart, & H. Morphy (Eds.), *Aboriginal religions in Australia: An anthology of recent writings* (pp. 171–184). Burlington, VT: Ashgate.

Paul Carter
Deakin University

SECTION I: CREATIVE PLACE MAKING

DORIS PATON AND LAURA BREARLEY

2. CO-CREATING A PLACE THAT LIES BETWEEN

Deep Listening Between Indigenous and Non-Indigenous Knowledge Systems

We are like the tree standing in the middle of a bushfire sweeping through the timber. The leaves are scorched and the tough bark is scarred and burnt, but inside the tree the sap is still flowing and under the ground the roots are still strong. Like that tree we have endured the flames and we still have the power to be re-born. Our people are used to the struggle and the long waiting. We still wait for the white people to understand us better. We ourselves have spent many years learning about the white man's ways; we have learned to speak the white man's language; we have listened to what he had to say. This learning and listening should go both ways.

Miriam Rose Ungunmerr 1999

DORIS' INTRODUCTION

Firstly I want to acknowledge my Ancestors of my Country and I want to acknowledge where I come from. My parents are both Elders and they have passed their knowledge on to me. My way of knowing comes from them. Looking out of the window now I can see the tarook on the lake. My Indigenous knowledge tells me that in the spring, it comes back green, and that's when you can pick the tarook.

When I look out the other window, I can see the wattles are in bloom and I know through my Indigenous knowledge from my parents and Ancestors that when the wattle is out, it's time to gather the eggs. That kind of knowledge wasn't privileged through my education process. My schooling experiences were non-Indigenous and I really only learned one way of thinking, doing and being.

In the doctoral research I am currently undertaking, I wanted to start with an Indigenous viewpoint. I have wanted to tell stories using the voice, epistemology and ontology of my being as an Indigenous person. I have looked for Indigenous researchers to support my journey and to help me to build my knowledge and understanding (Wilson 2004).

M. Somerville, K. Power and P. de Carteret (eds.),
Landscapes and Learning: Place Studies for a Global World, 37–52

Figure 1. Tarook.

Shall we sit together

And see what we might share?

Where is it we've come from

And what has brought us here?

Werna ninbar nalu

Il tackan nannane werna woor-dungin

Jillun werna back na ingga munga

Il nannane yara-bah tinkara?

DEEP AND RESPECTFUL LISTENING IN RESEARCH

We are part of a cross-institutional project called the Koori Cohort of Researchers. The Koori Cohort is a group of Indigenous artists and educators who are undertaking their Masters and PhDs. Koori is the generic name for Aboriginal people from the South East of Australia. The Koori Cohort has attracted a community of students and staff who are committed to exploring ways in which universities and Indigenous people can learn collaboratively. In our research, we are working with different kinds of text and forms of representation beyond the written word.

There is a concept which appears in many Aboriginal languages which describes a process of listening deeply in ways which build community. In the Ngungikurungkurr language it is called *Dadirri* (Ungunmerr 1999) and in Yorta Yorta, it is *Gulpa Ngawal* (Hamm 2008).

We use this concept as a research methodology and as a way of being together. It describes a way of listening and learning from each other in new ways. Deep and respectful listening lies at the heart of this approach to research. It is central to the process of building trust.

When applied as research methodology, Deep Listening provides an approach which facilitates a recognition of shared interests and concerns, as well as differences. In a Deep Listening methodology we learn from and with each other through the stories and experiences we share. "Stories are the way humans make sense of their worlds," writes Carolyn Ellis (2004, p. 32). They open the way for new meanings, questions and avenues of inquiry (Bochner & Ellis 2002).

What is it we look for

And what would make us whole?

What songs and stories

Live inside us all?

Nannane werna batha ma koote

Il nannane nulla glugan koote

Nannane wirnwirndook

Il nambur wandyin

Deep Listening changes people. Indigenous researcher Russell Bishop acknowledges the impact we have on each other in the research process,

> Simply telling stories as subjective voices is not adequate because it ignores the impact that the stories of the other research participants have on our stories. Instead (as researchers) we need to acknowledge our participatory connectedness with the other research participants and promote a sense of knowing in a way which denies distance and separation and promotes commitment and engagement (Bishop 1996, p. 23-24).

INDIGENOUS PERSPECTIVES IN RESEARCH

Shawn Wilson explored Indigenous methodology in his own doctoral research. In his thesis, he quotes another Indigenous methodologist Lester Rigney, "Indigenous people think and interpret the world and its realities in differing ways to non-Indigenous people because of their experiences, histories and culture" (Rigney in Wilson 2004, p. 8). In his research, Wilson used a qualitative research approach informed by the principles of Deep Listening (Dadirri), described by Judy Atkinson as an approach to research involving respect and checking your heart (Atkinson 2001). He drew on the concept of relational accountability which required him to form reciprocal and respectful relationships in the community where he was conducting research. His approach to data gathering followed proper community protocols for working with the community.

The ontological underpinning of my own approach is that the 'reality' of the Indigenous experience differs from that of those in other communities (Atkinson 2001). In my research I have had to look for other Indigenous voices. During this search, I found that the women of Peru were storytelling through quilting. I am a quilt maker too and in my PhD I have incorporated a methodology of using quilts to tell stories.

The making of quilts has created an opportunity for me to share stories in an engaging way. I could write a book but my family and my community relate better to a story represented on a quilt. They will not read a big, thick book so my quilt is an artifact for storytelling. I want to share stories with my community and my family in ways that will have an impact.

The site of my doctoral research is an Indigenous School known as Woolum Bellum, located in the regional town of Morwell in Gippsland, Victoria. For the first ten years of its establishment, the school flourished, with strong community support and culturally congruent curriculum. Sadly, in the last two years, the school has been in crisis and community members have been withdrawing their children from the school.

In my research, I have been working with research participants in the community to learn from this experience and to identify the enablers, barriers and critical success factors in creating sustainable learning environments for Indigenous children which encourage success and cultural understanding (Lawrence 1994).

If we listen deeply

And feel the trust begin

We could open up the doors

And let each other in

Werna wariga molla

Il mud-wud-gun gingin woonda

Nalu glurbety moolo

Il ya-wurn kinaway

Tier wootae nalu yail

PRINCIPLES OF RESEARCH

Through the course of my study, five principles have emerged as important for me as an Indigenous researcher. They are:
– Cultural ways of knowing
– Reciprocal and respectful relationships
– Talking circles as a place where everyone has a chance to speak
– Stories in conversation
– Community protocols

The five principles are central to who I am and are not separate to my ways of knowing and being. They are the ways of my parents, grandparents and Ancestors. They have provided guidance to all of our lives.

1. Cultural Ways of Knowing

Cultural ways of knowing are deeply embedded in my psyche. They lie at the core of the way I think, the way I look at the world and the way I live my life. My cultural ways of knowing have taught me how to listen deeply. My maternal grandmother used to tell us to "listen properly". She meant for us to not just hear what she was saying but to listen deeply and respectfully and to learn from what she said.

Cultural knowledge goes beyond the human and includes animals as well as the physical and spiritual worlds. It includes the sun, the moon, the mountains, the rivers and the sea. As I grow older these things grow stronger. I apply this knowledge to the world I live in and relate to it every day. I am sometimes torn between the two ways but I have learned to walk in two worlds and still remain true to myself.

In the development of my quilts I have wanted to share knowledge through culturally congruent ways of knowing. The quilts are the creative expression of knowledge and can be understood in different ways.

2. Reciprocal and Respectful Relationships

I acknowledge the guidance of our Ancestors and our old people who teach us how to live together, how to live with the land and to respect the physical and spiritual worlds we share. These ways have been passed on in stories through the generations. Our relationships with our children, our Elders and our community reflect our understanding of having respectful and reciprocal relationships with each other.

Russell Bishop (2005) discusses this relationship in *Kaupapa Maori* which means 'being and acting Maori' (2005, p. 114). He states that it is through the Kaupapa Maori approach to research that the researcher is in a participatory mode of consciousness in which they become part of the process. In my own experience, understanding the process of reciprocal and respectful relationships underpins my work as an Indigenous researcher. My approach to working with research participants, gathering data and representing my findings is predicated on having healthy relationships. To be congruent with my ways of knowing, I need to be connected and engaged with the people participating in my research.

3. Talking Circles

Talking Circles are the ways of our old people. They are a place where everyone can speak. Whilst they can be confronting for some, they provide equality. Respect and valuing the rights of others is a principle upon which Talking Circles operate.

41

In Talking Circles, language is spoken and unspoken. Deeply listening to each other encourages full discussion to flow. The core characteristics of Talking Circles are to show respect to each other and to avoid power struggles and domination of the discussion. Listening is done respectfully and properly, with everyone engaging in learning and discussion. Decision making is carried out in a consensual manner. This is the way we like to do business.

In my own research, data gathering is underpinned by the values of a Talking Circle and is embedded in the process of being in relationship with our Elders and the community. In the early days of the Woolum Bellum School, the Talking Circle provided a critical element in the planning and decision making processes of the school.

4. Stories in Conversation

Narratives are imbued with multiple meanings. Listening to the different voices within narratives is a culturally appropriate ontology for Indigenous people. Benham (2007) refers to Bakhtin (1986) who speaks of the power of the narrative to open up a space for voice where power, authority and representation can be heard, in particular the voices of the most vulnerable, those most often not heard. Benham says that fundamentally different from Western academic knowledge, most Indigenous ways of knowing define power to bring about change "not as individual power but as a sacred power passed on through story and ceremony. Indigenous narrative is not solely personal but is deeply communal" (2007, p. 519).

The stories in conversation are the tools for teaching and learning and are reinforced and passed on through the generations. In my family, we have a tradition that has been sustained for many generations. Each year, the great-grandparents, parents, children, grandchildren and great-grandchildren camp at Mystery Bay in NSW. It is a place of renewal of the spirit and restoration of the body for the year ahead. It is a place and space in our busy lives for all of us to practise storytelling, to share knowledge and to teach our ways of knowing to our future generations. This year four generations shared this time together.

At Mystery Bay my mother sleeps in a caravan and her great-granddaughter, like me, has learned from her mother about the *dooligah* (a little hairy man). She likes the little caravan that her great-grandmother sleeps in. On one of her many visits to the caravan, she told her great-grandmother that she had better close the curtains because the dooligah could see in and might come and get her. While she was there she learned that the dooligah lives in the mountain behind where we camp. She has learned through the stories the ways of our old people in discouraging children to wander off alone, just as her mother did and all those who have gone before us.

In my research, the stories in the quilts have multiple layers and allow the community to have a visual representation of the content of the research. Representing narratives of the school in the quilts provides an opportunity for the sharing of knowledge with community through conversation and discussions.

5. Community Protocols

Understanding community protocols is critical to getting things done. Knowledge of how the community will behave in certain circumstances and conditions is central to having respect for knowing the right way to behave and to respond. It also helps in understanding why the community may behave in a particular way. For example, 'talking with their feet', or saying 'yes' to avoid being pressured into agreeing to do something or not wanting to be hurried into making a decision. It is important to respect people for their knowledge, to understand community responses and to follow proper consultation processes.

My involvement and commitment to the Woolum Bellum School is well known across the community and the time and effort I give is acknowledged. In my research, this has assisted me in engaging the community to talk about the school. The community knows who I am and where I am coming from. They know that I am knowledgeable in community ways.

Deep listening, being part of the community and learning the ways of relating to the community help get things done. We look at everything in an inter-related and inter-connected way. We don't see things in isolation, which is sometimes why it takes us a long time to make decisions and why we sit and think sometimes rather than speak.

When I began the research, I knew that I would have to find a way to try and make someone understand where I was going and where I was coming from and for me the Koori Cohort has provided that space. It has given me the opportunity to put that knowledge into that environment and to be supported to do it.

QUILT-MAKING AS A SITE FOR STORY-TELLING

Having a place in the Koori Cohort of Researchers has enabled me to be true to my ways of knowing. It has provided me with the opportunity to tell the stories in a way that the community can share. It is important to me as an Indigenous researcher to share stories in ways which are culturally relevant and useful for learning. The quilts I am making as part of my research are a visual representation of stories grounded in knowledge.

In my research I am telling stories of the Woolum Bellum School through three quilts:

Quilt Number One   Indigenous Knowledge: Foundation of the School

This quilt represents a visual story of Indigenous ways of knowing about country, in the physical and spiritual world. The knowledge given to us by our Ancestors as custodians is passed on through story and ceremony. The relationship of the land and its people is told through the generations. This knowledge provides us with laws for living, for relationships, for healing, dance and song. This knowledge is shared in this quilt for the benefit of the community.

Quilt Number Two   Unmasking the Issues

This quilt represents the journey for the Woolum Bellum School thus far. The original vision of the school was to create a place of learning that acknowledged Indigenous ways of knowing and strengthened our individual and collective identities. There are positive stories from the Woolum Bellum experience but the current internal and external struggles are threatening its future. These issues have created many cracks within and outside of the school; power plays, a dismissal of Indigenous knowledge; a pretence by the system to listen.

Quilt Number Three   Listening Properly: Indigenous Voices in Education

This quilt represents the place for Indigenous ways of knowing in learning. It reflects the many dimensions of what is needed to make the school a success for the children, including factors such as the environment, management, curriculum, community support and understanding. The Woolum Bellum School has the potential to be a place that achieves change for Indigenous students, strengthening and reinforcing identity. It can help students achieve success and transform their lives. Other schools, the education system and the community can all benefit from a school that makes a difference.

THE STORY OF THE QUILT: INDIGENOUS KNOWLEDGE: FOUNDATION
OF THE SCHOOL

This quilt is about Indigenous knowledge. I have made the quilt as a way of sharing knowledge in a visual form. It brings Country to people and people to Country.

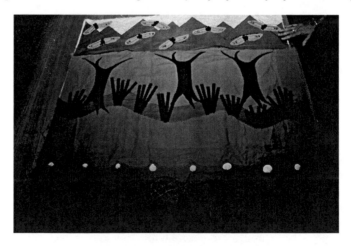

Figure 2. Woolum Bellum School quilt.

The quilt tells the story of the philosophy behind the Woolum Bellum School. In this quilt, I want to incorporate Indigenous knowledge because that has been so important to the development of the Woolum Bellum School. The School has given us an opportunity to share cultural knowledge with Koori kids.

I always remember when we were first asked if we wanted to put in an Expression of Interest for the School. We recognised that mainstream schooling was not servicing our kids' cultural needs and sense of identity. We saw it as an opportunity to bring back cultural knowledge and Indigenous family values into a learning environment. We also saw it as a way of reviving language and cultural knowledge and having ownership of how that knowledge was shared.

A key strategy we used in doing this was the development of the Bataluk Trail and curriculum. We went through a process of getting permission for the Bataluk Trail with the community and developing curriculum around the sites of significance on the Trail. This included the Lake Tyers Mission, The Nob Reserve and the Morwell Wetlands with its bush food, birds and plants. We developed a curriculum around language, stories and local history. It built up a lot of knowledge that these kids would never have got in mainstream schools.

DESIGN OF THE QUILT

The design of this quilt did not come easily. It is different from other quilts I have made which have been designed with particular people in mind. This quilt is a bit about me and that can be hard to represent. It requires me to ask myself what I stand for, what is important and what the quilt means.

The knowledge of how people survived on Country and passed on that knowledge to others comes from my own family. I wanted the quilt to represent that knowledge. This knowledge has been passed on in the development of the curriculum at Woolum Bellum to provide a culturally relevant learning for our Koori kids. What is represented on this quilt reminds me of one the places I take people to show them knowledge. It has trees and a creek and is called the Nob Reserve. It is like a classroom of knowledge.

Figure 3. My mother's representation of the Bogong Moths.

My mother (Aunty Rachel Mullett) has both Gunnai and Ngaraga knowledge. Her images of the Bogong Moths are my inspiration for using the moths in this quilt.

The Gunnai people used to go up to the mountains and feast on the Bogong Moths. People travelled to the mountains and feasted on the Bogong Moths for three months of the year and traded. They shared knowledge and exchanged artifacts and wives.

The scarred trees on the quilt represent the shields and canoes that came from the trees. They symbolise the knowledge about how those things were used on Country and what was important for living on Country. The trees represent the knowledge about living on Country and the making of artifacts such as coolamons which were used for carrying water and for gathering food.

The canoes were used on the Gippsland Lakes to gather swan eggs and to help people to fish and to move from place to place. The trees were also used in making the fishing nets.

The creeks and the rivers provided an important source of food for my people. The grasses represent the Cumbudgee or the Tarook which was a significant plant and used for many purposes. The quilt shows the fish in the lakes and the sea. The fish were trapped by using the string from the trees. The fishhooks were made by the women from kangaroo bones.

Figure 4. My representation of the Bogong Moths on the quilt.

Figure 5. The middle tree on the design of the quilt is the Canoe Tree.

Figure 6. Fish detail from quilt.

Figure 7. Bush food – Women's knowledge.

Figure 8. Bogong Moth detail.

The shells represent the seafood that was eaten along the coastline. The shells represent the importance of the water and the seafood that came from the water.

Knowledge has been passed on to me that I feel I can represent in the quilt. It shows men's knowledge as well as women's knowledge. The bark canoes were used by both men and women for fishing. The coolamons in the trees were used by women. Both the men and the women went up the mountains.

Figure 9. Edging detail.

The gathering of the bush food is mostly women's knowledge so that is probably more about me.

The inspiration for the stitching on the white material has come from the work of my brother who has passed on. He was a significant artist.

The designs that are around the edge of the quilt represent the male and the female.

SHARING CULTURAL KNOWLEDGE

This is the level of knowledge that I generally share with people. There is another level of knowledge that I do not share because it has not yet been permitted for me to do so.

Both my parents are Elders and the knowledge has been passed on through my grandparents. I am still learning. While I am learning I am being trusted. This knowledge is something I have been learning since I was little but it has developed much more strongly as I have got older.

For me to be able to pass knowledge on and share it with the kids and adults of this community is very important work for me to do. I have been privileged to learn it and it is a privilege to pass it on. I take it seriously. It is also a huge responsibility.

How much longer must we wait?

To recognise and co-create

A space between where we connect

In understanding and respect

Wunman wragliman werna targut

Jillianga kalanganinga il gallamda

Nindethana quarenook booth

Nguttay il woonda

The Elders do not give you knowledge if they do not trust you with it. I have seen people come up to Elders and say "Tell me about this" but they choose not to. You have to wait. It's all about waiting and listening and if you miss it they may not say it again. It's about sitting, listening, waiting and making sure that you remember. They expect you to listen the first time.

I'm getting older now and I am a grandmother. It is important for me to pass on knowledge on to my children and grandchildren. They are wanting to know more now. They are ready for it because they have grown up with it.

MAKING A DIFFERENCE THROUGH RESPECTFUL RELATIONSHIPS

Indigenous scholars George Sefa Dei, Buff Hall and Dorothy Rosenberg (2000) write that those of us who "wish to work with, learn from, and interact with Indigenous knowledges while based in dominant institutions must transform our way of understanding knowledge, learning and teaching ... Indigenous knowledges are not learned in isolation from the Earth or from other people" (p.7). They argue that we need to recognise that "knowledge is produced and acquired through collaborative processes" and that "no individual, group, community, or nation can justifiably claim ownership of all knowledge" (p.3). In this approach to research, there is a valuing of story-telling and listening and a recognition of the importance of family and community dialogue (Bishop 1998; Collins 1990).

Non-Indigenous researcher and autoethnographer, Carolyn Ellis, holds a similar view about the importance and value of story-telling in research. "Stories are the way humans make sense of their worlds" she writes, (Ellis 2004, p. 32). She poses key questions about the use of stories in research, "Does the story help others cope with or better understand their worlds? Is it useful, and if so, for whom? Does it promote dialogue? Does it have the potential to stimulate social action?" (Ellis 2000, p. 275).

We share an interest in telling stories which make a difference.

This space in the Cohort is a ripple and the opportunity for other community members to be drawn into the ripples echoes loudly across the waters. There are many Indigenous researchers emerging and finding the space to be true to themselves. Lester Irabinna Rigney (1997) proclaimed his methodology as 'indigenist research', making the Indigenous researcher responsible to the Indigenous communities and their struggle. In doing so, it is research which gives voice to Indigenous people.

In the work we are doing in the Koori Cohort of Researchers, we are working together in ways in which an "ethic of care is paramount" (Denzin 2003, p. 122) and where we can make a difference through our relationships, as described by Heshusius,

> We need to move from an alienated mode of consciousness that sees the knower as separate from the known to a participatory mode of consciousness. Such a mode of consciousness addresses a fundamental reordering of understandings of relationship between self and other (and therefore of reality), and indeed between self and the world, in a manner where such reordering not only includes connectedness but necessitates letting go of the focus of self (Heshusius 1994 in Bishop 2005, p. 15).

In our work together, we are co-creating a place that lies between Indigenous and non-Indigenous knowledge systems, as described by the Indigenous researcher Leilani Holmes,

Some of us will need to find a space 'in between' where both the knowledge of our Elders and the knowledge of our colleagues or professors may enter, live and be voiced (Holmes 2000, p. 50).

Norman Denzin and Yvonna Lincoln (2005) describe the development of research through a framework of eight overlapping 'moments'. What Denzin and Lincoln call moments are the appearance of new sensibilities, times when qualitative researchers become aware of new issues. "Moments are appearances of new sensibilities, ruptures in the fabric of our own histories, in which we are irrevocably changed." (Denzin & Lincoln 2005, p. 1116). The moments overlap and simultaneously operate in the present.

Denzin and Lincoln contend that we are in a moment of discovery and rediscovery in which "new ways of looking, interpreting, arguing and writing" are being debated and discussed (2005, p. 20). This approach to research incorporates new kinds of text which do not simply describe but which make a difference. It criticises how things are and imagines how they could be different. The idea of making a difference through respectful relationships is, in our experience, the key to the work needing to be done to co-create a place where we can work together in sustainable and sustaining ways.

When we listen deeply

And feel the trust begin

We can open up the doors

And let each other in

Werna wariga molla

Il mud-wud-gun gingin woonda

Nalu glurbety moolo

Il ya-wurn kinaway

Tier wootae nalu yail

The Deep Listening Song   *Molla Wariga Wirnwirndook*

Music/Lyrics   Laura Brearley
Gunnai translation   Aunty Doris Paton

Shall we sit together
And see what we might share?
Where is it we've come from
And what has brought us here?

Werna ninbar nalu
Il tackan nannane werna woor-dungin
Jillun werna back na ingga munga
Il nannane yara-bah tinkara?

What is it we look for
And what would make us whole?
What songs and stories
Live inside us all?

Nannane werna batha ma koote
Il nannane nulla glugan koote
Nannane wirnwirndook
Il nambur wandyin

If we listen deeply
And feel the trust begin
We could open up the doors
And let each other in

Werna wariga molla
Il mud-wud-gun gingin woonda
Nalu glurbety moolo
Il ya-wurn kinaway
Tier wootae nalu yail

How much longer must we wait?
To recognise and co-create
A space between where we connect
In understanding and respect

Wunman wragliman werna targut
Jillianga kalanganinga il gallamda
Nindethana quarenook booth
Nguttay il woonda

When we listen deeply
And feel the trust begin
We can open up the doors
And let each other in

Werna wariga molla
Il mud-wud-gun gingin woonda
Nalu glurbety moolo
Il ya-wurn kinaway
Tier wootae nalu yail

Vowel Key
O is o as in orange
A is a as in father
I is i as in ink
E is e as in learn
OO is oo as in look
U can be oo or u as in gunnai

REFERENCES

Atkinson, J. (2001). *Privileging Indigenous research methodologies.* Paper presented at the National Indigenous Researchers Forum, University of Melbourne.

Bakhtin, M. M. (1986). *Speech genres and other late essays.* Austin, TX: University of Texas Press.

Benham, M. K. P. (2007). Mo'o lelo: On culturally relevant story making from an Indigenous perspective. In D. Jean Clandinin (Ed.), *Handbook of narrative inquiry: Mapping a methodology* (pp. 512–533). Thousand Oaks, CA: SAGE Publications.

Bishop, R. (1996). *Collaborative research stories: Whakawhanaungatanga.* Palmerston North, NZ: Dunmore Press.

Bishop, R. (1998). Freeing ourselves from neo-colonial domination in research: A Maori approach to creating knowledge. *International Journal of Qualitative Studies in Education, 11*(2), 199–219.

Bishop, R. (2005). Freeing ourselves from neo-colonial domination in research: A Kaupapa Maori approach to creating knowledge. In N. Denzin & Y. Lincoln (Eds.), *The SAGE handbook of qualitative research* (3rd ed., pp. 109–138). Thousand Oaks, CA: SAGE Publications.

Bochner, A., & Ellis, C. (2002). *Ethnographically speaking: Autoethnography, literature and aesthetics.* Walnut Creek, CA: AltaMira Press.

Collins, P. H. (1990). *Black feminist thought: Knowledge consciousness and the politics of empowerment.* New York: Routledge, Chapman and Hall.

Denzin, N. K. (2003). *Performance ethnography: Critical pedagogy and the politics of culture.* Thousand Oaks, CA: SAGE Publications.

Denzin, N. K., & Lincoln, Y. S. (Eds.). (2005). *The SAGE handbook of qualitative research* (3rd ed.). Thousand Oaks, CA: SAGE Publications.

Ellis, C. (2000). Creating criteria: An ethnographic short story. *Qualitative Inquiry, 6*(2), 273–277.

Ellis, C. (2004). *The ethnographic I: A methodological novel about autoethnography.* Walnut Creek, CA: AltaMira Press.

Hamm, T. (2008). *Reconnecting with family: Exploring individual and community stories of Aboriginal identity through narrative and artwork.* PhD Thesis, RMIT University, Melbourne.

Heshusius, L. (1994). Freeing ourselves from objectivity: Managing subjectivity or turning toward a participatory mode of consciousness? *Educational Researcher, 23*(3), 15–22.

Holmes, L. (2000). Heart knowledge, blood memory, and the voice of the land: Implications of research among Hawaiian elders. In G. Sefa Dei, B. Hall, & D. Rosenberg (Eds.), *Indigenous knowledges in global contexts.* Canada: University of Toronto Press.

Lawrence, H. (1994). Aboriginal children in urban schools. In Issues, *Educational Research, 4*(1), 19–26.

Rigney, L. (1997). Internationalisation of an Indigenous anti-colonial cultural critique of research methodologies: A guide to Indigenist research methodology and its principles. Paper presented at the HERDSA Annual International Conference: Adelaide, South Australia.

Rigney, L. (2004). In S. Wilson (Ed.), *Research as ceremony: Articulating an Indigenous research paradigm.* Unpublished Doctoral Thesis, Monash University, Australia.

Sefa Dei, G. (2000). African development: The relevance and implications of 'Indigenousness'. In G. Sefa Dei, B. Hall, & D. Rosenberg (Eds.), *Indigenous knowledges in global contexts.* Canada: University of Toronto Press.

Sefa Dei, G., Hall, B., & Rosenberg, D. (Eds.). (2000). *Indigenous knowledges in global contexts.* Canada: University of Toronto Press.

Ungunmerr, M. R., & Isaacs, J. (1999). *Spirit country: Contemporary Australian Aboriginal art.* San Francisco: Hardie Grant Books.

Wilson, S. (2004). *Research as ceremony: Articulating an Indigenous research paradigm.* Unpublished Doctoral Thesis, Monash University, Australia.

Laura Brearley
Monash University
Doris Paton
Terry Melvin (Photography)

KATRINA SCHLUNKE

3. POSSESSION ISLAND

Pedagogies of 'Possessed' Place

POSSESSION ISLAND

Let me begin, not with Possession Island but with another island. An island that isn't an island anymore. An island right in the heart of Sydney, a mere five minutes by ferry from the Opera House, that is also a naval base and a museum, joined to the mainland now by an artificial isthmus. It's here that one Captain Cook died. In Australia, if you want to know about place you have to know about people and if you want to know about white people, you have to know about Captain Cook.

ANOTHER ISLAND (GARDEN ISLAND)

There is more than one story of Cook and some of them are known as the Cook sagas that come from northern and central Australia via their tellers, Paddy Wainburranga, Joli Laiwonga, Hobbles Danaiyairi and others on behalf of the Rembarrgna, Ngalkgun and Yarralin peoples through the recordings and dissemination by Chips Mackinolty, Penny Macdonald and Deborah Bird-Rose (Bird-Rose, 1984; Mackinolty & Wainburranga, 1988, pp. 355-360; McDonald, 1989). These different stories tell many nuanced accounts of Cook but most have some idea of two laws: Cook's law; oppressive, unprincipled and immoral and the true or Dreaming law that is based upon and assumes Indigenous ownership of land. In the telling of these sagas, numerous white figures - missionaries, pastoralists and Protection Officers - appear as Cook figures, continuing his law. In this sense Cook is not understood to be dead but very much alive in the form of all his followers who continue to "make themselves strong" (Bird-Rose, 1984, p. 35) through the exploitation of Indigenous labour, land, minerals and knowledge. This sense of Cook as a process of perpetual reproduction without difference obviously differs to so many historical efforts to freeze Cook in a particular moment, to insist he is dead when he continues in Australia to be highly productive, very much alive.

Perhaps the best known of the Cook sagas is that told by Paddy Wainburranga and Joli Laiwonga which was titled by Chips Mackinolty as 'Too Many Captain Cooks'. This saga begins with the good Cook from Mosquito Island (another tiny island, just off the big mainland of New Guinea on Milne Bay) who travels all about the place with his two wives and who knew not to interfere. He came to Sydney Harbour to build his boat and he made Sydney Harbour but not Sydney

M. Somerville, K. Power and P. de Carteret (eds.),
Landscapes and Learning: Place Studies for a Global World, 53–63

Harbour Bridge, just a "blackfella bridge out of planks first time" (Mackinolty & Wainburranga, 1988, p. 357). The devil lived on the other side of the Harbour and was able to start seducing Cook's two wives because Cook was always working. The devil who was also Satan got the two wives to help hide him so he could kill Cook and take the wives away. Cook and Satan eventually fight hand to hand and Cook kills the devil and throws him into a hole, the hole we now know as the Cahill Expressway. That was temptation defeated. Cook then went back to Mosquito Island but something happened and Cook was speared by his relations so he came back down to Sydney Harbour where he died of his wounds and was buried on the island which is known as Garden Island. It was on Garden Island that the then Prime Minister John Howard met the America President George Bush in 2007 because it could guarantee the highest level of security. It is to the Captain Cook Graving Dock within Garden Island naval base that the ships that defend Australian territory are sent to be repaired and restored so that Australia cannot be invaded by sea - again. At the Naval Base entrance the signs says: "It is a condition of entry to these premises that all persons present, upon request, any vehicle, bag, briefcase, or other container for security inspection on entering and leaving the island".[1] On the other side of the island you may land by ferry and walk along a small, fenced section of the shore and visit the museum outside the official gates. It is said the first tennis court in Australia was built here.

After this old Captain Cook came all the new Captain Cooks. As Wainburranga puts it (Mackinolty & Wainburranga, 1988, p. 359):

> They just went after the women. All the New Captain Cooks fought the people. They shot people. The New Captain Cook people, not old Captain Cook. He's dead. He didn't interfere and make a war.

> That last war and the second war. They fought us. And then they made a new thing called 'welfare'...

> They wanted to take all Australia.

> They wanted it, they wanted the whole lot of this country. All the new people wanted anything they could get. They could marry black women or white women.

> They could shoot people.

> New Captain Cook mob!

You hear in Paddy Wainburranga's acute legal diagnosis, his epic poem, the expansive scale of the destruction that was wrought. This is a myth of good and bad Cooks where the bad Cooks are still on the loose, only lessened by each act of restoring culture. The great power of Wainburranga's story is that he articulates the possessive force of the new Cooks. A force that maps and names but also shoots and legalises – literally transforming through a possessive rite one thing into another – the east coast of New Holland into Australia, a silencing into a discovery, the presence of people into an absence. All the weird magic of colonialism, all that giving into the temptation to possess this place.

THE COMFORT OF POSSESSION

In 2007 the Belvoir Theatre Company put on a play called 'Toy Symphony' written by Michael Gow (2008) and in it the main character Roland is suffering, perhaps some lifelong distress about what is real and what is writing and he is asked by his therapist to remember a moment when he was perfectly comfortable, joyful, open. He remembers a scene (which comes to life on the stage) from his primary school at Como within The Shire (this is the Sutherland Shire which includes Botany Bay where Cook landed in 1770 and also Cronulla site of the beach 'race riots' in 2005). In this scene his richly voiced third grade teacher stands behind the earliest version of the overhead projector and shows slides of the history of Como. This history begins with Captain Cook who after observing the transit of Venus came to explore the east coast thus paving the way for the founding of Como. The palpable pleasure the small boy feels in the semi dark, with the soothing rattle of plastic overheads and his perfectly reliable primary school teacher recounting, again, how his world, his known place has come into being. And we know it is an 'again' because the boy keeps bursting across her listing, possessed by knowledge: "And Cook went to observe the.." she says and is over-shouted by the excited boy ending her sentences "TRANSIT OF VENUS", and she goes on "he came on to" and the boy again; "BOTANY BAY, BOTANY BAY" and the teacher goes calmly on (Gow, 2008, p. 14). She hears his excitement, she knows he knows and she continues quietly, repeatedly, comforting him with Cook.

TAKING POSSESSION

In Australia, possession as named by Cook is marked by an island, a place; Possession Island. This is the island where Cook reported he carried out the following:

> Notwithstand I had in the Name of his Majesty taken posession of several places upon this coast I now once more hoisted English Coulers and in the Name of His Majesty King George the Third took posession of the whole Eastern Coast from the above Latitude down to this place by the Name of New South (Wales written in above) together with all the Bays, Harbours Rivers and Islands situate upon the same (*crossed out and said inserted*) said coast after which we fired three Volleys of small Arms which were Answerd by the like number by (*by crossed out and from inserted*) from the Ship[2] (National Library of Australia, 2008a).

Everything is claimed, even the harbours like Sydney that he hasn't seen and the rivers, the bays and all the islands. There is a pre-echo of Wainburranga's rhetoric here. Taking women, marrying anyone, shooting, wanting anything they could get, rivers, bays, harbours and islands. Was Cook comforted by this expansionist rhetoric? Finally, had he done enough? This tiny island, just off the tip of Cape York bears a huge representational burden. The seeming irony of an island as Carter pursues and displays with his italics. *An island* symbolically securing a whole coast and so eventually a continent. An island! But as Carter goes on to explain for Cook this island was not peripheral to his navigational journey but "stood as a symbolic centre, a jewel crowning his outline of names" (Carter, 1987, p. 27). And it was here Cook 'took' possession, here that in the taking of possession recognised that possession was already in the hands of others.

Possession seems never to have been an easy word. It seems always to have held within itself ideas of violence, settlement and transfiguration. Cook 'possessed' various islands and 'situations' in his voyages in the name of the King but the most usual use of the word in his journal was to designate items of property. These items of property in turn often appeared in relation to stories of finding bits and pieces from his ship or crew in the hands of Indigenous peoples. That is, Cook bought not only possession but also theft, for how else could he insist that property existed unless it has the possibility of being given to, sold or taken by others? This originating, expansive word is then taken to island. Possession Island. Island with its seeming isolation, island in its separation from land by sea. But islands are also doubled movements as they are created and contained within the sea. As Deleuze tells us, "geographers say there are two kinds of islands". These two kinds of islands are the continental and the oceanic. "The oceanic form from coral reefs and underwater eruptions and the continental are separated from a continent, born of disarticulation, erosion, fracture; they survive the absorption of what once contained them". Possession Island is continental. The oceanic island reminds us that the earth is still there, alive, active, erupting. The continental island reminds us that "the sea is on top of the earth". "Humans cannot live, nor live in security, unless they assume that the active struggle between earth and water is over, or at least contained". So "that an island is deserted", Deleuze (2004, p. 9) argues, "must appear *philosophically* normal to us". Islands *should* deter people.

To come onto Possession Island is to find what white possession has done in its writing over of its earlier namings as Bedanug and Tuidin. Here there is active deterrence. A set of prohibitive symbols beneath the legend: Possession Island National Park - no shooting, no dogs, no fires –watch out for crocodiles. Each warning insisting that the island be uninhabitable. Without a gun no larger mammals or reptiles to eat, without a dog no friend to please, without a fire no cooking of food and no way of warning the crocodiles to stay away. So no traditional practices are to occur here, no official reconnection of this island with its neighbours and peoples. But these signs are also a warning to the white escapee for they forbid exactly the things Robinson Crusoe had, dog (remember he even had cats), guns and fire. That bourgeois Crusoe, still needing his wrecked ship as a bank of tools to render his island habitable, that Crusoe as Deleuze notes who should have been eaten by Friday. These signs insist that officially only the perpetual re-enactment of Cook's path will be allowed. Officially we must only come across for a moment, confirm where we are by looking and re-confirm the island's importance in relation to Cook's navigational trajectory, to the mainland, to the whole of Australia, right to this very point beyond the tip - as possessed. And these re-enactments do occur in the helicopter flights from Horn Island that deliver people to the tip of Cape York, land them there to enable them to add one more stone to the cairn and on the way back buzz the Cook monument – that thing beyond all land, the possessor of Possession Island. But what is official up here? What vehicle could stop any night time camp fires when the tide has gone right out and the rocks ring us? Who will know if a turtle is taken or crab collected or oysters eaten? In this place local knowledge makes ordinary all those European fantasies of the self producing island cornucopia.

What does it mean that this island seems to have at least two other names; Bedang and Tuidin? Perhaps one from the mainland peoples and one from the island peoples? What kind of name does that make "Possession"? A third place name? As Moreton-Robinson puts it so succinctly in her introduction to 'The House that Jack Built: Britishness and White Possession' (Moreton-Robinson, 2005), the right to take possession was embedded in British and international common law and rationalised through a discourse of civilisation that supported war, physical occupation and the will and desire to possess. Underpinning property rights, possession entails values, beliefs, norms and social conventions, as well as legal protection, as it operates ideologically, discursively and materially. Property rights are derived from the Crown which in the form of the nations-state holds possession. We make as we take 'possession'.

But the kind of white possessiveness that Moreton-Robinson sees people being encouraged to invest in is, up here, ambiguous at best. To be white on Possession Island would be to starve. To constantly be calling up the importance of Cook in this place would put you against the reality of an almost complete area of native title. To think of ideas of discovery as foundational would be to deny not only what you would see day after day but what you would feel as a minority group, as 'European' here. Non-Indigenous Australians practice possession – we walk, talk, buy and sell within possession. But the actual naming of an island, naming something that is meant to be natural, intrinsic – throws too sharply into relief its shadow. It reminds us how far from Perth, from Melbourne, from here, from there was Cook's path. How did this small island make all of Australia a British possession and then a possessive nation?

ISLANDS OF THE MIND

This island might also be the real. It might be that which cannot be seen except in difficult, fraught glimpses—it may be the "impossible" of Jacques Lacan that does not belong to the wishful nor to the unconscious and yet pulls those constructions toward it. It has the force of existence. At first reading, the island is simply the national unconscious and needs to be properly interrogated as such. Cook used language to bring forth his place as a named certainty and at that point gave white Australia an unconscious. This is the "chapter of (our) history marked by a blank or occupied by a falsehood" (Lacan, 1977, p. 125). But as Lacan suggests of the individual, the truth can be rediscovered, for it will be written down elsewhere, in monuments, archives, traditions, and the traces preserved by the necessary distortions to keep the falsehood alive. The trace that lies in the act itself "took" possession when possession was itself taken from another. The archive shows us Cook knew the land belonged to others as "we" (the white nation) still know it.

Through this naming, this "languaging," the nation is granted something like an unconscious (the distorting falsehood) that leads to the national need to confirm our "reality" of possession. This is a daily, naturalised practice, the ordinariness of which belies the uncontrolled, unlawful things it is. A part of the ordinary confirmation of possession is the concomitant domination of the white human over plant, animal, sea, and sky through the language that defers an ultimate meaning and orders our knowing into an us and other through the naming of place. This island is simultaneously a confirmation and a question: Why possess if we already possess? So mostly we disappear this place. For this is a fight against truth, against the censoring of the unconscious, and so the island does not appear—not on our daily national weather maps nor on most maps of Australia nor in our consciousness— a reality beyond navigation, a symbolic centre of nation/home that we will not see, or more accurately we see and forget, see and forget. Possession Island is a naming that could reveal the very structure of colonial language and cease the hysterical symptoms of obsessive ownerships and reenactments that maintain the national mythology of total possession. This is the legacy of Cook—a national unconscious— and an unconscious both names and forgets. And names because it fears that it might forget. But something that Cook brought is not all the island is. It is also itself. A being outside, beyond, and before Cook's claim. How to write that?

GOING TO THE ISLAND

Possession Island began on Horn Island (the airport island of the Torres Strait) at 2 am when Susan turned the light on to check the time, then at 3:40 am when I woke for no reason. Perhaps it was the drone of the air conditioner keeping us awake; in the middle of winter we were still needing air conditioning like the thin skinned southerners we are. And then at 5 am we woke up properly to be at breakfast as we had been told by 6am. But at 6 am everything in the dining/bar area was in the murky greyness of shutness except for two casually business suited men in Aquaculture, one from Thailand, one from Canberra who were waiting with their rollaway bags and mobile phones for something to happen. We were meant to leave at 6:45 and at 6:30 a not very communicative woman came out and began laying out breakfast things. We rush through our 'Just Right' and cornflakes and run for the mini bus worried about missing it. The time arranged to meet Tony at the wharf was 7am to catch the tides. We have no idea where the wharf is, having flown in late the night before, and time is ticking as we wait for the bus to go. It is 6:45 and suddenly the bus is going. The driver, the same quiet woman who laid out breakfast and so we scramble on and travel exactly two minutes around the corner to the wharf. No one had suggested we could have walked. It is not assumed you would want to in the heat and perhaps they are right. Even in drizzle we are hot. At the wharf we wait for a while, always half worried we have somehow managed to miss our boat. The boats at the wharf are pink and purple and the surrounding sea is aqua blue even as the clouds came over. We re-read the crocodile warnings.

We know where the island is and we have Tony Tisaye to take us in his fast boat with a promise of food, swags and tents for the rain. The 'we' is my partner Susan and I. 'Susan' is important here in the western folklore of islands: 'Suzanne and the

Pacific', the *Lovely Susan* of 'Palm Island Adventure' (Strang, 1923; Giraudoux, 1923). So we know where we are going but we do not know when or how. When Tony comes Susan worries about the boat and the supplies. It seems small and un-full for all that we might need for our single night on the island. And the sea from inside the boat looks big. Will we be all right? There are more squalls moving in and it is darker for a moment than before. Tony does the mock exaggeration – hey, we get lost we'll be crocodile food and his quick punch line – 'only joking'. We get in the boat.

To approach the island from the sea is to move toward a rounded shape, the pleasure of that approach, of coming across rather than into something, and landing clumsily into sand and walking up upon a beach. The island as a whole island has been in my mind for a long time and when we arrive it takes up a wholly sensational existence. It refuses writing and description; never becoming small enough in memory to be seen and recorded with the words that would vivify it. It remains intensely, sensorally concrete. I can't make up an idea of this place that can fit in my forehead which is how Scarry says we remember.

Even now I can't remember Possession Island as an island. It refuses to become memory as one would usually understand it - as a set of brief vivid snapshots, momentary experiences, a single flower, a patch of rock. It is instead a presence. It is connected to but not the same as standing at one end of the long, long paddock of the not quite ruins of Birkenau and feeling most profoundly things fall into place. There, there was thin-clad shed after thin-clad shed stretching away from the gas chambers, across a wide, long expanse of green grass where so many people had been and where all the words of another, European unconscious fell out and could be seen—in place. And I was left with a look. Knowing I could look, knowing I was one part of what remained. That as an Australian of a "settled" nation things had been put in place for me. This island too remains. It does not resolve itself into piecemeal remembrance, but like a wide, wide-angle shot remains completely across the mind. On it Australia falls into place. There are hardly any white words about it but those two: "Took possession".

But here national possession seems not merely incommensurate with lived Indigenous sovereignty but ludicrous. The journey into the heart of whiteness finds not an ultimate barrier, the original fence to domesticate the wild but a small island, a National Park: no dogs, no guns, no fires, watch out for crocodiles – and the other mark of national possession - the Cook monument.

THE MONUMENT

The monument depends on its contextualising language. Physically it looks faintly military—its squat, boxy cement shape a mixture of flag base and machine gun mount or gun pillbox. It feels defensive. Its peeled white paint and rusted front pole suggest an uncared-for public convenience. But the first written plaque is clear and clean. The words well spaced, eyes to front, staring into the uncaring sea: "Lieutenant James Cook RN of the Endeavour landed on this island which he named Possession Island and in the name of his Majesty King George the Third, took possession of the whole eastern coast of Australia from the latitude 38 degrees south to this place" (National Library of Australia, 2008b). This place. On the side is a more detailed set of particular acknowledgements. The ship's crew who built it, the bicentenary committee who funded it, the historical society that initiated it, and the bishop who blessed it. And here we learn that this is also a monument to the defacement of the first: "[The] Torres Strait Historical Society initiated reconstruction of this monument after the original cairn, erected by the federal government earlier this century, was vandalised". Fiona Nicoll has written about the ways in which Indigenous sovereignty works as a "public secret" using Michael Taussig's ideas on defacement: the public secret that can be defined as "that which is generally known but cannot be articulated". He asks, "Then what happens to the inspired act of defacement? Does it destroy the secret or further enhance it?" (Taussig in Nicoll, 2002, p. 3) His example was the naked statue of Queen Elizabeth II and Prince Phillip installed as part of the National Sculpture Festival in Canberra in 1995 that was then beheaded, the double defacement that he believes led to a reinforcement of the public secret of monarchical power in Australia. But what of this Cook example? A defacement officially recognised in a plaque recording a monument's (now only ever partial) restoration, never replication? Is this the historical continuation to the original opposition to Cook at Botany Bay? Is it in this small sentence, in small writing on the side of this raggedy monument, that Indigenous sovereignty is quietly named aloud? Reconstructed, monument, earlier, vandalised. The monument looks toward the northeast and so toward the island of Mer. Eddy Mabo's Mer, where the idea of Australia being a land occupied by no one, possessed by no one before Cook, was proven legally to be incorrect. What is now known as the Mabo decision was begun by three people (including Eddie Mabo) from the Murray Islands (of which Mer is the largest) asking the High Court of Australia to declare that their possession, ownership, and occupation of their land had not been extinguished by colonisation (National Archives of Australia, 1992). Although their plea was not entirely accepted, the case resulted in a legal and moral breakthrough—Australian common law recognised a form of native title. Where such title had not been extinguished, "native title rejects the rights that the laws or customs of the Indigenous inhabitants give them to their traditional lands" (Butt & Eagleton, 1993, p.91). This was the first true recognition in Australia of a 'before' Cook having a continuance in Australian law. The success of the case partly depended on the very clear markers of possession and continuous occupation that the small island of Mer could provide. Tony tells us Mer is one of the most beautiful islands, rich and bountiful: "It makes you happy just to go there". Mer that began to undo the state of possession—Dispossession Island?

TREES

I went to Possession Island to find a tree that I knew could not be there. This is the tree painted by Gilfillan and turned to print by Calvert. It is the originary, possessory tree; shading the conquerors, providing their food and extending its limbs over the coming domain of the British in Australia. The great Australian imaginary. This print is called in part, 'Taking possession of the Australian continent'. This, as you now know was meant to take place on Possession Island.

My failure to make memory of this island is connected perhaps to a failure to imagine. Elaine Scarry (1997) makes a lovely case for the ways in which imagination and the flower are interrelated. Her flowers are soft, near translucent, filmy – not the solid felt of the Australian flannel flower or the engaging force of the banksia –but a specific geographical imagining that arises from the cool climate, wet sclerophyll in the relatively new and mud-based soil of her country. Those flowers are the right size to fit in our foreheads, the right softness, the right innocence of culture. But how do we imagine here then? All of us who have grown up with the solidly defined, baroque curlicles of the banksia and the flashing metallic sheen of the eucalypt leaf that have left their mark on us? How do we describe the force of this imagining we have learnt to call nature but is the worked upon, storied up place of Indigenous occupation?

I found my tree. Not a tree of possession but a mangrove tree, *rhizomorpha stylosa*. A hint of the island as real. You know it by its exposed roots (pneumatophores) which come up for oxygen where there is none in the muddy, sandy tidal flat. *Rhizomorpha*, literally the transmitter; the bearer of the root, the rhizomes that move horizontally. Roots that don't simply dig down and hold on but take up the sea, shed the salt and breathe. The roots holding the sediment that

Figure 1. Samuel Calvert after J. A. Gilfillan, "Captain Cook Taking Possession of the Australian Continent on Behalf of the British Crown, AD 1770, Under the Name of New South Wales," 1865, nla.pic-an7682920, National Library of Australia

nurtures crabs and molluscs, enemy and friend alike and stabilise the wind-blown side of the island. It is not really in opposition to anything. It draws humans to it for what further food it might support, to take the crabs that destroy its seedlings and the bark that is used for ulcers and yaws. Some say these trees began up here. Beyond language. For Scarry, "The felt experience of imagining, the interior brushing of one image against another, is the way it feels when two petals touch one and other" (Scarry, 1997). But why not here another experience of imagining? The natural histories of Captain Cook, the real that happened all the time outside his languaging of place. The brushing of water and root, wind and sand, polystyrene and human hand? The moments of potential place within the mangrove tree, reaching up for air out of possession? Another kind of imaginary. Another kind of pedagogy. Another kind of place.

Figure 2. Mangrove tree, Possession Island, Australia, 2007

ACKNOWLEDGEMENTS

Many thanks to the editors and readers of this paper and to Margaret Somerville for the opportunity to teach a place story. Thanks to Susan Brock for being there and Jan Idle (Research Assistant on the Cook Project) for getting us there.
An extended version of this chapter exists in the *South Atlantic Quarterly* (Schlunke, K. 2009, 'Home', *South Atlantic Quarterly*, *108*(1), 1-26).

NOTES

[1]   Author's on-site transcription, Captain Cook Graving Dock, Garden Island, September 18, 2007.
[2]   Spelling per original.

REFERENCES

Butt, P., & Eagleton, R. (1993). *Mabo: What the High Court said*. Sydney, NSW: Federation Press.

Carter, P. (1987). *The road to Botany Bay*. London: Faber and Faber.

Deleuze, G. (2004). Desert islands. In *Desert islands and other texts, 1953–1974*. Los Angeles: Semiotext(e).

Giraudoux, J. (1923). *Suzanne and the Pacific* (B. Redman, Trans.). New York: G.P. Putnam and Sons (Original work published in 1921).

Gow, M. (2008). *Toy symphony*. Sydney, NSW: Currency Press.

Lacan, J. (1977). Function and field of speech and language in psychoanalysis. In *Écrits: A selection* (A. Sheridan, Trans.). London: Tavistock Publications.

Mackinolty, C., & Wainburranga, P. (1988). Too many Captain Cooks. In T. Swain & D. B. Rose, (Eds.), *Aboriginal Australians and Christian missions: Ethnographic and historical studies*. Special Studies in Religion 6. Bedford Park, SA: Australian Association for the Study of Religions.

McDonald, P. (1989). *Too many Captain Cooks*. Sydney, NSW: Ronin Films.

Moreton-Robinson, A. (2005). The house that Jack built: Britishness and white possession. *Australian Critical Race and Whiteness Studies Association Journal, 1*, Retrieved 2008, from http:// www. acrawsa.org.au/ejournalFiles/Volume%201,%20Number%201,%202005/AileenMoretonRobinson.pdf

National Archives of Australia. (1992). *Mabo v. The State of Queensland No. 2 1992 (Cth)*. Retrieved June 11, 2008, from http://www.foundingdocs.gov.au/item.asp?sdID=105

National Library of Australia. (2008a). *Cook's journal: Daily entries, April 29, 1770*. Retrieved June 22, 2008, from http://nla.gov.au/nla.cs-ss-jrnl-cook-17700429.

National Library of Australia. (2008b). *Cook's journal: Daily entries, April 29, 1770*. Retrieved June 18, 2008, from http://nla.gov.au/nla.cs-ss-jrnl-cook-17700429

Nicoll, F. (2002). De-facing Terra Nullius and facing the public secret of Indigenous sovereignty in Australia. *Borderlands, 1*(2). Retrieved June 18, 2008, from http://www.borderlandsejournal. adelaide.edu.au/vol1no2_2002/nicoll_defacing.html

Rose, D. B. (1984). The saga of Captain Cook: Morality in Aboriginal and European law. *Australian Aboriginal Studies, 2*, 24–39.

Scarry, E. (1997, Winter). Imagining flowers: Perceptual mimesis (particularly delphinium). *Representations, 57*, 90–115.

Strang, H. (1923). *Palm Tree Island*. London: Oxford University Press.

Katrina Schlunke
University of Technology Sydney

EMILY POTTER

4. FOOTPRINTS IN THE MALLEE

Climate Change, Sustaining Communities, and the Nature of Place

PLACES UNDER STRESS

Whatever places are, they have come to be associated with the presence or absence of sustaining conditions. American academic bell hooks writes that "talking about place, where we belong, is a constant subject for many of us. We want to know if it is possible to live on the earth peacefully. Is it possible to sustain life?" But the reality, she argues, is disconsolate: "Many folks feel no sense of place. What they know, what they have is a sense of crisis, of impending doom. Even the old, the elders… [say] our world today is a world of 'too much' – that this too muchness creates a wilderness of spirit…" (hooks, 2009, p. 1) The 'too much' that hooks describes, a culture of over-production, over-consumption, and time poverty, is also a problem of too little, at least as far as the fate of place seems to go. The environmental crisis that frames hooks' remarks on the sustenance of life, and its relation to belonging, is most recognised through increasing absence: the loss of species, the loss of forest, the loss of water, the loss of community. Climate change – the result of an overabundance of carbon dioxide in the atmosphere – is widely registering as a deficit, and the future of place, as a nexus of human and non-human life, is at the forefront of this concern.

In the Victorian Mallee country, the loss associated with changing climates and environments has been bureaucratically noted. According to the Victorian Department of Sustainability and Environment, communities here are on the cusp of becoming "Australia's first climate change refugees" (Ker, 2009). The implications of this displacement, in the context of postcolonial history especially, are complex. The Mallee has long been a site of loss, dispossession, and unsustainable practice. But it is also a place of creativity. While years of drought and diminishing populations have come to fundamentally inform these communities and their relation to place, in recent years so has the widespread development of new environmental literacies. Initiatives that seek to address environmental ignorance, inappropriate agricultural practice, and ameliorate environmental damage are flourishing, and communities are re-forming around these.

Such attempts to remake place, under the threat of catastrophic climate change, work to forestall displacement by renegotiating belonging – a belonging that remediates loss through creative engagement. Landcare schemes, water-saving initiatives and carbon sequestration industries all forestall a dispossession from place.

M. Somerville, K. Power and P. de Carteret (eds.),
Landscapes and Learning: Place Studies for a Global World, 65–74

The concern of this chapter, however, is that this focus upon place, and the threat of displacement, relies upon and yet obscures the question of time. With creative endeavours oriented toward improved environmental futures, there is an implicit disconnect from damaging pasts. Despite intentions, this perpetuates an unsustainable logic which evacuates place of a temporal dynamic and, as a consequence, multiple other creative forces that unsettle an opposition between absence and presence, loss and 'much-ness'.

The calculative rationalities of mainstream environmental practice work very much in a Foucauldian mode of governmentality, where territory is managed as part of a project to secure the optimum well-being of populations. The stated purpose of remedial activity is first and foremost to sustain life, but the implementation of these technologies, because of their grounding in modern discourses of public administration, excludes the incalculable, messy and ephemeral aspects of place and its constitution that are crucial to sustainable futures. Such futures depend upon a recovery of time – history – and the stories through which temporalities are enacted as non-linear, generative and always relational. What I hope to describe is not a drought-affected Mallee perched perilously between loss and creative redemption, but a place continually composed through acts of discursive recollection that materialise hidden geographies of life and community in the face of their erasure.

MALLEE CLIMATES

The Mallee is a semi-arid region in the south-east of Australia, spreading out through the north-west of Victoria and across the borders into South Australia and New South Wales. It takes its name from an indigenous variety of Eucalypt collectively known as Mallee: a multi-stemmed, low-height tree well adapted to the sandy soil of the region. Mallee species develop an extraordinarily tough and dense subterranean lignotuber or 'Mallee root' which stores water, enabling the tree to be self-sustaining through periods of drought and bushfire. The Mallee region's climate is characteristically hot and dry; rainfall is infrequent. When the surveyors arrived in the mid nineteenth century, their impression was bleak: according to A.J. Skene, "this district presents a scrubby, sandy waste, almost entirely destitute of fresh water and grass, and therefore unavailable to human industry" (Durham, 2001, p. 17). Regardless, and despite the tenacity of the Mallee root whose hold in the ground required adaptation of existing agricultural technologies, it wasn't long before the clearing of the Mallee for agriculture, particularly wheat production, began in earnest and this continued well into the twentieth century. With widespread deforestation, the severity and length of drought periods has increased. Soil erosion, rising salinity and dust storms are pervasive. And now the particular impacts of climate change are manifesting in the Mallee.

Mean temperatures have risen by 0.1 degree per decade since 1950 (Victorian Department of Sustainability and Environment, 2004). In the area around Lake Tyrrell in the north-east of the Victorian Mallee, local farmers have noted more erratic rainfall and the disappearance of faunal species over the last ten years (Pook, 2007). The only reliable source of freshwater for the region is the Murray River which is itself under severe stress from irrigation and lack of rain. The Murray-Darling Basin is recording its lowest levels of inflow on record, prompting the Murray-Darling Basin Authority to warn that "water for critical human needs could not be guaranteed forever" in this region (Ryan, 2009, p. 8). Under the conditions predicted as the climate warms, this situation will worsen. Years of low rainfall and poor crop yields have meant that farming families are leaving the land; the rate of farmer suicide has risen and depression is common. With economic prospects bleak, communities are losing their youth to the cities or regional centres. Members of the shrinking Wycheproof community made the pointed gesture, in July 2009, of offering out a rental farmhouse for $1 per week in a bid to increase town numbers. The local school has seen a 30% decline in year 12 students since 2005 (Cooper, 2009).

The vision of a bleak and dispossessing Mallee is not a new creation; in 1902 the *Guardian* newspaper reported that "the Mallee was never in a worse state than it is at present since settlement... It is rumoured that some of the settlers will experience great difficulty in pulling through". Echoing the situation today, the paper went on to report that "[s]trenuous efforts are being made on all sides to induce the government to inaugurate a scheme for [the] permanent supply of water" (Ouyen Local History Resource Centre, 1998, p. 102). Carrie Tiffany's 2006 novel *Everyman's Rules for Scientific Living* describes the grim consequences of post World War One settlement in the Mallee: returned soldiers were encouraged to take up a life of farming in this environment, informed by modern techno-scientific discourses of efficiency and reasoned progress. "Your first duty as a farmer is to completely clear the land", to remove all impediments between "yourself and the soil" (Tiffany, 2005, p. 33), explains one of the novel's protagonists, Robert, who subsequently watches his farm degrade under the winds and dry skies of the Mallee. "Fences mark one man's crop from another" reflects his wife, Jean, "but they have no power over the land itself. They can't contain the sandy soil that blows and blows in vast rolling clouds most afternoons... Soil clouds roll right through the house, in at the back, out at the front. There is always soil in our cups when I pour the morning tea" (p. 160).

In recent years, however, efforts have been mobilised to address and repair this environmental degradation and its social effects. The recognition of the inappropriate nature of traditional farming methods, such as tilling, as well as the importance of retaining native vegetation has seen the introduction of significant changes in agricultural and environmental practice in the region. Initiatives including sustainable property management planning, no-tillage agricultural practice (supported by educational organisations such as Vic No-till), and a 'whole of landscape' approach to vegetation management focus on minimising water use, sustaining the soil and keeping salinity down; membership of Landcare groups – collectives of land owners committed to the remediation of environmental damage – is close to 100% in some areas of the Mallee. Complementary social programs have focused on re-educating farming families on life after farming (Stephens & McGuckian, 2004) and re-skilling farm workers, while government and welfare sector organisations provide a range of financial and emotional resources to communities.

Yet it is not only through transformations in agricultural practice that the redemption of the Mallee is taking place. The native ecology, for so long considered aberrant by colonisers, has been recuperated as 'useful' by an emerging industry for carbon sequestration. In a place that so visibly records the legacy of inappropriate environmental practices, and is degrading further under the influence of rising temperatures, corporate carbon sequestration initiatives are thriving. Across the Mallee, in both Victoria and New South Wales (and also in other agricultural areas of Australia where these trees thrive, such as Western Australia), Mallee trees are being planted in earnest. In exchange for financial remuneration and as an added means of improving land fertility and managing groundwater, farmers are leasing parts their property to these burgeoning plantations. Mallee trees are exceptionally good at soaking up carbon, have a long life span, and keep groundwater low, thus minimising salinity.[1] Businesses invest in the planting and maintenance of the trees by way of purchasing carbon credits and thus negating their 'carbon footprint': a relative measure of resource consumption and waste production.[2] CO2 Australia, a company that establishes and manages these 'carbon sinks', oversees 12,500 hectares of Mallee trees in south-east Australia and Western Australia as part of their carbon sequestration scheme.

CALCULATED RELATIONS

The concept of off-setting carbon emissions with the purchase of credits applies a calculative approach to human/environment relations that reduces natural processes to units of exchange. As an essentially economic activity, with environmental benefit, this is not surprising. The techno-scientific solutions that dominate our culture's responses to environmental change tend to complement and enable the calculation of economic value and its attachment to all aspects of environmental change. As a result, sustainability is framed in terms of a problem to be managed or fixed; as well as capturing and trading in carbon, we undertake water 'audits' and 'restore' water flows to our parched rivers. We train and recruit 'sustainability leaders' and develop 'sustainability strategies'. The dominant discourse of sustainability itself invokes calculability, emphasising balance, linear development and an orientation towards future security: pursuing economic growth in the present "without compromising the ability of future generations to meet their own needs" (United Nations, 1987).

Security is central to the discourse of sustainability, and it connects to the neo-liberal traditions of governance and regulation that underpin much sustainability practice in the west today. These traditions, as Clarke and Stevenson contend, bind the contemporary "quest for environmental justice...[to] dense networks of calculation, regulation and monitoring" in which "a new wave of surveillance, discipline and self-monitoring... inheres in the ideal of the good ecological citizen" (Clark & Stevenson, 2003, p. 238). Carbon counting, and the calculative management of one's carbon footprint (whether an individual or an entity), is an example of this.

According to Foucault's concept of biopower, calculation is a central technique of modern liberal governance, employed for both the management of populations and their spatial territories. To these ends, calculative strategies (technologies such as measurement and statistics) work to administer security and consequently – in the logic of liberalism – to "assure living", which is the object of biopolitics (Elden, 2007, p. 575). In Foucault's analysis, security is understood not in terms of discipline and confinement, but rather through the capacity for circulation, connectivity and distribution – all key aspects of a modern market system. The spatial conception of security thus historically involved the administration of territory so as to facilitate the movement of people and the optimum circulation of goods. Here, territory is not considered a "static entity", but rather a composition of "specific qualities", all of which can be individually measured (p. 575). This rationalisation of territorial elements enables environmental components to be identified and rendered discrete from one another, as well as divisible in terms of economic ownership. The concept of environmental flows, for instance, allocates portions of a water resource to 'the environment', while other portions are allocated for industry and domestic use.

For colonial Australia, the settler ideology of land mapping, clearance and division is clearly informed by calculative reason in the name of security and governance. This reason also performed an ontological function, ensuring a sense of stability and rightfulness in place, necessary to quell the uncertainties of colonial occupation of an unfamiliar country. Paul Carter has described how the colonial gaze theatricalised the Australian environment, reading into it a raft of prescient and supernatural signs that could thus be repressed with the certainties of reason. Conceptualising the conquered land as a passive surface affording unencumbered movement to the coloniser-body was an important strategy. Land clearance signified "unimpeachably firm foundations" for the colonial self in its newly claimed place (Carter, 1996, p. 2).

While such security conferred a licence to push back the frontier and claim more territory, a metricalised environment provided ontological assurance in the midst of external 'chaos'. As Carter argues, the colonial "eagerness to remove every vestige of vegetation" from a landscape, as well as dispossessing and silencing its indigenous inhabitants, staged its own vision of the environment as empty (p. 9). In the smoothing of ground and the laying out of fences and boundaries, the shadows of instability could be pushed back, with knowledge and certainty kept in and uncivilised and threatening forces shut out. As non-indigenous settlement extended its presence in the Australian landscape, a primary intention remained to stabilise the ground, and provide a secure place for the colonial project to unfold.

BAD TIMES

The making of colonial places thus depended upon a profound historical repression – the erasure of prior human and non-human ecologies. This was a poetic as well as a practical project. In works such as *The Road to Botany Bay* (1987), Paul Carter traces the poetic colonisation of Australia through modes of naming and story-telling which brought a doubling of identity – an overlaying of indigenous landscapes with the histories of other places, far away and quite distinct – and an attendant disease to Australian places that had disastrous consequences for local ecologies. What this meant in practice was that settler Australians set about remaking the land in an image of elsewhere – redirecting rivers, clearing land, and establishing agriculture as if environments of the Southern hemisphere were no different to those of the North. The stories that oversaw this activity were ones that we recognise today but – because of the manifesting realities of environmental damage – are beginning to lose their potency: myths of "golden soil and wealth for toil" (we know this from our national anthem), of unlimited land to be mastered and harvested, and of social progress built upon this economic base. A double dispossession faced by Indigenous peoples lay in the fact that while their own histories of place were discounted and suppressed by the dominant culture, the environments so entwined with Indigenous life and well-being began to seriously decline.

There is thus a significant parallel between colonial strategies of place-making, techniques of modern governance and contemporary sustainability practice: a parallel which demands a rethinking of how we conceive of sustainability as a concept and a range of strategies. If environmental degradation is to be truly addressed then it makes sense to break from, rather than perpetuate, the prevalent logic of modern liberal society. Indicative of this continuance, the 'carbon footprint', as a political tool, affirms the individualising and rationalising nature of dominant environmental governance discourse. As a poetic device, the footprint measure is conspicuously uni-vocal and concerned with flat topographies. While the carbon footprint has become associated with progressive environmental politics, and is seen by some as a marker of ecological citizenship – where a traditional focus of citizenry rights shifts to the responsibility, or obligation, of humans to care for the non-human world[3] – the story of human/non-human relations embodied in the carbon footprint does nothing to generate new practices, or new ways of being in place. It is the same kind of narrative retold, one in which we understand the world as composed of – and through – discrete objects rather than dynamic processes that enrol both humans and non-humans. Indeed if, as Whatmore and Hinchliffe argue, citizenship means "a capacity to act in relation... in the multiplicity of relations through which civic associations and attachments are woven", then the metaphor of the carbon footprint falls short on this count too (Hinchliffe and Whatmore, 2006, p. 135).

The security imperative that characterises governmentality in both colonial and contemporary Australia is therefore as much about the management of immaterial resources as material; the administration of life is pursued through both the calculation of space and time, and their poetic manifestations. The future-facing nature of mainstream sustainability discourse and practice reinforces a cultural obsession with linear time, as if, in cleaning up the environment, we also clean away the 'bad things' of the past – those things that haunt, unsettle or disrupt prevailing narratives of place. The "intergenerational economy" imagined by sustainability discourse, "extending between present and futures [as] a matter of heritage and inheritance to be shared and handed down across time and space", is configured in one direction only (McKee, 2007, p. 551). There is no going back.

CREATIVE GEOGRAPHIES

Yet as the work of economist Michel Callon reminds us, calculation is never a neutral process; instead it is a performance that produces its own object (Callon, 1999). That is, calculative techniques cannot fix reality. They participate, along with a host of other devices, in its making. This hinterland (Law, 2004) of devices is what a politics that privileges calculation in a bid to gain certainty over the future, and at the expense of the past, will fail to acknowledge. All that falls away from calculative regimes – the uncalculable, ephemeral, messy and a-temporal – is where a new approach to sustainable place-making may be found: an approach in which 'bad things' figure too. Central to our unsustainable present is its discursive and materialised rupture with the past. It is therefore in the recollection, or re-admittance, of the past into our making of the present that environmental initiatives must lie.

Sarah Whatmore's concept of "hybrid geographies" is helpful for thinking through the reincorporation of what evades metrical analysis into political projects. Whatmore introduces this idea as an attempt to extricate geographic inquiry from positivist rationalities that promote a dichotomous world-view of nature/culture, human/non-human, and presence/absence. She advances "hybrid mappings" as a creative, generative and ethical way of understanding reality: these are "closely textured journeys" through the assembling "socio-material imbroglios" that make manifest everyday life (Whatmore, 2002, p. 4). Hers is an argument against epistemic traditions in which passive nature is rendered ontologically distinct and thus observable and wholly knowable to the human mind – something that spatial practice and visual culture are seen to confirm. An inheritance of Cartesian logic, whereby humans construct meaning from the "dead matter" that surrounds them, this tradition situates the perceiving subject outside of time – an "observer", as Barbara Adam notes on the subject, that "cast[s] no shadow" (Adam, 1999, p. 142).

In contrast, the concept of hybrid geographies draws upon alternate philosophies emergent from STS (Science and Technology Studies) and Actor-Network theory to insist that humans are always caught up in networks of non-humans – poetically, physically, and politically – thus distributing agency and fundamentally reconfiguring the terms by which we come to know the world. It has profound implications for how we think about environmental change, and in particular, what we mean when we talk about environments or environmental constituents. In the assembled reality apparent in hybrid geographies, it becomes impossible to talk about place, climate or water in a drought-ridden Mallee, as singular, temporally stable things. Instead, they ask to be considered as continually composing, hybrid forums, where immaterial and material, human and non-human, and past and present elements gather in a dynamic set of relations. According to Whatmore, there is a "distribution" of ontology and agency here that – suggestively for thinking about the poetic production of place - "refuse[s] the choice between the word and the world" (2002, p. 3).

The application of this thinking to the current situation in the Australian Mallee opens up to an expanded understanding of what sustainable places might be, and, importantly for an era in which the urgency of environmental issues is prompting a surge in sustainability practices, highlights the repetitive logic that underlies many of these. While the privileging of linear time under modernity makes a clear distinction between life and death, presence and absence, a non-linear approach to time challenges these boundaries. Outside the calculative frames of governmentality and liberal reason, the hybrid geographies of life in the Mallee give voice to alternate histories, not of loss or triumph alone, but of encounters, entanglements, and unresolved arrangements of 'words and worlds'. Sustainable places need sustainable stories. But more than this, stories need the incorporation of what was already known and has been forgotten or repressed: the re-narration of history is a predicate of making sustainable places.

SUSTAINABILITY RECONCEIVED

Given this, what constitutes a water source in the Mallee? Where do the creative work of recollection and the material manifestation of water coincide? Hybrid geographies suggest an alternate way of proceeding to rewater an environment degraded by human-centred and instrumentalist logic, where a mapping of water across forms and manifestations materialises new water stories and, more importantly, water sources – sources for thinking and living with water differently. For, despite its absence registered so visibly in failing crops and diminished communities, the presence of water here is palpable: in Indigenous histories, other local histories and the traces of pre-colonial ecologies; in the design of architecture and streetscapes; in the instruction boards for boating and swimming that overlook the Mallee's long dry lakes; in local practices of water conservation, social programs and community initiatives; in archives and artefacts. These assemble with the work of narration to trace out a pattern that is both water's history and its possible future. A water source is as much a creative as a 'natural' product.

While techno-scientific tools have their affordances, they have their limits too, addressing only certain aspects of human and environmental reality. Moreover, they do not exist in a void. There are other kinds of tools that we have at our disposal, tools whose work evades the quantification and rationalisation of mainstream sustainability speak, and which – in a hybrid view of the world – operate on the same, shifting surface, of assembling reality. These tools are poetic: they involve a way of thinking about the world which is fundamentally creative, predicated on making connections and materialising associations between things with the proviso that such connections are never made final. They also centralise the work of discourse, and the narration of place and its ecologies, in foregrounding different ways of thinking that highlight our cultural predilection for unsustainable logic.

The recollection of our hybrid geographies generates new stories and place cultures in which humans and non-humans are understood to work together. In this alternate ontology, where reality is composed of assembling relations, saving water – or rewatering a country – would mean a new practice of place-making, where expanded histories enter new designs for the future. For place is not a creation of humans alone; it is practised by more-than-human actors, too, and is a dappled construction, shifting always in and out of the light. In these terms, place lies between a world of 'too much' and 'too little'. It emerges in the spaces outside the firm footprints of a positivist tradition that seeks to secure our environmental claims, and is woven through the rhythm and always negotiated placing of footsteps instead. In this movement we encounter sustainability – and life – on a different, more uncertain and untimely ground, vibrant in its composition and always exceeding calculations: "sustainability without guarantees" (McKee, p. 574).

NOTES

[1] See the website of CO2 Ltd, which heads up the carbon sequestration industry in Australia, http://co2australia.com.au/default.aspx?d=136101.
[2] See http://www.carbonfootprint.com for a more detailed description of the concept.
[3] See for example Angela Crocombe, *A Lighter Footprint*, Scribe, Melbourne, 2007.

REFERENCES

Adam, B. (1999). Radiated identities: In pursuit of the temporal complexity of conceptual cultural practices. In M. Featherstone & S. Lash (Eds.), *Spaces of culture: City-Nation-World*. London and Thousand Oaks, CA: SAGE.

Callon, M. (1999). Actor-network theory – the market test. In J. Law & J. Haddard (Eds.), *Actor network theory and after*. Oxford, UK: Blackwell Publishing.

Carter, P. (1987). *The road to Botany Bay*. Chicago: University of Chicago Press.

Carter, P. (1996). *The lie of the land*. London: Faber and Faber.

Clark, N., & Stevenson, N. (2003). Care in the time of catastrophe: Citizenship, community, and the ecological imagination. *Journal of Human Rights, 2*(2), 235–246.

Cooper, M. (2009, July 3). Town offers $1 rents to break resident drought. *The Age*. Retrieved from http://www.theage.com.au/national/town-offers-1-rents-to-break-resident-drought-20090702-d6l8. html

Durham, G. (2001). *Friends of Wyperfeld: Australia's first Mallee National Park*. Elsternwick, Vic.: Friends of Wyperfeld National Park Inc.

Elden, S. (2007). Governmentality, calculation and territory. *Environment and Planning D: Society and Space, 25*, 562–580.

Hinchliffe, S., & Whatmore, S. (2006). Living in cities: Towards a politics of conviviality. *Science as Culture, 15*(2), 123–138.

hooks, b. (2009). *Belonging: A culture of place*. New York: Routledge.

Ker, P. (2009, March 18). Exodus fears for Murray Towns. *The Age*. Retrieved from www.theage.com.au/environment/global-warming/exodus-fears-for-murray-towns-20090317-911h.html

Law, J. (2004). *After method: Mess in social science research*. London and New York: Routledge.

McKee, Y. (2007). Art and the ends of environmentalism: From biosphere to the right to survival. In M. Feher, with G. Krikorian, & Y. McKee (Eds.), *Nongovernmental politics*. New York: Zone Books.

Ouyen Local History Resource Centre. (1998). *A Mallee album: Reflections on Mallee life*. Ouyen, Victoria.

Pook, J., Interview with Emily Potter and Paul Carter, Lake Tyrrell, 7 March 2007.

Ryan, S. (2009, April 8). Murray inflows slow to a trickle. *The Australian*, 8.

Stephens, M., & Mc Guckian, N. (2004). *There is still a life after farming: A resource book for farmers considering leaving farming*. Bendigo, Victoria: North Central Rural Financial Counselling Service.

Tiffany, C. (2005). *Everyman's rules for scientific living*. Sydney, NSW: Picador.

United Nations. (1987). *Report of the world commission on environment and development.* Retrieved from http://www.un.org/documents/ga/res/42/ares42-187.htm

Victorian Department of Sustainability and Environment. (2004). *Climate change in the Mallee.* Retrieved from www.climatechange.vic.gov.au

Whatmore, S. (2002). *Hybrid geographies: Natures, cultures, spaces.* London and Thousand Oaks: SAGE.

Emily Potter
Deakin University

ANNA HICKEY-MOODY

5. MAKING CREATIVE PLACES

INTRODUCTION

In Australia's current political climate, audible strategies for promoting creative curriculum development and for considering the cultural implications of moves for regional renewal are greatly needed. In taking up this research agenda, I focus on interdisciplinary places of learning that cross boundaries between informal educational sites, communities and creative industries. Such a cross-disciplinary focus is intended to contribute to understanding the educational, social and economic benefits associated with different places. I advance this project via theoretical means that allow a discursive re-positioning of the politics of place-making and fostering creativity in youth. Specifically, I take up Deleuzian concepts of creativity and spatiality to explore the work of two UK arts companies and one Australian youth arts company, each of which seeks to foster creativity in young people through particular place-making projects.

CREATIVITY AS THE DIFFERENTIAL BECOMING OF THE WORLD

Deleuze argues that the context in which creation takes place is problematic, or difficult to 'define' in located terms (1994). However, his philosophy is highly responsive to environment. For Deleuze, society grows through affirming the fact that the slippery nature of creativity, and life, can leave us 'blind' to understanding the central features of environments in which creativity is produced. We know that environments impact on creativity, but our set, or 'striated', conscious means of understanding creativity and the world, obscures our chance to see environments as creative triggers. Deleuze and Guattari describe striation as a process "which inter-twines fixed *and* variable elements, [and] produces an order and succession of distinct forms" (1987, p. 478). For the most part, our consciousness occupies a striated space-time relation. In order to counter the capitalist model in which fixed modes of financial value are bound to the becoming of creativity, social formations must grasp the creatively significant aspects of our environments, by expressing them in new ways. Expression will also inevitably change these aspects of our environments (Williams, 2000, p. 202).

Deleuze adopts becoming as a way to affirm the processes of differentiation, or constant change, which are misapprehended in our perception of apparently static things (1994). He puts forward an ontology of becoming, in which 'reality' is in a permanent state of flux, or *continual differentiation*. This true 'flux', or the differential becoming of the world, is obscured by the illusions of fixity and identity

M. Somerville, K. Power and P. de Carteret (eds.),
Landscapes and Learning: Place Studies for a Global World, 75–86
© 2009 Sense Publishers. All rights reserved.

that become key features of our subjectivity. The aspects of our environment that are necessary to creativity are an inseparable part of these processes of becoming.

A creative endeavour combines an unconscious registering of the reality of flux and change with a conscious recognition of this process. Because reality is primarily in flux, a creative affirmation of this becoming is a resistance to our acceptance of a determined world around us. This positive resistance is activated, when, for example, an architect expresses the becomings at play in an actual site through the design of a new building (Williams, 2000, p. 203), or when an artist actualises possibilities for new aesthetic vocabularies by painting an image that evades the clichés embedded in a blank canvas. This creative engagement with potentiality, and resistance to unconscious clichéd perceptions is also referred to by Deleuze as a "resistance to the present" (Deleuze & Guattari, 1994, p. 108). The ontology of becoming turns against 'progress' as development towards an ideal. Instead of progress, there is an expression of pure movements, defined as *variations,* or *differentiations.* Reality is a flow of variations that need no relation to different identities or fixed reference points. It is the constructed human subject that needs reference to identities or fixed points.

Deleuze's ontology and affirmation of becoming is justified on the basis of relations between actual movements or processes (1994). He would contend that we are overly occupied with proving our imaginings of the *way things are* and that because of this we lose the capacity to pay attention to *what things are becoming.* If we perceive our identity as embedded in place, we take away from our capacity to understand place and self as actualising individual potentials. People and places *are* folded into one another at different points of their constitution, yet they are also part of assemblages in which they are not connected and, rather, become quite separate things. While we need to acknowledge and understand the points at which places fold in to constitute our subjectivity, we should not lose sight of the potentials held within places and ourselves, outside these points of connection.

For example, Australia is a sovereign nation. Yet if one was to believe that Uluru was only a tourist attraction, generations of Aboriginal knowledge and connection to country, and the force of these connections, would be discounted. Uluru is a multiplicity. In some social assemblages it is a tourist attraction, where it is connected to ideas of 'authentic Australia' and is positioned as an attractive gem in the crown of our ruling monarch. In other social assemblages, Uluru articulates knowledges that cannot be understood by whitefellas, let alone the Sovereign head of State, to whom they claim allegiance.

If creativity is seen, as Deleuze (1994) presents it, to be an active engagement with the differential becoming of the world and resistance to cliché, then it is this awareness, this resistance to the present that we must nurture through social formations. In order to begin such a venture, I look to open up conceptualisations of the work of youth arts projects as forms of making creative places.

I begin this trajectory with the work of Creative Partnerships; an initiative that brokers placements for arts practitioners in socially and economically disadvantaged schools. I focus on a site in Margate, a coastal town in Kent, UK; which is a place with an ethnically diverse population. The neighbouring town of Dover is a primary entry point for asylum seekers and illegal immigrants to the UK. Creative Partnerships explore issues of identity, tolerance and equality as articulated in the social fabric of Margate. The project I examine is one in which the public art organisation ArtAngel collaborated with filmmaker Penny Woolcock in staging 'The Margate Exodus'. As a contemporary re-working of the Biblical tale, this film explores a community's search for a 'Promised Land' and the social pressures that such journeys can produce. The work offers a mediation of macro and micro social movements, as biographies, landscape, culture and traditions are pleated into one text through filming live performance. The Margate Exodus was made in conjunction with the display of a photography project called 'Towards a Promised Land', in which banner photographs hung across the centre of Margate. This involved twenty-two young people who migrated to the UK from places affected by war, poverty or political unrest. With photographer Wendy Ewald, the children re-conceptualised their diverse experiences of moving. The photographs produced were shown on the walls of buildings in public spaces across the city, re-territorialising the de-industrialising architectural space of the town. Buildings became canvasses, and the faces of minoritarian children were accorded new levels of visibility.

Folding this re-inscription of town space into the social politics surrounding migration in Margate, The Margate Exodus is a now a major feature film screening in cinemas across England, that has been created with, and features, the people of

Figure 1. Image from 'Towards a Promised Land' by Wendy Ewald.

Margate. Across the film text, the contention that social policy on immigration needs to be rethought is articulated through the moving image and through community involvement.

In late 2006 I interviewed Anna Cutler who was then the Artistic Director of Creative Partnerships. I began our conversation by asking her about how social context had been taken up as an inspiration for the 'Exodus' project. Cutler responded that:

> When I came here (and I had come from Belfast) what I knew to do was to ... just absorb for a bit and go around and talk to people and find out what was going on, so I could ... see what kind of social situation was going on here and what kind of deprivations there were. And probably one of the worst ones here is lack of aspiration and hope. And that is across the whole East Kent coast which, because it is next to the very wealthy rest of Kent, it makes it even worse somehow. ... so the language that people use to talk about ... [Margate] has lack of hope and aspiration associated with it. ... I thought my whole program should be about place and identity because my feeling is that the place, its geography, helps to shape and what has happened economically, shape the identities of those who live there – and the identities of those who live there will shape will the place .... And this is key to what we are doing in Creative Partnerships, ... So we're working with young people ... in a geographic place that is run down, things are boarded up, it's physically miserable, there are spikes on the pavement, there is a lot of wiring around, [outsiders] ... know that they are not invited.

Cutler is aware of the ways in which the suffering, de-industrialising economy of coastal Margate folds in to constitute a sense of isolation in its residents, many of whom are immigrants. She notes how this isolation is re-articulated geographically by "things being boarded up ... spikes on the pavement ... a lot of wiring around". It was because Cutler was separate enough from these connections between economy, geography and community, having just arrived in Margate from Belfast, that she was able to see these connections so plainly, and to follow the trajectories they form; to inquire as to what it is that these connections *produce*, and what other assemblages they could become part of. As a way of resisting the inertia of the present, the re-telling of the Exodus was taken up by Creative Partnerships to connect people and places in Margate with the global market of media consumption and to argue that the politics of immigration (and located feelings of disenfranchisement) have never been more meaningful than they are today.

Cutler continues, explaining that:

> You have to inspire the imaginations of people, if you can't imagine an alternative, I don't know how you will ever get there. ... If you can't see it, if you can't imagine it, ... you won't ever do it. And people have lost that sense that anything is possible here. In Auston, they have been offered things and they haven't happened, so that is the history of Margate in particular, that offers have been made and they haven't turned out, ... so there is a lot of frustration here and people feel that they don't deserve anything because it gets reiterated through people's practice.

As for the architecture of the place, it signals terrible poverty, there is rubbish in the streets; sometimes we don't get our rubbish picked up for ... week[s] ....

Three years ago I was having a conversation with ArtAngel, about starting a project, I'd worked with Michael West from ArtAngel before, ... So Michael came down to have a look at the place to begin with, and I knew he would love it because it is a poor place with lots of boarded-up buildings, but it is also beautiful. It has the most beautiful Georgian architecture and fabulous Victorian buildings ... and the beaches are staggeringly gorgeous. And he really saw that juxtaposition between the mess and the arcades and the flashing lights, and these other ... beautiful things. And it makes it a[n] ... interesting place to be and it also has lots of natural theatre space to it ... he came back and said that what he really wanted to do was to get this filmmaker ... to come and make a film, and it was about the whole community, and because a lot of refugees and asylum seekers [are here]... it seemed like a point of entry and a point of exit ...

... what we have been doing is planning it since then, and gradually bringing in the community and we've been working ... in schools with 20 local artists ... on the concept of 'what a plague is'. The kids have been doing plagues of apathy, plagues of exclusion, plagues of cabbage locusts (because we grow cabbages around here), but it has been extraordinary because ... we've got ... professional gallery spaces to exhibit the children's work ... We are looking at bands who are going to join in, ... we are going to have plagues songs that famous writers have written ... we've got a layer of the international artists ... working with the community to produce a broadcast film that will be shown ... [in cinemas and on BBC TV]. So it's ... high profile, I think that ... one of the important things is [having] high-stakes, because everybody moves up to them.

After the broken promises, and the disillusionment that comes once opportunities have been lost, such a large invitation, and such a brave act of saying 'stand up now because the nation is looking' has certainly proved reason to rise to an occasion. The Margate Exodus has been a critically acclaimed success and it has brought the community of Margate into the public sphere in a range of ways. Margate, as a community, has been pushed to grasp the defining features of its environment – the juxtaposition between the mess and the arcades, the flashing lights and the boarded-up buildings, the Georgian architecture and the beaches. Paradox between possibility and historicity has become the creatively significant aspect of this community's context. Expressing these paradoxes in new ways, folding virtual futures into the space of the present, the landscape of Margate has been modulated. It is becoming. The features of Margate's environment that are necessary to creativity are an inseparable part of these processes.

Articulating the importance of links between place, community and creative industries is what Creative Partnerships does well. The exploration of such connections is socially significant because it generates broader understandings of interdisciplinary places of learning that cross boundaries between informal

Figure 2. Exterior of the Stratford Circus Building.

educational sites, communities and creative industries. However, it has been, and remains, a source of concern to me that the sustainability of the creative cultures generated by Creative Partnerships is limited. The programs they initiate do involve communities and certainly effect change in communities, yet they are not community driven and do not have the capacity to run without expertise brought in from outside the community. A similar critique of the lack of sustainability of the Creative Partnerships programs has been advanced by Hall and Thomson (2007). Certainly, this difficulty with sustainability is an enduring shortcoming of such specialist- run programs.

Now I move on to discuss an institutionalised example of macro and micro scales of social value being re-imagined through a place-based aesthetic. I turn to the education provider 'NewVIc', which is the Newham Sixth Form Arts College at Stratford Circus. The Circus is a centre for the performing arts and moving image, managed by NewVIc in collaboration with five professional arts organisations

The Circus is a thoughtfully designed, well-equipped building in East London. It has a large, circular structure with three floors that circle around an open, central community space. One enters the well-lit community space in the foyer, to see that the ceiling goes up three levels, and one is automatically part of an open cafe space in the middle. The stairs to different levels run along the outside of this open space. The architecture pays attention to the importance of flexibility in the respect that many of the regular studio rooms can also be rehearsal and audition rooms, meeting places, small exhibition spaces, but there are also large performance areas, theatre stages, a capacity to cater for big scale events. So proximity and spectacle are both possible.

The Circus is run by NewVIc as a site of arts education, yet it also houses professional dance, music, theatre and new media studios, and facilitates a range of adult education programs. The companies that NewVIc leases the building facilities to are: East London Dance, a design and urban music firm called Urban Development, Theatre Venture, NewCEYS (which is the performing arts bloc of Newham's community education and youth service), and the 'Circus Media' Centre.

The Circus Media Centre is also affiliated with NewVIc and it supports emerging freelance artists and production companies in delivering broadcast media. Through the Circus, local community members, artists and educators are brought together.

In 2006, in a café on Canary Wharf in London's East End, I spoke to Graham Jeffrey, a lecturer in Creative Industries at the University of East London, about the role that he played in establishing the Circus. Our conversation examined how social policy and political climate informed, and was also affected by, the Arts Centre at Stratford. The project at Stratford has taken on social context in a comprehensive way, in the respect that it is part of a broader push to creatively redesign London's East End and Docklands. The local student community does not have a history of performing well academically, and the practical training offered by the performing arts and new media programs at The Circus, alongside the links to industry that are part of these programs and a part of the building itself, provides its students with a creative model of education which has been developed in response to their needs. I asked Graham to comment on this responsiveness to context, and he suggested that such reflexivity is:

> ... absolutely critical. The idea was always ... that every aspect of our work ought to have a really clearly articulated relationship to the communities that we were working in, ... [and] that's partly out of necessity, because we work in a borough like Newham, [so in terms of] the social context, you can't take [any student engagement] as a given because the levels of deprivation are really high, [and]the level of diversity is ... amazing,

> so you can't make any assumptions about the young people that you have to work with ... Some of them may have arrived in the UK in the last six weeks, others might come from families who have lived in the East End of London for generations, others might be second generation immigrants, [who are] profoundly religious, some of them might be profoundly ... disadvantaged in all sorts of ways ... that sort of ... diversity leads you to be much more conscious of ... social context than you would be if you just worked in a suburb, where ... there is ... a relatively 'mono-culture'. ... [C]ommunity education has always been the sector in education that's ... done more than schools or universities to engage with learners that don't fit the traditional mould.

Here, Graham envisages the politics of community as inseparable from his art education practice. Furthermore, it seems that there are certain ideas of creativity associated with working in such a diverse student demographic. I am reminded that for Deleuze, the point of creativity is to break out of the everyday, the 'familiar'. The question of producing creativity is the same question as *how difference is possible*? How can we go beyond the coordinates of our constitution? Graham takes up the political utility of creativity in a (perhaps unintentionally) similar manner, musing that:

> The other thing I'm interested in is that creativity, ... inevitably, implies deviance, implies breaking the rules, implies criticism, and it implies challenge. It's not about working within the framework of "what if [this actually]"

exists, except to say "what if?". So, creativity to me is essentially bound up with the notion of social change, with the notion of trying to alter things, and of course that brings it inevitably into conflict with institutions, because that's not what institutions are in the business of doing. On the whole, institutions ... are in the business of regimenting, of disciplining, of ordering, of cataloguing and creating taxonomies and systems which bind people to certain ways of being. ... you've got to understand how it works in order to subvert, you can't hack an organisation if you don't really get [into] the politics of it.

Decades before this statement is made, Deleuze quotes Nietzsche in *Difference and Repetition* (1994, p. 136) as an impetus for his definition of creativity, as a situation in which new values and the recognition of established values are both affirmed as having different utilities. In a Deleuzian model of creativity, relationships between the new and the old are redesigned while they are being affirmed. In terms of accommodating this fractured and expanding experience of spatiality and folding it into the design of the Circus, Graham says:

We wanted to have an awareness of ... [a fractured experience of spatiality] in the work that we were doing, and not hold up school or college as the centre of the universe, but to understand that in fact people have multiple places they identify with, and multiple kind of selves almost in relation to those places, so they've put on one face to do this thing and perform in a different way [and then another face for another thing] ... with somewhere like Stratford Circus, the idea was to create a ... flexible sort of place, but it could be lots of different things, so that for example, Friday evenings are grind night, and it's like the East London masses, ... everybody comes down and it's pretty ... noisy and most people are between 16 and 22, ... it's really hardcore grind music, and at an earlier time that day, there might have been a tea dance in the same space, so it's a hybrid space. ... it becomes a place where it's possible to bring groups of people together who otherwise would have sod all to do with each other.

Intergenerational contact is difficult to facilitate outside families, hospitals and educational institutions. It seems to me that this is one of the ways in which the Arts Centre at Stratford Circus is exploring what a notion of creative place making might be. In the respect that the Arts Centre fosters exemplary teaching and learning practices that enable diverse groups of people, including young people, to become more innovative in the ways they think about their relationships to community.

Across the globe, in a starkly different physical and political environment, I spent some time researching a youth arts hub with parallels to Stratford Circus. The Courthouse Youth Arts is a regional youth arts centre in Geelong, Victoria that has been designed specifically to respond to the social and environmental issues that are specific to young people in rural and regional Victoria. I now contextualise my discussion of the two UK projects described above in relation to this regional Victorian case study. The time I spent at the Courthouse was in late 2004 and 2005. The Howard Government had been in power since 1996, arts funding had received unprecedented cuts during this period, and rural Victoria was in severe drought. This social context holds in relief the value accorded to, and appreciation of, arts projects that became part of English culture under the late Blair Government. This stark difference was brought to my attention recently when I was speaking at a University Symposium that brought together industry professionals and academics. The Symposium was in Australia and one attendee was a British artist who had travelled to Australia on a UK arts research scholarship. She made the point that the Australian Arts and Disability scene was ten years behind Britain at least four times across the course of two days. I was never sure quite what the utility of making this point was, though I assumed it was her way of expressing frustration and making quite plain the fact that she wasn't feeling overly stimulated or excited to be there. Australian arts practices have been remarkably under resourced in comparison to the United Kingdom. Yet, this has not led to a poor quality arts scene, rather, an unlikely arts scene: resilient, interesting and low budget.

The Courthouse Youth Arts Centre operates on the premise that music and movement bring people together. Community is formed through sense: senses of belonging, of being known and recognised. Music and movement are two media through which individual recognition and collective enjoyment are facilitated. Increasingly over the past three decades, street beats: hip-hop, rap, R'n'B and movement styles which have evolved with these sounds have brought together communities from a range of ethnic backgrounds and social classes. Wathaurong Koori people, Sudanese refugees, Lebanese, Greek, Italian and Anglo-Australian young people in Geelong come together through street beats and dance styles under the umbrella of Courthouse Youth Arts. Here community isn't about nationality, sexuality or money as much as it is about movement and style.

The Youth Arts Centre occupies a spacious 1950s style courthouse. The Centre's pastel coloured art deco facade is one of the more eye-catching buildings in the heart of Geelong, as the refurbishment of the building celebrates the old with a

Figure 3. Exterior, Courthouse Youth Arts Centre, Geelong.

contemporary flavour. A sense of place and an understanding of social context are critical when looking at the work Courthouse is doing. Local, regional sites are kept in focus through the Centre's outreach programs and through the multi-disciplinary focal lens of the Centre, which has been designed to embrace a diverse cross section of young people living in and around the rural centre of Geelong. Courthouse runs programs that focus on music, dance, visual arts, film, arts management and theatre making. The Courthouse's theatre making program currently includes street dance, break dance and MC-ing; tools of performance-making with which young people are particularly keen to engage.

The Courthouse is an exceptional place, the heart of an active arts community in Geelong; a town that has come a long way since it began as a wool distribution port. A successful textiles trade built upon the wool distribution at the financial heart of Geelong and at times this is reflected in the ways young visual artists approach their work here. However, the old Geelong wool stores are now campus buildings for Deakin University and while Geelong is still an industrial town, the focus of labour has shifted distinctly. Alongside Deakin's growing contribution to the community here, the Ford engine manufacturing plant and local Shell oil refinery are, and have been, Geelong's primary financial sources for decades.

Beyond the smoking refinery pylons, Geelong enfolds pockets of the 1950s alive and well in the new millennium, and a broad community demographic. In-between the production buildings there are cottages that sell home made gollywog dolls and potted irises. There are sushi shops, Lebanese restaurants and schools for Sudanese refugees. Some people take break dance classes a few nights a week. Other people grow their own vegies and have chooks. It's the country and the city at the same time. It's an in-between place that feels distinctive in comparison to the grey streets and over-filled trams of Melbourne. There are some funky young people in Geelong. Many of their mums and dads work for Ford, and these young people are living on the cutting edge of a very different kind of cultural production – jamming acrobatics, street dancing and rhymes, sourcing new stories of their own and giving them platforms. These folk are making it pretty clear that while some parts of Geelong tell tales of car engines, petrol and gollywogs, there is another level of cultural production going on. In a Deleuzian model of creativity, relationships between the new and the old are redesigned while they are being affirmed. Deleuze states:

> Nietzsche's distinction between the creation of new values and the recognition of established values should not be understood in a historically relative manner, as though the established values were new in their time and the new values simply needed time to become established. In fact it concerns a difference which is both formal and in kind. The new, with its power of beginning and beginning again, remains forever new, just as the established was always established from the outset, even if a certain amount of empirical time was necessary for this to be recognised. What becomes established with the new is precisely not the new. For the new –in other words, difference – calls forth forces in thought which are not the forces of recognition, today or tomorrow, but the power of a completely other model, from an unrecognised

and unrecognisable terra incognita . What forces does this new bring to bear upon thought, from what central bad nature and ill does it spring, from what central ungrounding which strips thought of its 'innateness' and treats it every time as something which has not always existed, but begins, forced and under constraint? By contrast, how derisory are the voluntary struggles for recognition (Deleuze, 1994, p.136).

The Courthouse embraces and produces *terra incognita* just as much as it re-inscribes dominant discourses of the arts helping youth at risk. The centre publicises itself as being concerned with engaging marginalised and disenfranchised young people and as offering opportunities for creative types to build their skills and excel. Courthouse is a community-based organisation where the concerns of Geelong's youth community are reflected in its programs and in turn, the programs produce works that appeal to Geelong's youth.

My first class at the Courthouse was one of the weekly *HeadSpin* master classes held for eight young emerging visual artists, writers and theatre makers. The *HeadSpin* master class program had a focus on theatre making and it applied this focus broadly to encompass all aspects of theatre production. The project invited eight emerging artists to work in teams to devise and stage three short performance works, roughly twenty minutes each in duration. These works were then presented as a triple bill in May 2005. *HeadSpin* consisted of weekly master classes with the Courthouse coordinator of the theatre making program, Naomi Steinborner. Naomi mentored *HeadSpin* recipients until December, at which point specialist mentors in different disciplinary areas came on board the project. These additions to the artistic team individually supported the eight young *HeadSpin* artists through the finalisation of their performance concepts, auditions, rehearsals, design, production and presentation.

The *HeadSpin* class were an interesting and diverse bunch. After completing Drama Studies at Adelaide University, Naomi Steinborner studied animatuering at the Victorian College of the Arts. Her background in thinking through space and visual, conceptual design is evident in her approach to fostering new talent. A sculptor, a design student, a visual dramaturge, two writers, a sound designer, a puppeteer and two directors made up the HeadSpin team. While I was on board, the community theatre company Somebody's Daughter ran a workshop with *HeadSpin* that looked at working with disenfranchised people and sourcing performance material from community participants' lived experiences. The *HeadSpin* team worked in a very welcoming and engaging way with *Somebody's Daughter;* a company who offer a model of community theatre which has been slipping out of focus a little since the late 1980s. After *HeadSpin* many of the young artists being mentored in this program wanted to turn their focus to community cultural development (CCD) work. Indeed, some of the participants were already actively engaged in CCD work with young mums. *HeadSpin* produced some striking and diverse works: a puppetry fantasy about a young boy's journey through a gypsy forest, a contemporary satirical perspective on parlour games and an affective atmosphere / soundscape of adolescence. These works appealed to a broad cross-section of Geelong's community.

One of the most important things about youth arts work is the ways in which it can include, speak to and be modelled around, marginalised community groups, yet theatre work by its very nature is not marginalising. Making theatre is about getting along with people. It's about working together and *getting out there*. It's also about an irreducible humanness. Whatever the specific difficulties of people's lives, people get along as people and laugh and cry at similar 'human' things. While some contemporary social theorists argue we are now living in an age of post-humanism, I think collectives like the Courthouse show us otherwise. We are living in the age of a new humanism, a place where your aesthetics are your ethics; where sense, atmosphere and affect take precedence over the binary ruts of identity politics.

My analyses of these three place-making projects gestures towards the respective utility and need for a critical reconsideration of the educational work that youth arts programs undertake. While the connections drawn together here span a broad range of discourses, I want to outline some of the force, complexity and cultural significance that lies at the intersection of youth arts work and place-making projects. Deleuzian theories of creativity and place show us that the intersection of youth arts work and place-making projects can be taken up in order to redefine −and speak back to− dominant discourses of place and creativity. As sites of public pedagogy, such youth arts projects promote diverse conceptions of creativity and place. They show up the instability of our everyday uses of these concepts. Perhaps most saliently, they involve many young people who can become imaginatively captured, skilled and inspired.

ACKNOWLEDGEMENTS

A modified version of this chapter was first published as 'Youth arts and the differential becoming of the world' in *Continuum: Journal of Media and Cultural Studies 24*(1).

REFERENCES

ArtAngel. Retrieved January 12, 2008, from http://www.artangel.org.uk/

Creative Partnerships. Retrieved December 19, 2007, from http://www.creative-partnerships.com/

Deleuze, G. (1994). *Difference and repetition* (P. Patton, Trans.). New York: Colombia University Press. (Original work published 1968)

Deleuze, G., & Guattari, F. (1994). *What is philosophy?* London: Verso Publishers.

Deleuze, G., & Guattari, F. (1987). *A thousand plateaus: Capitalism and schizophrenia* (B. Massumi, Trans.). Minneapolis, MN: University of Minnesota Press. (Original work published 1980)

Hall, C. J., & Thomson, P. L. (2007). Creative partnerships? Cultural policy and inclusive arts practice in one primary school. *British Educational Research Journal, 33*(3), 315–329.

Margate Exodus. Retrieved December 19, 2007, from http://www.themargateexodus.org.uk/home.html

NewVic Sixth Form Arts College. Retrieved September 10, 2009, from http://www.newvic.ac.uk/

Williams, J. (2000). Deleuze's ontology and creativity: Becoming in architecture. *Pli: The Warwick Journal of Philosophy, 9*, 200–219.

Anna Hickey-Moody
University of Sydney

SECTION II: LANDSCAPES OF LEARNING

JENNIFER RENNIE

6. "IF YOU SEE A BUBBLE COMING UP"

Reading and Writing the Landscape

In the water you just go down to the sandbar. You can see the big brown black thing and you walk a little bit closer. If you see it move, that's when it's a crab. In the creek, there is just a little hole and if you see a bubble coming up. Like there's a hole there and you can see clean water but if you see dirty water it just ran in hiding from us.

Darcy is one of the children who participated in an extensive study that generated detailed case study information about the transition experiences of seven Aboriginal and Torres Strait Islander children as they moved from Year 7 in their community school to Year 8 in their new urban high school (Rennie, Wallace, & Falk, 2004). In particular the study documented the literacy and numeracy practices valued in the home community, community school and urban high school and highlighted the continuities and discontinuities between them (Lincoln & Guba, 1985). Discontinuities were found in the ways in which children engaged in the various activities. Further, the data highlighted a lack of understanding, valuing and acknowledgement of the various community literate and numerate practices by schools. The results of the study suggested that student identities embodied different forms of knowledge and skills and these qualitatively different identities played key roles in the students' effectiveness as 'westernised' learners. In the opening vignette Darcy explained how to find crabs in the oceans and creeks. All of the children who participated in this study actively read and wrote their landscape. They read their environment, the water and their bodies and they represented this through story, art and dance. As they moved to urban high schools these different literate practices were not valued.

The paper will explore another example from the data, where Darcy shared his highly developed knowledge of place, self and significant others at the local art centre as he took the researcher from the story of his favourite Grandmother's painting to his late father's pottery. Finally, it will highlight the need to redefine literacy, so we might acknowledge, value and use different reading and writing practices in productive ways.

READING AND WRITING DIFFERENTLY

In this study literacy was approached from a socio cultural perspective which means it was not simply understood as a discrete set of skills but rather as variable forms of social practice, see for example, "New Literacy Studies" (Barton & Hamilton, 1998)

M. Somerville, K. Power and P. de Carteret (eds.),
Landscapes and Learning: Place Studies for a Global World, 89–100

"social literacies" (Gee, 1996; Street 1993), or "situated literacies" (Barton, Hamilton, & Ivanich, 2000). Literacy enables us to 'do' things, to learn about ourselves and others and to communicate our knowledge, thoughts, understandings and feelings. Most importantly the process of becoming literate and the kinds of literacy practices engaged in demonstrates aspects of the individual, place and cultural, social and community identities (Falk & Balatti, 2004; Ferdman, 1991; Guofang, 2000).

Literacy occurs through a range of different modalities including the visual, oral, kinaesthetic, digital and written. The multiliteracies framework described by Cope and Kalantzis (2000) is helpful for thinking about literacy in this way. They argue that we need to think about literacy differently because of the advent of new technologies and the increasing awareness of cultural diversity in a globalised world (Somerville, 2009). Since the introduction of mass schooling the literacies of reading and writing print based texts has been privileged. According to Cope and Kalantis (2000) literacy teaching and learning has been carefully restricted to "monolingual, monocultural and rule-governed forms of language". They believe that:

> the most important skill students need to learn is to negotiate regional, ethnic, or class based dialects; variations in register that occur according to social context; hybrid cross-cultural discourses; the code switching often to be found within a text among different languages, dialects or registers; different visual and iconic meanings; and variations in the gestural relationships among people, language and material objects. Indeed, [they say] this is the only hope for averting the catastrophic conflicts about identities and spaces that now seem ever ready to flare up (p. 14).

Somerville (2009) also highlights a need to redefine literacy. She discusses body and spatial literacies which evolve from a highly developed learned understanding of our own identities in relation to the places and spaces in which we work and live. According to Somerville (2009) literacy is something which occurs in the translation between these embodied knowledges and different textual forms. In the context of this study a broad definition of text was adopted to include kinaesthetic, oral, visual, print and digital text forms. The child at the centre of the discussion in this paper was not considered literate in the school space. Darcy had some difficulty reading and writing print based texts and was placed in an Intensive English class when he moved into high school. Despite this I found Darcy to be highly literate with an embodied knowledge about self and place which he comfortably conveyed to me through different modalities.

BACKGROUND TO THE STUDY

The study referred to was funded through the Federal Department of Education, Science and Training as part of a broader initiative to fund small projects that investigated students considered at risk in the school environment.

A feature of many rural and remote communities in Northern Australia is the requirement for Indigenous students to leave their home communities in order to access secondary education.

According to the Northern Territory Department of Employment, Education and Training (DEET) (2002), there were 85 schools that serviced rural and remote areas of the Northern Territory. Sixty-two of these schools were relatively small primary schools with one to five teachers. Three were Area Schools that provided formal education to Year 10 and a small number were trialing the delivery of secondary education to Year 12. Generally these schools in remote locations did not provide any formal secondary education and most students were required to leave their home communities to attend urban boarding schools in order to access secondary education (DEET, 2002). The majority of children in these schools were of Aboriginal and Torres Strait Islander descent and the retention rates of Aboriginal and Torres Strait Islander children in high school according to Collins (1999) and Ramsey (2004) were reportedly significantly lower than that of non-Indigenous children. Problems associated with providing 'good' education to children living in remote areas of Australia are not unique to the Northern Territory. According to Barcan (1965) this has been an ongoing problem since settlement (as cited in Reid, Edwards, & Power, 2004).

Whilst there has been a serious commitment toward improving the delivery of secondary education in remote communities in the Northern Territory, it will be some time before all Indigenous students living in rural and remote areas have access to secondary education in their home communities.

According to Ramsey (2004), in 2001, the Northern Territory had the largest proportion of students attending schools in remote areas in the country. Forty-four percent of all students attended remote schools compared to the national average of less than 5%. However, in the same year only 21% of these remote students attained the Year 5 reading benchmark. Similarly, students enrolled in regional Northern Territory schools fared worse than their urban counterparts. Despite a slight improvement in Northern Territory figures in recent years reported Indigenous literacy outcomes continue to remain well below non-Indigenous outcomes. In 2006, for example, 36.5% of Indigenous students in Year 7 met the national literacy reading benchmark compared with 90.2% of non-Indigenous students. Similarly in the same year 26.1% of Indigenous students met the Year 7 writing benchmark compared with 78.9% of non-Indigenous students. In 2006 there were 3,635 Indigenous students and 6,073 non-Indigenous students enrolled in high schools across the Northern Territory. In the same year 92 Indigenous students graduated with their high school certificate compared to 632 non-Indigenous students (DEET, 2007, p. 53).

Amongst other things, this study was interested in better understanding the kinds of literacy practices that constituted the daily lives of these children and to see how these connected with the kinds of literacy practices that these students were required to engage with in school.

THE RESEARCH SITES

The two communities in this study are situated in the Tiwi Islands approximately 100 kilometres north of Darwin in the far north of Australia. Each community has a population of approximately 400 people and is serviced by a local store, bank, primary school, recreation hall, sporting facilities, social club, police, women's and men's centre, library, post-office, art and health centre. Both communities are very traditional with the children and their families participating in hunting and ceremonial activities regularly.

Each of the two community primary schools investigated had a student population of approximately eighty students. The seven children that participated in this study were chosen because they were relocating to the same urban high school in Darwin.

The urban high school in this study had a population of about 800 students, the majority of which were day students. The school provided boarding places for Indigenous children from over forty different remote locations in the Northern Territory. At the time of this study Year 8 was streamed into three different programmes, which included mainstream, supported secondary and intensive English classes. Students placed in mainstream worked with the mainstream curriculum, those placed in supported secondary were being assisted so they could later be moved into mainstream classes and those in intensive English classes had a strong focus on the teaching and learning of literacy and numeracy. Initially, one of the seven students was placed in a mainstream class; three were placed in supported secondary and the remainder in intensive English classes.

The data found that the parents and caregivers of the children in this study had high expectations of the school system and of their children in relation to learning, community and school involvement and future career opportunities. The community clearly valued learning and what the education system represented. Learning was an integral part of community life. Parent and community members expected their children would learn during the various community activities such as hunting, ceremony and sport and most importantly the children knew that they too would be required later in life to pass this knowledge on to younger family members. Similarly the school also had high expectations in relation to learning; however, these students were positioned as being unsuccessful learners before their school journey began and teachers said it was the exception not the rule that these children would leave the school system with their high school certificate.

Children in this study identified strongly with the various activities in which they participated in their home communities. They identified with them because the activities helped to construct who they were. Their totem, dreaming, language, family and special places were embodied and connected them to places and other members of the community. All of the children in the study had their own song, their own dance and their own country. They identified with some people in the community but not others. The teaching that occurred through their hunting adventures, their participation in ceremonies, their sharing stories around the campfire and their watching others paint and carve, helped them to understand who they were. It helped them to understand what their roles and responsibilities were in the community and it taught them how to do the same.

The research found that many of the discontinuities for these children lay in the fact that much of what the children knew and who the children were, what they preferred to do and could do was often not valued and acknowledged in the school setting. The irony of the latter point was clear in the data: Continuities in knowledge and identity can be seen to provide the bridges and connections (based on what the children can do and who they are) that build learning and new knowledge and identities. Discontinuities in knowledge and identity prohibit effective and engaged learning.

This research was specifically designed to identify some of the continuities and discontinuities for these children so that schools might better help these children to become successful learners in school.

RESEARCH DESIGN

The study referred to in this paper generated detailed case study information about the transition experiences of seven Indigenous students from their home community and school to their new urban high school in relation to the literacy and numeracy practices of these different contexts (Dyson, 1997; Lincoln & Guba, 1985).

Ethnographic techniques of observation, document analysis and interviews were used during the data collection phases. Qualitative techniques were used to analyse the data. In the initial phase of the analysis, data collected from the home, community school and urban high school were analysed separately. After the various interviews and observations were transcribed, coding of the data sets occurred (Miles & Huberman, 1994).

The second phase of the analysis involved an ethnographically grounded approach to discourse analysis. Gee and Green (1997, p. 139) identified four dimensions of social activity: World building, Activity building, Identity building and Connection building. World building referred to how participants assembled "situated meanings about reality, present and absent, concrete and abstract" (p. 139). Activity building described the construction of situated meanings connected to the activity itself. Identity building concerned the identities that were relevant to the situation and included ways of knowing, believing, acting and interacting. Finally, Connection building related to how interactions connected to past and future interactions (Gee & Green, 1997, p. 139). Gee and Green (1997) suggested a number of questions relating to each of these dimensions. The research team selected a number of questions that could be answered through the data. The questions provided a framework to analyse the various data and provided a rich description of the activities investigated.

The third phase of the analysis involved constant comparative analysis between the data sets to assist in identifying discontinuities between the data (Guba & Lincoln, 1981; Lincoln & Guba, 1985). This assisted in identifying the extent to which school literacy and numeracy practices reflected those valued by the community.

In this paper two examples from the data are discussed. A different approach to the analysis of these excerpts will be taken. The multiliteracies framework described by Cope and Kalantzis (2000) and Somerville's (2009) body and place literacies and ideas which describe literacy as an act of translation will be used. In the first example Darcy is in his place, the local art centre. There he reveals a highly developed knowledge about himself, others and his place by carefully moving between different knowledge systems and modalities to convey his story. In the second example Darcy is in a different space, his Year 8 English classroom. In this space he attempts to tell a similar story. However, in this space these ways of knowing and doing literacy are not privileged and so his story remained untold.

"YOU GOING TO BE POT MAN"

Darcy walked me down to the local art centre where we met his grandmother. She was busily working on one of her paintings at the table out the front. He told me how he comes here every afternoon after school and how he often drops in at lunch time to see his grandmother. Darcy explained that the painting she was working on was about gathering 'long bums' and 'mussels' and that the colours used in the painting were traditional colours. They included grey, black, yellow, brown and white. He then pointed to the shapes that represented the long bums and the shapes which represented the mussels. The local women and children on the community often gather long bums and mussels during their hunting activities.

He explained that the white colour represented body paint and that the white circle in the middle was to put an outline on it to make it "look outstanding". My understanding of traditional Aboriginal art was very limited and very 'white' and so I asked whether Darcy knew how to make the paint. He explained it was acrylic and came in containers, although he did say that sometimes they used ochre and that he did know how to make this. He told me you get some rocks and that you scrape them. He called this "woody woody". Then some powder falls off. You then mix that with a very "small amount" of something else that helps turn it into a "good" paint. He also explained that some products were "better" than others for making good paint.

Darcy then began talking about some of his grandmother's other paintings. He proceeded to take me to the art centre's show room so he could point them out to me. When we got inside he began looking through a pile of canvases that were stacked on the floor. He spotted the one he wanted to show me and asked the sales assistant to help him pull it out. He explained that it was his favourite painting and that it represented two snakes, a "girl and boy snake". He then explained it was his grandmother's dreaming, her totem. He reminded me that his totem was "Jungle Fowl" like his father and highlighted the fact that the colours were slightly different to the first painting we had looked at in that there was no grey, only white, yellow and brown. This was obviously a hugely significant point. He finished by telling me this was his favourite because it was one of the longest ones she had painted.

After we had looked at his Grandmother's painting he moved me towards the pottery displayed on the shelves. He told me that pottery he had made had sold and he mentioned that his father who had passed away also made pots. He then proceeded to show me a book about the pottery made on the island. He took me on a picture flick of the book pointing out all the people he knew and pieces of work his father had created. He pointed to the first picture and explained that it was Maria and his father when he was young. He then turned to another picture and said that this was his father making pottery when he was old. He showed me the kiln he was talking about on the previous day and told me he would show it to me after.

Following this he showed me pictures of several artefacts that his father made.

He then turned to a picture which he explained was a group of "famous people" at his father's opening exhibition. He said that he missed his father and showed me a picture which gave details about his country, skin group and dreaming. He also showed me where his name appeared in the book.

He then turned to a page which talked about his father's *Pukamani* which is a period of mourning that occurs after a person has passed away. During this time the deceased member is given a different name and family and other community members are forbidden to refer to the person using their birth name.

Finally he showed me a picture of several people and told me how they were related to him. He then turned to a picture of a plate which his sister had made and he explained that he had painted the plate. He was very proud of this piece of pottery.

Following this Darcy went on to the computer to show me the art centre's website. He explained that people from all over the world bought the paintings and that the artists made a commission on their work.

Darcy then proceeded to take me outside to where the pottery is made. He told me that this was the place he was talking about on the previous day. He showed me the potters' wheel, showed me where to put the clay and how to turn the wheel. He said that he often makes pottery when he is feeling bored. He pointed out some unfinished pots and walked over to the kiln and explained how the pots were fired. He showed me where the clay was kept. He then said he had been making pots since he was four years old and that he kept doing this until he was seven, the year when his father passed away. He said that his father used to tell the kids to go to school and to come down and help with the pots after school was over. He said he still makes some pots with his big sister. He took me outside and was very excited to show me the old brick kiln. He showed me where they stacked the pots. He explained that there used to be an iron sliding door where the heat came up. Finally he showed me where they put the wood to fire up the kiln. His closing comment was that his Uncle had told him that he was going to take "all this over" and that he, Darcy, would be the next 'pot man'.

During my time at the art centre Darcy took me on a journey through time from the story of the painting his Grandmother was doing when we arrived to the days when he was four watching his father fire the pots in the old kiln. I learned snippets about his family, his dreaming, how to make ochre, stories of paintings, the economic workings of the art centre, the old and the new. This place was part of Darcy's life. The paintings and the pottery helped to form his identity in the past, present and future. After all, he was told he would be the next 'pot man'. A few months later I sat with Darcy in a different place, his Year 8 English classroom.

wRiting REMOTELY DIFFERENT

I walked into the classroom and sat with two of the Tiwi children. Other students were busily taking out their English books and writing implements. The teacher supplied Darcy and Arnie with pen and paper and asked them to ensure they were better prepared for their next lesson. After the normal routine of re-establishing the classroom rules and procedures the teacher wrote "The Purposes of Writing" on the whiteboard. The students were orientated to the lesson and asked to write a list of all the different kinds of writing. Darcy and Arnie began their list which included shopping list, email, timetable, newspaper, books and magazines. Darcy began to write the word 'painting' and looked to me for approval. I told him it was a good thing to include; after all, he had told me some of the stories in his Grandmother's paintings. Then Arnie said, "What about dance?" I told him it also was a very good example to include. I had seen their dances and they had told me how they represented their various totems. Both children became excited and started adding other less conventional forms of writing to their list including tracks, songs and the seasons. The teacher asked each group to call out their lists. She began to compile a list of all the students' ideas. Darcy and Arnie were pleased that their ideas were recorded. Following this the teacher chose four of the examples the class had offered and erased the remainder of the students' responses. The final list included novels, dictionary, map legend and email. She continued with the lesson and the groups were asked to think about purpose and audience in relation to the remaining four genres.

In a prior interview with the teacher she explained that this lesson was an introductory session for her writing program this term. She expressed concern about these students' preparedness for secondary school and said that it was important to "get back to basics". She aimed to have these children comfortable using a range of written genres by the end of term and to have them plan and draft their writing appropriately.

In the following section further discussion of the two stories is presented. The first example demonstrates how we might think about literacy as an act of translation and it shows how Darcy successfully helps the researcher in understanding and coming to know a different place. In this example Darcy carefully draws on a range of literacies. In the second example Darcy is unsuccessful in his attempts to use literacy as an act of translation. The resources available to him are limited and the translation between the different modalities such as print, visual, bodily, spatial and kinaesthetic are not afforded or explored in this context.

THINKING ABOUT LITERACY DIFFERENTLY

As stated earlier literacy enables us to 'do' things, to learn about ourselves and others and to communicate our knowledge, thoughts, understandings and feelings. It demonstrates aspects of the individual, place and cultural, social and community identities. Further it can occur through a range of different modalities including the visual, oral, kinaesthetic, spatial, body, digital and written. Somerville (2009) argues that literacy is always an act of translation which begins in childhood.

She suggests it is something that begins at birth as we move from "inchoate sensory experience to forms of representation, expressed initially in gesture, then sounds, and finally marks on a page later differentiated into drawing and writing" (2006, p. 5). She argues further that the movement from inchoate experience through to marks on a page should not be conceived as a developmental pathway where we lose all that precedes print literacy, but that all forms need to be maintained so that we can move freely between these different modalities. In order to understand how we might acquire print literacy we need to understand the "acts of translation" that occur between these various modalities and need to facilitate these translations.

I further argue that privileging one mode of literacy has the tendency to produce barriers making it difficult for all cultural groups to participate equally in our society. Cope and Kalantzis (2000) also suggest that thinking about literacy differently is the only hope for "averting the catastrophic conflicts about identities and spaces that now seem ever ready to flare up" (p.6).

POINTING TO THE MUSSELS

I draw attention back to where Darcy was telling me about the painting his Grandmother was working on when we visited the local art centre. When I first viewed the painting it resembled other Aboriginal artworks I had seen. The shapes, colour, lines and texture were similar. Like other artworks it was pleasant to the eye but beyond this meant nothing to me. Darcy knew about this painting in ways that I did not. He read it like I read a novel on a Sunday afternoon. The shapes, colours and lines told a story about people and place. For me to understand this Darcy used a range of modalities. He pointed to things, explained things orally and directed me to other artworks which held similar storylines. This painting revealed stories about places and people. It told the story of the women collecting mussels and long bums. The shapes, colours and lines all represented aspects of the individual, place and country. It was easy for Darcy to tell this tale. He had experienced it. It was part of who he was and what he did. Darcy's literacies were embodied and emplaced. They arose from a particular place and particular bodies connected to that place. Similarly when he pulled out his favourite painting of the two snakes he revealed the iconic meanings to me. He read the symbols and the colours in the painting and explained what they represented. Darcy's grandmother like many other people on the community recorded their stories about self, community and country in their paintings. These stories remain untold without some act of translation. Darcy was able to facilitate this translation through the use of a range of different modalities including oral, body and kinaesthetic literacies. He facilitated the translation from visual to oral literacy so that I would understand.

MY FATHER: THAT'S HIM THERE

After I had learned about Darcy's grandmother he then proceeded to unveil the story of his late father. Similar to any other 12 year old he began by showing me the pottery he had made and then casually mentioned that his father had also made pots.

He was proud of his father and showed me the book on the shelf that documented aspects of his father's life. It is interesting that he used the book to do this. It made it easy for me to understand by reading the various passages and examining the visual images Darcy had selected. He also unlocked other secrets that were not readily accessible in this print representation of his father's life. In his careful selection of text and images, including samples of his father's artwork, important gatherings, his connections to other people and extra information he provided I was able to gain a sense of how Darcy was part of this text. Like the paintings, he explained how the pottery told stories about people and places. To complement this he showed where his father used to work. In his vivid explanation of the old and new kiln you could almost smell the fire. Similarly I could almost feel the clay between my fingers as he showed me how to work the clay and use the potters' wheel. This knowledge Darcy had was embodied and through this brief encounter he figured out ways to make me understand by drawing on a range of literacies including body, spatial, print and oral. Literacy was an act of translation.

THE PURPOSES OF wRiting

In the Year 8 English classroom Darcy and the other students were asked to make a list of all the ways we use writing. Darcy and his Tiwi friends began by listing conventional writing forms. Darcy then turned to me and asked whether he could include painting on the list. I told him I thought this was a good idea. In this encounter Darcy and his friends were exploring other possibilities in relation to writing. They were challenging writing in its traditional form. Their teacher recorded their ideas on the whiteboard with other less conventional forms such as dance for a short period. These ideas were then erased. In this lesson, writing, learning about writing and 'doing' writing were constructed from a school-based view of literacy. There was no space to discuss these ideas or to explore how we might understand the translation from these visual forms to more conventional print based literacies. A different view of literacy was presented in this space. It was not used as a means to 'do' things, to learn about ourselves and others or to communicate knowledge, thoughts, understandings and feelings. There was no context for choosing or using different literacies and students learned little about themselves or others. Literacy in this context was disembodied and place-less. The lesson had been constructed in such a way that nothing could be told and nothing could be learned, it had no purpose. Ironically it was called the "Purposes of Writing".

This was in complete contrast to the intricate tale that Darcy told me at the art centre where I learned about traditional colours, totems, dreaming and family relationships. Where I was told about making "good paint", about how the website took their artwork to the rest of the world and that his favourite painting was the "longest one". Further he gave me insight into the character of members of his family. He told me how his father told the children to go to school, how he was famous and he told me how he made pots with his sister. In the telling of his intricate tale, Darcy utilised a range of literate practices. He told his story orally, he showed me the things he was referring to and he revealed how his grandmother's identity was represented in her paintings. He showed me where aspects of his family's life had been recorded in a printed text and he showed me where the art centre went out to the world digitally. He moved from oral story telling, to giving explanations about how things worked, to using procedural discourse to tell me how to make things, to navigating websites. Darcy presented as being highly literate in this place, using different forms of literacy to tell me about his connections to the local art centre.

In contrast the observed lesson in Darcy's Year 8 English classroom presented literacy in a more conventional way. Despite Darcy offering different ways to think about writing, these ideas were not explored. This lesson constituted a missed opportunity. It was an opportunity for Darcy and Arnie to tell their stories. It was an opportunity for other children to learn. It was an opportunity to redefine literacy. It was an opportunity for the children who were considered to be struggling with literacy to be positioned as experts. It was an opportunity for the teacher to better understand these students' literate competence. It was an opportunity to explore the translations between different literacies. The teacher missed it because her definition of literacy was driven by a curriculum constructed within a culture which privileges its own view of learning and literacy.

REFERENCES

Barton, D., & Hamilton, M. (1998). *Local literacies: Reading and writing in one community*. London: Routledge.

Barton, D., Hamilton, M., & Ivanich, R. (Eds.). (2000). *Situated literacies: Reading and writing in context*. New York: Routledge.

Collins, B. (1999). *Learning lessons: An independent review of Indigenous education in the Northern Territory*. Darwin, Northern Territory: Northern Territory Department of Education.

Cope, B., & Kalantzis, M. (Eds.). (2000). *Multiliteracies: Literacy learning and the design of social futures*. South Yarra, VIC.: Macmillan.

DEET. (2002). *Annual Report 2001-2002*. Darwin, Northern Territory: Department of Employment Education and Training.

DEET. (2007). *Annual Report 2006-2007*. Darwin, Northern Territory: Department of Employment Education and Training.

Dyson, A. H. (1997). Children out of bounds: The power of case studies in expanding vision of literacy development. In J. Flood, S. Brice Heath, & D. Lapp (Eds.), *Handbook of research on teaching literacy through the communicative and visual arts* (pp. 167–180). New York: International Reading Association.

Falk, I., & Balatti, J. (2004). *Identities of place: Their power and consequence for VET*. Paper presented at the Learner and practitioner: 'The heart of the matter', Canberra, ACT.

Ferdman, M. F. (1991). Literacy and cultural identity. In M. Minaami & B. P. Kennedy (Eds.), *Language issues in literacy and bilingual/multicultural education* (pp. 347–373). Cambridge, MA: Harvard Educational Review.

Gee, J. (1996). *Social linguistics and literacies: Ideology in discourses*. London: Taylor and Francis.

Gee, J. P., & Green, J. (1997). Discourse analysis, learning, and social practice: A methodological study. *Review of Research in Education, 23*, 119–169.

Guba, E., & Lincoln, Y. (1981). *Effective evaluation*. San Fransisco: Jossey-Bass.

Guofang, L. (2000, Winter). Family literacy and cultural identity: An ethnographic study of a Filipino family in Canada. *McGill Journal of Education*, 1–14.

Lincoln, Y. S., & Guba, E. G. (1985). *Naturalistic inquiry*. California: SAGE Publications.

Miles, M. B., & Huberman, M. A. (1994). *Qualitative data analysis* (2nd ed.). California: SAGE.

Ramsey, G. (2004). *Report on future directions for secondary education in the Northern Territory*. Darwin: Charles Darwin University, Department of Employment Education and Training.

Reid, J. A., Edwards, H., & Power, K. (2004). Early literacy education in rural communities: Situating development. *Australian Journal of Language and Literacy, 27*(2), 128–141.

Rennie, J., Wallace, R., & Falk, I. (2004). *Discontinuities in literacy and numeracy practices between Indigenous community schooling and urban high school*. Canberra, ACT: Department Education, Science and Training.

Somerville, M. (2006). *Literacy as translation*. Paper presented at the Australian Council of Adult Literacy Annual Conference, Adelaide, SA.

Somerville, M. (2009). Re-thinking literacy as a process of translation. *Australian Journal of Language and Literacy, 32*(1), 9–21.

Street, B. V. (Ed.). (1993). *Cross-cultural approaches to literacy*. Cambridge, UK: Cambridge University Press.

Jennifer Rennie
Monash University

.

DEBRA HAYES

7. PEDAGOGIES OF PLACE AND POSSIBILITY

INTRODUCTION

The outcomes from schooling of the children of low-income families are consistently less than those of middle and high-income families. In this chapter, I draw upon a three-year longitudinal study of four schools characterised by high levels of poverty and difference to illustrate the scale and nature of the problem of inequity in educational provision in Australia. Using descriptions of practice (recounts) produced in this study, I show how some teachers challenge taken for granted perceptions about what children from low income backgrounds are capable of achieving by making uncommon pedagogical choices. It is not surprising that these choices are uncommon because our society often places young people who most rely upon schooling under the care of the least experienced in the most unstable conditions. Even so, some possibilities for human agency are explored in this chapter.

ASSESSING NEED AND SUPPORTING SUCCESS

Every four years public schools in New South Wales are invited to take part in a survey administered by the State education system that identifies the twenty per cent of schools with the highest concentration of students from low-income families. Under the Priority Schools Program these schools are provided with additional equity-based funding which includes a cash grant to support literacy, numeracy and participation, as well as a staffing supplement and additional consultative support. This assessment is based upon a combination of factors related to the Aboriginality, employment status and educational achievement of parents. The number of sole-parent families and those receiving government benefits and pensions are also taken into consideration, along with a weighted score of occupation. Participating schools are required to draw upon their own resources to distribute and collect the survey, and they must also rely upon the cooperation of parents. Some of the poorest schools may not be identified through this process as they are unable to commit time to its administration. Even so, in 2004, more that fifty percent of the 2,223 schools in NSW considered that their students were from sufficiently disadvantaged backgrounds to apply for some of the additional funds available. Given the time and resources required to undertake the survey, it is unlikely that these were ambit claims but rather an indication that the actual levels of disadvantage are greater than those identified by equity-based funding categories.

M. Somerville, K. Power and P. de Carteret (eds.),
Landscapes and Learning: Place Studies for a Global World, 101–117
© 2009 Sense Publishers. All rights reserved.

Elsewhere in Australia, this type of equity-based redistribution of public funding for schooling has dried up since the federally funded Disadvantaged Schools Program was discontinued in the first budget of the Howard Government in 1996. Throughout its eleven years in office, Howard's conservative Liberal government favoured strategies that delivered targeted support to individuals rather than groups, thus prioritising individual choice over ameliorating the structural disadvantage experienced by some groups in society. During this same period, Australia experienced significant real income growth, the real income of less well off Australians grew, and the real wealth per person increased as reported by the Australian Bureau of Statistics in a report that provides information about whether life is getting better in Australia, Measures of Australia's Progress (2004). Despite this progress, according to successive results in the OECD's (2003, 2006) international comparative assessment (Programme for International Student Assessment or PISA), the relationship between social background and achievement in Australia is stronger than in similar countries such as Finland and Canada. In other words, if you are disadvantaged in Australia, the education system does not serve you as well as systems in other comparable countries.

A commonly held view is that good schools have good teachers who get good results. That is, it is generally believed that success or failure at school is largely due to the quality of teaching. While we can be fairly confident that we know what high quality teaching looks like (Darling-Hammond, 1997; Newmann & Associates, 1996; Wrigley, 2000), the findings of one of the largest classroom based studies to be conducted in Australia (Queensland School Reform Longitudinal Study, 2001) showed that high quality teaching was uncommon, and generally limited to a small number of classrooms in the participating schools. There is little variation in classroom practices across different school types, and most of the classrooms (numbering almost 1,000) observed in this study showed limited intellectual demands and connections to the world beyond the classroom. These kinds of classroom practices are more likely to work with middle class children who are better equipped to endure the routines of schooling because they have an understanding of the rewards that it will deliver, and they have access to resource rich homes as supplementary learning environments. The pattern of distribution of classroom practices observed during the QSRLS suggests that low-income families, for the most part, receive the same kind of education as other children but the education they receive is less likely to support their success at school. In the next section, I develop this argument with reference to four cases studies conducted in NSW Priority High Schools during the period 2005-7.

THE UNIVERSE OF SECONDARY SCHOOLING

About five years ago, the executive team at a western Sydney high school embarked on an ambitious plan to improve the school's literacy and numeracy results. They decided to adopt a common language to talk about learning and a consistent approach to handling discipline problems. This dual platform for learning was driven hard by the leadership team; every teacher received professional development in the principles underpinning these approaches, ongoing support through professional learning teams and one-on-one coaching in classrooms. The school's leaders were unwavering in their commitment to this approach, and did not countenance resistance. Additional equity-based funding was used to support professional learning, the establishment of key positions to support teaching and learning and time for professional learning teams. Before long, the Year 10 results on State wide standardised tests in literacy and numeracy started to improve, and in following years increased further.

By the time the school joined our research study, the executive team that had been responsible for this success had started to move on and were taking up promotions elsewhere. The school went through an extended period of instability with an acting head before the appointment of a new first-time principal. At the first executive conference led by this new leader, the faculty heads were united in their criticism of the scale of past reform efforts, and what they described as its coercive nature. As a group, they set about clarifying the purpose of the numerous programs that were still running in the school. There was widespread agreement that the dual platform for learning had become hollowed out, having lost its 'essence', and they began to make new plans for how to address the perceived needs of students at the school. Little attention was paid to analysing or explaining the improvement in outcomes of Year 10 students in the preceding years. This time had passed, as had those responsible who led the changes.

'Western High School', the name we gave this school, was one of four secondary schools in NSW that participated in the Changing Schools Changing Times 2005-7 research project. We worked closely with these schools to describe the conditions under which they were operating and the approaches they were developing to change their classroom and leadership practices to improve students' learning outcomes. As well as all being Priority Schools, there were high levels of cultural difference among their students.

When we first visited Western HS, it stood out from the other three schools in our study because it had achieved so many of the things the others were striving for, such as regular timetabled opportunities for teachers to engage in professional learning, a focus on learning and a common language to talk about it. Yet, within the space of a few months during which we saw the departure of key leaders, cracks started appearing in the school's resolve and commitment to its dual platform for learning. Watching this decline illustrated the difficulties associated with sustaining innovative practice, even when it establishes a small foothold.

What is perhaps most disturbing about this example is how unremarkable it is because it is generally taken for granted that the overall direction of schools may swing dramatically with the departure and arrival of key personnel. Indeed, it is just such a dramatic swing that is considered to be necessary in schools that have been placed in 'special measures' in the UK. These measures might include 'parachuting in' a hand-picked leadership team. In contrast, new leadership appointments at high status selective schools with long and highly valued traditions are likely to be chosen for their ability to maintain and strengthen the existing school culture. These differences highlight the vulnerability of schools facing challenging circumstances, and the taken for granted instability of their cultures.

THE GAP

For the most part, the appointment of new personnel in 'hard-to-staff' schools in NSW is determined by system-wide formulas that are largely insensitive to local variations and needs. As Borman *et al* explain: "The general spirit of today's reform efforts continue to articulate top-down standards, which dictate many of the changes in the content of schooling, but fundamentally leaves the process of school change up to the discretion of local educators" (2003, p. 126), and up to the availability of resources, particularly human resources, at the local level. This was evident in the schools in our study which faced many challenges: they all served predominantly low income communities; there were high levels of difference among the students; the rate and scale of teacher and student turnover was extremely high; many teachers were in the early stages of their careers; school executive members were often newly appointed to their positions of leadership; and student performance outcomes were persistently low. In recognition of these contexts, the term 'school in challenging circumstances' is sometimes used in the school improvement and school effectiveness literature (see for example Levin, 2006).

Undoubtedly, all schools face particular challenges but schools facing challenging circumstances are generally equipped with less to deal with more. Consequently, they occupy different relative locations from schools for whom success comes more easily within what Teese and Polesel describe as the "universe of secondary education" (2003, p. 188). These researchers apply Bourdieu's theory of capitals (1986) to explain that "where a school fits within the institutional geography of the school system" is largely due to the gap between the demands of the curriculum and the cultural and pedagogical resources available to students. There is a tendency to attribute a school's location within this universe to lower levels of student motivation and less support from parents. But Teese and Polesel's articulation of the problem supports ways of understanding how schools are positioned differently that do not require young people, their families and communities to be understood in deficit terms.

In settings where students achieve consistently weak or at best modest outcomes, teachers develop powerful sets of explanatory logics to explain and justify the apparent limits of their collective practice. These logics of practice (Bourdieu, 1998) reflect their perceptions of the capabilities of students, their understanding of the demands of the curriculum, and their confidence in the potential of their efforts to make a difference; in other words, the relative likelihood of their collective success in improving the outcomes of students from schooling. These logics frequently attribute lack of success at school to perceived limitations in the cultural and social backgrounds of students. In other words, students are to blame for not being able to close the gap because they have inferior cultural backgrounds. The concept of a culture of poverty (see for example Payne, 2003) has broad-based popular appeal among some teachers and school leaders who are struggling with the hard work that equity demands. This approach claims that a culture of poverty has distinct values and forms of social organisation. Poor families are considered not to value education as much as more affluent families.

It conceptualises socio-economic disadvantage as a choice that arises from the values and beliefs of those in poverty, thus ultimately making the poor responsible for their own conditions (see critiques by Osei-Kofi's, 2005; Ng & Rury, 2006).

Such deficit ways of thinking about students and parents from high poverty and high difference backgrounds are commonplace in Australia. A decade of neo-liberal and robustly anti-multicultural policies of the conservative Howard government have added legitimacy to these views, but they have been systematically challenged in research in the sociology of education (Lareau, 1987; Connell, 1994; Anyon, 1997), research into cultural and linguistic differences (Delpit, 1995; Gardiner, 1997), and large scale studies of school reform (Newmann & Associates, 1996; QSRLS, 2001). For example, American sociologist Annette Lareau (1987) has for many years challenged commonly held views about parents with low incomes. Also drawing upon Bourdieu's (1986) theory of capitals, which explains that schools draw unevenly on the social and cultural capital of members of society who possess different economic capital, Lareau demonstrates that parents have unequal resources to comply with teachers' requests for parental participation. Although both middle- and working-class parents in her study valued educational success, wanted their children to do well in school and all saw themselves as supporting and helping their children achieve success at school, schools take for granted certain linguistic patterns, authority patterns and types of curricula. Consequently, the children of middle-income families whose experiences at home resonate with those at school are more likely than low-income children to adjust to the cultural and other curriculum demands of schooling, thereby transforming cultural resources into economic capital. Lareau's explanation takes into account how power operates in society to value some cultures over others, and to create institutions that support success for the children of the already powerful.

The other side of the gap is the curriculum, and lack of success at school by children from low-income families is sometimes seen as a problem with an overcrowded and intellectually demanding curriculum. In this case, the gap is considered to be due to what the curriculum demands and the solution is making the curriculum more relevant, practical, and hands-on. While there is nothing wrong with these goals per se, they are often accompanied by an expectation that achieving these goals requires making the curriculum less demanding. This response limits students' access to the kinds of cognitive tasks that are increasingly demanded in a globalised world (Rizvi, 2006) and involves a capitulation of efforts to close the gap between what is demanded in the actual curriculum by providing an alternative curriculum.

Achieving a more relevant, practical, and hands-on curriculum could also be achieved by making the curriculum more responsive to the resources that young people from diverse backgrounds bring to school, what Thomson refers to as their "virtual schoolbag" (2002). Researchers working in the field of critical literacy argue that the curriculum needs to be more flexible and that it needs to focus less on the transmission of knowledge and more on the skills and multi-literacies associated with accessing, manipulating and communicating knowledge (The New London Group, 1996). At the same time, conservative politicians and commentators are calling for a return to the basics and traditional content. In the current political climate in Australia, it is unlikely that progress will be made on this front but it is certainly possible to move the curriculum towards young people in ways that maintain intellectual demand but make it more deeply relevant and connected to who they are, and who they are becoming.[1]

The other side of the gap described by Teese and Polesel relates to the pedagogical resources available to students. Previously it was stated that in schools facing challenging circumstances, these resources are particularly low due to the inexperience of teachers and leaders. In these situations, there may be a majority of first-time leaders, or 'reserve teams' of leaders who are filling vacancies by acting in positions, and it is common for most teachers to be in the early years of their careers. In one school in our study, a faculty was made up of two first year out teachers, who were being led by an Acting Head Teacher in her second year of teaching (having spent her first year as a casual), and two unfilled vacancies were being taken up by casuals.

How the gap between the curriculum and the cultural and pedagogical resources available to students is understood tells us something about the logics of practice of teachers and the collective responsibility they assume for making a difference in the lives of young people who are generally not well served by schooling. It is easy to blame children and their families for their lack of success at school but this diminishes the role of the curriculum and pedagogical resources in producing inequities in education and diverts attention away from what can be changed and improved. The difference between the understanding derived by conceptualising some cultures as less valued because they are marginalised within the power dynamics of society, rather than less valued because they are viewed as inferior or weaker to the dominant culture is significant, and results in very different responses by teachers and schools in challenging circumstances. However, the complexity of the problem is such that it will not be solved by simply changing how teachers think about their students. Frustratingly, we know all too well what schools in challenging circumstances look like, as well as what we would like them to look like, but very little is known about how to turn the former into the latter and keep them there. In the following section, I describe a longitudinal study that was set up to investigate this dilemma.

CONDUCTING RESEARCH IN CHALLENGING CIRCUMSTANCE

In the Changing Schools Changing Times project, we acknowledged from the outset that the conditions under which we were conducting our research were also the conditions under which the participants were attempting to lead and teach. We therefore assumed that our efforts to generate knowledge and understanding within these contexts might provide us with opportunities to better understand the challenges faced by the participants since, like them, we too had to find ways of getting people together in one place to have an uninterrupted conversation; and we had to find ways of accommodating constant change, frequent interruptions, a focus on procedures, and discontinuity as the norm.

In an attempt to facilitate communication within this context, we started to write up our field notes into an evolving description of each school that was brief enough to be read when we met with participants. We limited each story to a single page (about 400 words). These "School Stories" (see Hayes, 2006) provided us with a means by which to check the information we were gathering, and to provide ongoing feedback to the schools on our observations.

In the first year, we spoke mainly with the senior executive in each school and as a result the School Stories gave us insights into whole school issues, particularly as they related to leadership practices, but classrooms and other sites remained in the background. We had conducted some classroom observations in this first year of the study which confirmed that they were sites of great interest to our research because of the challenges faced by teachers engaging students in learning, but we had not written up the observations in a way that involved the participants sufficiently to speak about what we had seen.

In the second year, we decided to look into classrooms with the assistance of teachers and leaders in each school. We recognised that we needed to work with school-based personnel to produce authentic artefacts and to interpret what was happening. As a result, we developed what we have called 'Day Diaries' which recount the classroom practices experienced by one Year 8 class over the course of a single day in each school. As much as possible, we refrained from making assessments, providing explanations or drawing comparisons in what we observed. Through facilitated conversations with the research participants, we checked the details and filled in some gaps in the recounts, and asked teachers and leaders in each school to read and interpret the Day Diaries with us.

These recounts document a pervasive set of classroom practices visible across all the schools in our study (Hayes, Johnston & King, in press). For the most part, teachers across the four schools drew upon a limited range of classroom practices, what we have previously referred to as "default practices" (see Johnston & Hayes, 2007). They also used similar logics of practice (as discussed earlier) to explain why this was necessary. The Day Diaries thus provided insight into the pedagogical choices of teachers as well as their understandings of what works 'here and now'. Power is exercised through this practical reasoning because it determines the limits of collective practice or in other words what is considered to be possible within the context of the school.

While the default practices we observed may be adequate in some contexts, the Day Diaries illustrate how inadequate they are in challenging circumstances. In these circumstances, a complex hope is needed that "begins from a realistic and sophisticated assessment of the structural pressures against social justice and the possibilities of human agency in relation to those pressures" (Thrupp, 2006, p.270). We acknowledge that the logics of practice we encountered were the realistic and sophisticated assessment of teachers of the possibilities for human agency in their schools, but we wanted to investigate if there were teachers who believed in other pedagogical possibilities; were there teachers who held a complex hope.

In the third year of the study we set out to locate teachers who operated outside the default practices and investigate their logics of practice. We selected teachers whose classroom practices stood out as different from those described in the Day Diaries because they spent very little time establishing order and negotiating behaviour, and more time on what they had planned to do. Their students had a clear understanding of what was expected of them in terms of behaviour, and in terms of the quality of work that they were to produce, even though these teachers hardly spoke about the former but were explicit about the latter. Issues of control operated in the background while the acquisition of knowledge was foregrounded. In contrast, default practices required constant maintenance and there was very little time left to do anything else.

Below I describe the classroom practices of three teachers, Julie, Tim and Sean, who exhibited different types of classroom practices but each attempted to create knowledge producing relationships with their students, thus providing them with access to useful and/or valued learning.

Julie

Julie taught Japanese and was the Year 7 adviser in a school located in a country town. She first came to our attention early in the research when we were speaking with the parents and carers of Aboriginal students. A number of them related how their children did not do any homework, except in Japanese. At this time, Julie had worked at the school for over five years and she had settled in the town. She had very few problems managing students' behaviours. She acknowledged that she liked high levels of control, and that being a long-term member of the teaching staff meant that she was familiar with the students (as they were with her). She explained that her own experiences at school shaped her approaches to teaching. For example, she reacted strongly to name-calling and put downs, and would relate personal experiences of having to overcome being labelled 'dumb' at school. She felt that this created opportunities for the students to connect to her as a person, not just as a teacher.

In many ways, Julie's classes were similar to those in our study which we have previously described as operating according to a particular script in which the students entered the classroom, sat down, paid attention to the teacher, answered questions, received a resource (usually a worksheet), listened to instructions, worked individually (or occasionally in groups) on a set task, handed in work or made it available to be inspected, packed up, and exited the room (Johnston & Hayes, 2007). However, in Julie's classes this script operated with little effort by her. She used the structure provided by the script as a kind of scaffold to the lesson and regularly explained to the class how it was framing the lesson: "All we're doing is reading at the moment"; "In approximately three minutes I'm going to go through all the answers with you"; "I want to mark this before we do the next thing"; "You have approximately nine minutes to finish this exercise". Her resources were also designed to signal to the students how they were to be used: pink sheets were about culture and were not to be written on because they would be handed back; white sheets were about grammar, they were extracted from the textbook and were to be completed and glued into workbooks, etc.

Julie's application of the script created moments when the students were working quietly, as well as moments when Julie had everyone's attention because she was setting a new direction in the lesson, or she was reviewing work. Julie used these opportunities to project photos on a screen and engage in unscripted dialogue; to provide interesting and relevant narratives, explanations and demonstrations; and to engage in personal exchanges with students that guided, encouraged, scolded and maintained their focus on the tasks that were set for the lesson. This dimension of her teaching was made possible because the script operated as a kind of invisible scaffold, rather than as something that needed to be continually reinforced and maintained.

In conversation with us, Julie explained that she fears losing control, and is reluctant to 'give away' too much. She talked about how the settlements she reaches with students have changed. No longer do they involve negotiating time on task in exchange for playtime. She digs in and expects students to complete the set tasks, and our observations of her classroom practice confirmed these expectations. For example, when the bell rang no one left until she checked each student's work. Departure from the room was gradual and orderly as each student finished.

Like so many of the teachers we have observed, Julie thinks of each class as a discrete experience rather than a connected and ongoing one. Each lesson the students begin and complete work on a specific feature of Japanese language or culture: "This lesson you'll learn about religion in Japan", activities don't generally carry over into the next lesson. Nevertheless, students are challenged each lesson to make connections between Japanese and Australian culture, language and society. By learning about another culture, Julie supports their reflection on their own culture and their place in Australian society.

In Julie's classes, knowledge is accessible to students through hard work – the same way she learnt to speak Japanese during a year living in Japan. She explained that it took her a long time to realise that by being creative and by putting more effort into her lesson preparation, she was better able to engage the students and to avoid problems with behaviour. Even so, she still feels the need to prioritise to keep a tight rein on students' behaviours. She is respected by the students for her knowledge, her fairness and her consistent classroom practices.

Tim

Tim taught Design and Technology and was the Head Teacher for this subject in the same school as Julie. We were particularly interested in a robotics project that he had adapted for use with students in Years 7 through to 9. Students worked in small groups to write simple programs that directed their robots around a set course. This unit of work extended over a whole term (ten week period), and the incorporation of design principles within project-based approaches to his classroom practices meant that Tim's students were able to begin work at the start of each class with minimal instruction. Explicit links between lessons were in stark contrast to the discrete experiences we had observed in most classrooms where students generally anticipated that what they did during one lesson would be different from the lessons that preceded and followed it.

Tim took his preparation seriously, and explained that it had to be done thoroughly before each class. This included having the necessary equipment on hand (as he did not have a technical assistant) but also thinking through and anticipating the problems that the students might encounter. Tim worked alongside the students as a co-producer of knowledge. He recognised the importance of tasks being connected to the world beyond the classroom, and in the case of the robotics project students learnt about the Defense Advanced Research Projects Agency (DARPA) which holds a competition to stimulate research into the production of fully autonomous land vehicles that are capable of completing on and off-road courses in a limited period of time.

Tim recognised the importance of providing students with compelling reasons to learn something new. He illustrated this by describing an example when a group realised that they needed to know how to work with fractions and to represent them with decimals:

> It was interesting that once there was a reason for doing it, there was all of a sudden a really urgent need to find out what half a second is, or if we've got 0.5 and that's too far then what number do we need, 0.25's lower than that so we can put that in. There was an urgent need to start learning something which was quite interesting and funny to watch: "What's half of .5? I need to know!"

Although Tim's classes did not follow the regular script, they were carefully planned and organised. He monitored students' work closely, and spent time during each lesson planning and discussing progress with each group. Tim felt that what worked for him would not necessarily work for other teachers, and he had some difficulty explaining what he did: he just did it. He acknowledged that he modified his approach and expectations when he worked with different groups, and he was reflective and considered about the things he'd like to improve in his practice. Perhaps most notably, he spoke respectfully about his colleagues and students. He acknowledged the importance of developing a good rapport with students, and of the challenges and necessity of creating learning experiences that engaged and challenged them.

Sean

Sean taught music at a metropolitan high school with a large number of Pacific Islander and Aboriginal students. He was a classically trained pianist and in his spare time he played with a jazz trio. When he was appointed to the school the Principal provided him with some funds to refurbish the music rooms, and with some of the money Sean cut an archway to connect two separate rooms. He also used the funds to block up the internal windows and build an acoustic buffer between the rooms and the corridor, and buy musical equipment. With the help of the art teacher, Sean created a bright ,colourful mural across one entire wall. The mural portrayed four distinct sets of figures, each one representing a period of musical creation. On the left was a musical scene from classical Greece, next to it an orchestral scene with a prominent figure of Mozart, then a jazz scene showing African-American musicians, and on the right of the room, a group of rap musicians using electronic musical gear.

One of the rooms had the usual school desks and chairs in the middle, around the walls were arranged 10 or so electronic keyboards with ear phones attached. The other room through the archway was more of a performance space. Along one wall there were several guitars and a set of drums connected to a sound system. A short space away there was a more sophisticated keyboard set up. At the back of the room there was a computer with software students used to compose their own music. Under the windows there was an old, comfortable leather couch and armchairs that Sean and a teacher friend picked up from the roadside during a recent council throw-out.

Sean designed this space to be inviting, relaxing and conducive to creating music. He spoke about the intuitive musicality of many of his students. He was particularly impressed by the Polynesian and Aboriginal students who had no formal knowledge but could pick up a guitar and harmonise and construct songs – a skill which he admired after developing it himself as the result of his formal training, and which he thinks the students acquire informally and unconsciously within their families and community. He worked with his students as knowledgeable producers of music.

Sean expressed a strong belief in hands-on learning. His ideal would be to develop his music room so that the keyboards could be complemented with a bank of computers with software that allowed students to compose their own songs. His preferred classroom would be one where individuals and groups were engaged practically on performance and composition and where he would move around as a facilitator. This style of teaching and learning, he commented, seemed to be more in tune with the kind of hyperactive, episodic engagement that young people have with the electronic environment of iPods, mobile phones, and Internet. "I can't seem to expect," he commented, "that these kids will stay on one task or activity for more than a few minutes – they move around from computer to keyboard to guitar. It seems to be the way they are."

While Julie, Tim and Sean demonstrated very different pedagogical approaches, they all engaged in different types of negotiations with their students from those that were generally recorded in the Day Diaries. A feature of all classrooms is that teachers and students continually negotiate what will be achieved, when it will be completed, who will be involved, what product is required, and what the implications of these negotiations are for future exchanges. Consequently, a range of bargains are made and various settlements are reached. In classrooms where behaviour and management issues are foregrounded, teachers sometimes secure time on task by limiting the demands of the task, or rewarding the completion of tasks with playtime or some other form of 'downtime', such as the use of computers for playing games or accessing the Internet. In these classrooms, 'content' is 'covered' through the application of the script that I described earlier, and since this operates to varying degrees of success, the means by which work is completed and its quality tend to be a secondary consideration to the maintenance of the script.

In the classrooms of teachers who were operating outside the default practices, these negotiations functioned in very different ways. For example, they usually started with the baseline assumption that all students would engage in learning related activities and that while the means by which tasks were to be completed was negotiable, all students were expected to complete the assigned work within a reasonable amount of time. In this way, the production of quality work was more taken for granted and less likely to be bargained away. The operation of the script slipped into the background or disappeared from view. In these classrooms, negotiations centred around how knowledge was positioned within the interactions of teachers and students - its forms of production, acquisition, application, transference, interpretation and manipulation.

Berlak and Berlak's (1981) use of what they refer to as "dilemma language", provides a helpful articulation of "how teachers through their schooling acts transmit knowledge and ways of knowing and learning" (p.144). They articulate a set of curriculum dilemmas which distinguish between personal knowledge and public knowledge; knowledge as content and knowledge as process; and knowledge as given and knowledge as problematical. These dilemmas illustrate some of the possible ways in which teachers position themselves in relation to students and knowledge through 'schooling acts' that demonstrate the choices they make about ways of knowing and learning in classrooms. These are not simple choices. Most of the teachers in our study resolved these dilemmas through the application of default practices which were derived from their shared logics of practice.

Seddon (2001) draws upon the work of Raymond Williams (1976) to explain how teachers' curriculum choices regulate students' access to particular knowledge, and thereby serve particular social ends. Although Seddon's focus is on curriculum at the national level, her explanation is just as relevant to the decisions that teachers make at the classroom level.

> What counts as a 'curriculum' is governed by the conscious and unconscious choices that are made in the process of determining what should be taught. The consequence of this official and unofficial decision-making creates a pattern of inclusion and exclusion in terms of the knowledge, skills and dispositions that are taught and, simultaneously, creates selective traditions that, in social and political terms, define 'useful and/or valued learning' that are passed on to the subsequent generations. Further conscious and unconscious choices about who should have access to particular knowledge, skills and dispositions, and how access should be distributed across society determines the character of educational provision. The effect of these decisions about content and distribution "shapes education as a social technology that serves particular social ends." (Seddon, 2001, pp. 308-309).

The Day Diaries illustrate how locally developed logics of practice shaped education as a social technology serving particular ends. Drawing upon Berlak and Berlak's dilemmas language, classroom practices that emphasise the first element of each dilemma (personal knowledge, knowledge as content, knowledge as given), while eliding the second element (public knowledge, knowledge as process, knowledge as problematical), provided weak support for student success at school, whereas classroom practices that included both elements provided stronger support for this goal. Our observations indicate that teachers who drew upon prevailing default practices tended to resolve these curriculum dilemmas in ways that offered students weak support for success at school, whereas those whose classroom practices operated outside the default practices created other pedagogical possibilities and were more likely to resolve these dilemmas in strong ways by engaging students in the type of knowledge, skills and dispositions that are needed for success at school and beyond. These teachers positioned themselves as brokers and facilitators of knowledge. They were more likely to work alongside students, as co-learners, to be curious and to engage in the kind of knowledge production that was more open ended, requiring problem solving, and the manipulation of information.

CONCLUSION

There is nothing particularly remarkable about the classroom practices that Julie, Tim and Sean deployed. As far as pedagogical technique is concerned, they were drawing upon fairly standard professional capabilities that might be expected of all qualified teachers. What is noteworthy are the relationships they developed and mediated between themselves, their students and forms of knowledge - its production, acquisition, application, transference, interpretation, and manipulation. Each teacher was making decisions about what should be taught as well as how it should be taught based on their personal and professional experiences in their subject area. They had done the hard work that is necessary to acquire deep understanding within their discipline areas, they had put in the time necessary to develop and practise the required skills, and they had developed the dispositions of experts in their respective fields, which informed how they understood learning and supported it through their teaching practices. Most significantly they expressed different logics of practice to the majority of their colleagues. They believed in their students' abilities to learn, and in their capacity to teach them. They held these beliefs deeply but spoke softly about them and were reluctant to set themselves apart from other teachers, even though the effects of their practices were distinctly different.

The challenge for educational leaders and systems that seek to improve teachers' classroom practices is how to make more teachers like Julie, Tim and Sean; in other words, how to make learning and teaching a central concern for more teachers. Recent large-scale school improvement efforts in Australia have focussed on developing pedagogical models that are 'rolled out' across systems accompanied by various means of pressure and support. The previously mentioned Queensland School Reform Longitudinal Study (2001) was utilised for this purpose. Core researchers in the study drew upon an extensive review of the literature to produce a twenty element observation instrument. The promotion of this tool as an idealised form of classroom practice was well underway long before the final report was written, and subsequently rippled out with varying strength across the country. The rapid take up of this research instrument may be partly explained by the composition of the research team who moved between high-level academic and State policy positions, while speaking directly to school-based personnel through targeted and large scale professional development (cf. Yates, 2004). Not surprisingly, the research tool also underpinned the strategic interests of the State system of education that had commissioned the research. At the time, the government was repositioning Queensland as the 'Smart State' by developing new industries and economic opportunities and moving away from its long established primary industry base.

Further analysis of the QSRLS results was used to justify the development of a more limited pedagogical model in NSW (NSW DET, 2003), but this also resulted in large-scale top down reform initiatives. The key problem is that such processes are unlikely to support change in classroom practice because these models were designed to describe practice not change it, and the local processes that are required to facilitate change are highly variable, and usually unsupported by large scale 'roll outs'. The issue remains, how to disrupt default practices and open up pedagogical possibilities.

The production of the Day Diaries provided us with numerous opportunities to talk with teachers and leaders about the pervasiveness of default practices and how difficult it was to break free of the patterns of classroom interactions that they established (Johnston & Hayes, 2008). We were struck by how the default practices of classrooms were mirrored in the practices of school leaders, and expressed through how they prioritised their time, managed meetings and set directions. Subsequently, we have applied the processes which produced the Day Diaries to recount executive meetings, which we came to understand as primary sites of practice of school leaders. These recounts highlighted the resonance between the default practices of classroom teachers and school leaders because they powerfully illustrated that the practices of most of the leaders in our study followed a script that was not unlike the script we had observed in teachers' practices. The leaders were consumed by crisis management, they spent large amounts of time dealing with behaviour issues and administrative tasks, and they rarely engaged in professional learning. Both teachers and leaders complained about not having enough time to do the things that mattered.

School leaders demonstrated through their practice what they valued and, for the most part, classroom teachers followed their lead. If school leaders are not making time for professional learning, and for practicing the pedagogical dimension of their leadership, then it is reasonable to expect that classroom teachers might also have difficulty supporting learning in their classrooms. Leaders related how the inexperience of teachers and constant turnover limited their capacity to bring about a stronger focus on learning and teaching across the school, while teachers related how the backgrounds of students and their high levels of mobility and absenteeism limited their ability to improve their learning outcomes. Leaders emphasised management and administrative issues in meetings, rarely providing opportunities for professional learning; and teachers emphasised control and routines that rarely provided opportunities for students to engage in the kind of learning that leads to success at schools. The more we explored these synergies, the more it became clear that school leaders should not expect teachers to be leading learning in their classrooms if they are not able to demonstrate it though their own leadership practices. Since both teachers and leaders work within the same contexts, both face similar challenges in changing their practice to be more centrally concerned with learning.

It is likely that these synergies can be extrapolated across systems, and that regional and State office personnel are likely also to be consumed with practices that are not primarily oriented towards supporting professional learning, either their own learning or the learning of those they supervise. This suggests that reform needs to be fundamentally reconceptualised as a question of inquiring into how to support a stronger focus on the pedagogical dimensions of practice at all levels within systems of education. Rather than viewing reform as changing the practices of teachers, reform needs to start with the practices of school leaders, as well as regional and State office personnel. Everyone, not just teachers, needs to inquire into what it takes to make pedagogy a core concern of their practice. Our initial explorations of how to realise this goal suggest that the top down imposition of pedagogical models (no matter how effective their elements may be shown to be) are unlikely to bring about improvements in practice because they continue to focus attention on what happens in classrooms, and to leave the prevailing logics of practice undisturbed. We suspect that small scale, local and sustained inquiries into the effects of classroom and leadership practices may provide teachers and leaders with the kind of knowledge that might help them to focus more on learning and the pedagogical dimension of their practices. Demonstrating other pedagogical possibilities within local contexts, and preferably through the practice of local teachers, is likely to be necessary in order to disrupt prevailing logics of practice.

ACKNOWLEDGEMENTS

The Changing Schools Changing Times research project was funded through the Australian Research Council's Linkage program in partnership with the NSW Department of Education and Training. The members of the research team included (in alphabetical order): Narelle Carey, Debra Hayes, Ken Johnston, Ann King, Rani Lewis-Jones, Kristal Morris, Chris Murray, Ishbel Murray, Kerith Power, Dianne Roberts, Kitty te Riele and Margaret Wheeler.

The teachers and schools involved in our study provided open access to their classrooms and other sites of learning, and were willing to work with us to interpret and describe what we saw there.

Dr Ken Johnston's field notes and reflections made a significant contribution to the development of the descriptions of Julie and Sean's classroom practice.

Naomi Brennan provided valuable feedback on the draft.

NOTES

[1] See for example the Redesigning Pedagogies in the North research project, http://www.unisa.edu.au/hawkeinstitute/cslplc/rpin/index.html.

REFERENCES

Anyon, J. (1997). *Ghetto schooling: A political economy of urban educational reform.* New York: Teachers College Press.

Australian Bureau of Statistics. (2004). *Measures of Australia's progress.* Catalogue No. 1370.0. Canberra, ACT: ABS.

Berlak, A., & Berlak, H. (1981). *Dilemmas of schooling.* London: Methuen.

Borman, G. D., Hewes, G. H., Overman, L. T., & Brown, S. (2003). Comprehensive school reform and achievement: A meta-analysis. *Review of Educational Research, 73*(2), 125–230.

Bourdieu, P. (1986). The forms of capital. In J. Richardson (Ed.), *Handbook of theory and research for the sociology of education* (pp. 241–58). Westport, CT: Greenwood.

Bourdieu, P. (1998). *Practical reason: On the theory of action.* Stanford, CA: Stanford University Press.

Connell, R. W. (1994). Poverty and education. *Harvard Educational Review, 64*(2), 125–149.

Darling-Hammond, L. (1997). *The right to learn: A blueprint for creating schools that work.* San Francisco: Jossey Bass.

Delpit, L. D. (1995). The silenced dialogue: Power and pedagogy in educating other people's children. In L. D. Delpit (Ed.), *Other people's children: Cultural conflict in the classroom* (pp. 21–47). New York: The New Press.

Gardiner, G. (1997). Aboriginal boys' business: A study of Indigenous youth in Victoria in relation to educational participation and contact with the juvenile justice system. *Journal of Intercultural Studies, 18*(1), 49–61.

Hayes, D. (2006). Telling stories: Sustaining improvement in schools operating under adverse conditions. *Improving Schools, 9*(3), 203–213.

Hayes, D., Johnston, K., & King, A. (in press). The disruptive possibilities of looking in classrooms: The use of day diaries to disclose the logics of practice in high poverty contexts. *Pedagogy, Culture and Society.*

Johnston, K., & Hayes, D. (2007). Supporting student success at school through teacher professional learning: The pedagogy of disrupting the default modes of schooling. *International Journal of Inclusive Education, 11*(3), 371–381.

Johnston, K., & Hayes, D. (2008). 'This is as good as it gets': Classroom lessons and learning in challenging circumstances. *Australian Journal of Language and Literacy, 31*(2), 109–127.

Lareau, A. (1987). Social-class differences in family-school relationships: The importance of cultural capital. *Sociology of Education, 60*(2), 73–85.

Levin, B. (2006). Schools in challenging circumstances: A reflection on what we know and what we need to know. *School Effectiveness and School Improvement, 17*(4), 399–407.

Lucas, S. R. (2001). Effectively maintained inequality: Education transitions, track mobility, and social background effects. *American Journal of Sociology, 106*(6), 1642–1690.

New London Group. (1996). A pedagogy of multiliteracies: Designing social futures. *Harvard Educational Review, 66*(1), 60–92.

Newmann & Associates. (1996). *Authentic achievement: Restructuring schools for intellectual quality.* San Francisco: Jossey Bass.

Ng, J. C., & Rury, J. L. (2006, July 18). Poverty and education: A critical analysis of the Ruby Payne phenomenon. *Teachers College Record.*

New South Wales Department of Education and Training. (2003). *A classroom practice guide. Professional support and curriculum.* Sydney, NSW: Department of Education and Training, Professional Support and Curriculum Directorate.

Organisation for Economic Co-operation and Development. (2003). *Education at a glance: OECD indicators 2003.* Paris, France: OECD Publishing.

Organisation for Economic Co-operation and Development. (2006). *Education at a glance: OECD indicators 2006.* Paris, France: OECD Publishing.

Osei-Kofi, N. (2005). Pathologizing the poor: A framework for understanding Ruby Payne's Work. *Equity & Excellence in Education, 38*(4), 367–375.

Payne, R. K. (2003). *A framework for understanding poverty* (3rd Rev. ed.). Highlands, TX: Aha! Process.

Queensland School Reform Longitudinal Study (QSRLS). (2001). *Submitted to Education Queensland by the School of Education.* Brisbane, QLD: University of Queensland, State of Queensland, Department of Education.

Rizvi, F. (2006). Keynote address to the Australian Association for Research in Education Annual Conference, Adelaide, 27–30 November.

Seddon, T. (2001). National curriculum in Australia? A matter of politics, powerful knowledge and the regulation of learning. *Pedagogy, Culture and Society, 9*(3), 307–331.

Teese, R., & Polesel, J. (2003). *Undemocratic schooling: Equity and quality in mass secondary education in Australia.* Carlton, VIC: Melbourne University Press.

Thomson, P. (2002). *Schooling the rustbelt kids: Making the difference in changing times.* Sydney, NSW: Allen & Unwin.

Thrupp, M. (2006). Editorial. *British Journal of Educational Studies, 54*(3), 269–271.

Williams, R. (1976). *The long revolution.* Harmondsworth: Penguin.

Wrigley, T. (2000). *The power to learn: Stories of success in the education of Asian and other bilingual pupils.* Stoke: Trentham.

Yates, L. (2004). *What does good education research look like?* Maidenhead, Berkshire: Open University Press.

Debra Hayes
University of Sydney

HELEN NIXON AND BARBARA COMBER

8. LITERACY, LANDSCAPES AND LEARNING IN A PRIMARY CLASSROOM

INTRODUCTION

For over two decades we have worked collaboratively with teachers to understand the histories and resources that students living in low-income areas bring to schooling, and the learning that they do inside and outside school. We have been equally interested in how teachers design curriculum and pedagogies that take account (or not) of children's different life experiences. Because we are literacy educators, we tend to privilege texts of various kinds in our attempts to understand the differential effects and take-up of pedagogy and school knowledges among different children. So we look at children's products to see what they indicate about what the students know about how texts work. We know that the capacity to work with language, in various media and genres, is integrally related to young people's academic success and life chances.

Our commitment to understanding the work that teachers do, in order to enhance the learning and life chances of poor children, has taken us back time and again to the same *places* in order to investigate literacy pedagogies which make a difference. Specifically, we return to the west and the north of Adelaide, suburban areas of South Australia now undergoing massive urban renewal. So inadvertently, as researchers concerned with class, we have become researchers concerned with place, and increasingly we are aware of place as more than a 'context' or 'background' to children's learning lives (Comber, 1998). In order to understand what was going on in these school communities within the wider landscape of urban renewal, we began to read theories of space and place, and to bring together our work on critical literacy and social justice with research about place-based pedagogies and eco-social justice (Comber, Nixon & Reid, 2007; Comber, 2007).

We have now engaged in several studies which foreground the relational aspects of pedagogy, places and literacy, and explore the affordances of landscape and place for literacy learning and identity work (Comber, Nixon, Ashmore, Loo & Cook, 2006; Kerkham & Comber, 2007; Nixon, 2007; Nixon, Comber & Cormack, 2007). In this chapter we discuss one recent project, 'Urban renewal from the inside-out'.[1] The project was multi-disciplinary and involved university researchers from architecture, communication and education. We discuss how the teachers and children located in a high-poverty suburb in the throes of urban renewal engaged in imagining, designing and making a garden on their school grounds. We suggest the importance of place-making projects, not only in nurturing

M. Somerville, K. Power and P. de Carteret (eds.),
Landscapes and Learning: Place Studies for a Global World, 119–137
© 2009 Sense Publishers. All rights reserved.

children's understandings of and attachments to place, but also in expanding their literate repertoires.

We begin by briefly outlining different kinds of research about children's relationships with place undertaken in several disciplines. The body of the chapter discusses our project as a case of place studies and place-making in a primary school. In particular, we discuss how a focus on the school landscape as a part of a wider landscape of urban renewal allowed young people to engage with specific spatial practices and fostered new knowledges and dispositions.

STUDIES OF SPACE, PLACE AND CHILDHOOD

In the main, theories of childhood have tended to ignore "the spatial dimensions of children's identity" (Scourfield, Dicks, Drakeford & Davies, 2006, p. 2). However, over the last decade, children's emotional responses to, and sense-making practices about, the spaces and places they occupy in everyday life have been of considerable interest to several fields of social science inquiry. For example, "the new social studies of childhood" (e.g. Corsaro, 2005; James, Jenks & Prout, 1998; Jenks, 2005; Prout, 2005), has insisted that children should not be considered as being in a state of 'becoming' or 'not yet adult'. Rather, children need to be understood as social actors and agents in their own lives, and active members of, and participants in their societies. Research in this tradition, and with a specific focus on space and place, includes studies of the "geographies of childhood" (e.g. Holloway & Valentine, 2000) which examine, for example, children's mobility and the spatial restrictions they experienced due to age and gender. Other work, for example, a study of children in a run-down East London council housing estate (Reay, 2000), suggests that class too, impacts on children's relationships to place, with working-class children likely to feel more bounded by, and fearful of, the potential dangers of the estates, than their more mobile and confident middle-class peers who ventured beyond.

The fields of ecological and environmental psychology have also focused their attention on children and place. For example, a recent collection of studies of "environments for children" (Spencer & Blades, 2006) focuses on the environments or "places in which children grow up, play and learn" (Spencer & Blades, 2006, p. 1), including the outdoors. Whereas *ecological* psychology is concerned to investigate "the properties and possibilities that places provide for users, whether or not those possibilities were originally envisioned by the designers and planners" (Spencer & Blades, 2006, p. 2), *environmental* psychology begins from the premise that *places* are fundamental to children's developing self-concept and identity. For example, surveys of what children learn from their environment suggest that, "through active place-making and place attachment ... they experience imagination, escape, safety, and creativity" (Derr, 2006, p. 109). Some research further considers how children might be involved in *active participation* in "sustainable development" (Heft & Chawla, 2006) and in the design and building of child-friendly places in which they can grow, play and learn (e.g. Francis & Lorenzo, 2006; Horelli, 2006; Sutton & Kemp, 2006).

studies where they could identify and address issues of concern
s traffic, conditions of local vegetation, and personal safety.
school embarked on a series of interlinked projects which focussed

ion
capacity building
munity literacies
ed curriculum
rticipation and representation in decision-making
d constructing the Grove Gardens.
rom our university research centre worked as collaborators on a
se projects as catalysts, co-researchers and as co-educators,
achers' positive and innovative work towards social justice and
(Comber, Thomson with Wells, 2001; Comber & Nixon, 2005;
r, 2006; Wells, Badger & Kimber, 2000).
Renewal project was informed by studies in high poverty areas
which indicate the importance of education, local action, and
th involvement in building sustainable and equitable communities
02; Browne & Jain, 2002). The need for reciprocal respect and
ne between school-based educators and community builders is key
McCloud, 2001; Thomson, 2002). The school community wanted
hanges to its own physical environment. In brief, there was an area
der preschool and the school that was bare, unwelcoming and unsafe
orated a car-park). The school community wanted to symbolically
link these spaces by designing a garden and/or a structure that
o, making this space aesthetically pleasing, and enhancing the safety
the children, their families and teachers. In designing the garden
cting structure, they wanted to represent the diversity in the
ddition, they wanted the enhancement of this space to contribute to
arning (Fisher, 2003). A survey of preschool children revealed that
to be a space where they could be active, and explore, touch and
rent textures and places.
chool principal, teachers, community members and school students
r a period of twelve months with a team of consultants, architecture,
ommunication academics and undergraduate students to negotiate,
truct a garden and structure that linked the preschool and school.
ators, we recognised that we did not have the expertise required to
oject, so we invited colleagues from architecture and journalism to
capitalise on new opportunities for our own learning about places
ether the teachers (Ruth Trimboli and Marg Wells), the architect
d the teacher educators (Barbara Comber and Helen Nixon) planned
a complex and evolving curriculum around the design of Grove
ion, the teachers built on their knowledge of the children and the
n to incorporate other elements as needed. As it eventuated, the
wo full school years and involved different groups of school and

Anthropologists too, have used participatory action research methods to investigate children's participation in urban planning and social sustainability projects (e.g. Chawla, 2002; Christensen & O'Brien, 2003; Malone, 2007).

Research in all these fields has potential implications for education. As educators we agree with Heft and Chawla (2006) that it is important to know more about "what experiences prepare children to value and care for their local environment and join in community decision-making" (p. 199). In order to research this question, we need to know more about "environmental learning as children engage with their localities, or about how children learn to take collaborative action *on behalf of* the places where they live" (Heft & Chawla, 2006, p. 199). After all:

The very possibility of sustainable development depends on nurturing a generation of children who recognise the connection between human action and environmental sustainability and, most critically, who can *imagine themselves as being participants* in achieving this end (Heft & Chawla, 2006, p. 213. Original emphasis).

We agree that being able to *imagine* being participants in building a sustainable world is only a first step; for us, the emphasis on fostering action by children *on behalf* of the places where they live has particular resonance. For example, what Francis and Lorenzo (2006) call "proactive process" in relation to city design, has many similarities with principles of critical pedagogy and critical literacy that are familiar to us (Comber, 2001; Comber & Nixon, 2005). Assisting children to develop the dispositions, skills and expertise to be able to *act on* the world in relation to topics that matter, locally and globally, is a key goal of critical pedagogical practice. Similarly, Francis and Lorenzo (2006) argue that the "most integrative and effective" way to "better engage children and youth and include their ideas in urban design" (p. 217) is to work with a proactive process which has the following dimensions:

- An inclusive process that involves children, adults, planners, designers, and decision makers
- Involves learning on the part of children and adults
- Involves active listening by adults and designers
- Includes the ideas of professional designers and planners
- Involves negotiation between children and adults
- Is not romantic about wanting to return to an earlier and more primitive form of childhood
- Addresses concerns of safety and security by getting children outdoors
- Uses new and interactive media as tools in the design process (Francis & Lorenzo, 2006, p. 233).

Finally, we agree that such a process is *pedagogical* – it involves "negotiation" and "learning on the part of children and adults" (Francis & Lorenzo, 2006, p. 233).

Another field of scholarship that foregrounds both the *pedagogical* nature of place and the importance of adopting a *critical* approach to place studies, is located within environmental education. Here scholars argue the importance of "place-based pedagogy" (Smith, 2002) and "a critical pedagogy of place" (Gruenewald, 2003b) in which we learn "to listen to what place is telling us" and "respond as informed, engaged citizens" (Gruenewald, 2003a, p. 645). Such scholars have explored how and why educators might assist students to be actively involved in learning and communicating about, and advocating for and acting on, their places and environments (e.g. Gruenewald 2003b; Martusewicz & Edmundson, 2005; Smith, 2002). Together, they make a powerful argument that, for the future of the planet, our changing relationships to our places is as important as techno-scientific solutions (Somerville, 2007).

SPACE, PLACE AND LITERACY STUDIES

Leading scholars in the field known as the New Literacy Studies (NLS) have studied the 'local' and 'situated' literacies of people living in particular communities (e.g. Barton & Hamilton, 1998; Barton, Hamilton & Ivanic, 2002; Prinsloo & Breier, 1996; Street, 2001). They argue that literacy needs to be understood locally and historically "both in terms of the histories of individuals and in terms of the histories of the places and social relationships in which they find themselves" (Barton & Hamilton, 1998, p. xiv). Accordingly, studies in NLS have used ethnographic approaches to document people's cultural uses of literacy; what people in particular places do with literacy, and what these practices mean to them. In this tradition, schools are "just one specialised context in which literacy is used and learned" (Barton & Hamilton, 1998, p. 21) in what Barton (1994) describes as an "ecology" of literate practices across home, community and school contexts.

Other literacy scholars have more directly brought *spatial* theory to bear on literacy research. Here, more often than not, the relationship between literacy, identity and 'social space' has been the phenomenon under investigation (e.g. studies collected in Leander & Sheehy, 2004), and a substantial sub-set of this research has paid particular attention to the challenges associated with researching the literacy practices surrounding young people's engagements with the virtual worlds of the internet and new media (e.g. Leander & McKim, 2003; Leander & Rowe, 2006).

Research that more directly focuses on the *material* spaces of schools and their communities as sites for learning is rare in the field of literacy studies. Education scholars have studied how children can be assisted to participate in the design and re-design of schools; here the emphasis has been on children's views about schools as *places for learning* and on children as co-participants in the design of schools as learning environments (e.g. Burke, 2005, 2007; Burke & Grosvenor, 2003; McGregor, 2004). However, such studies have paid less attention to the textual and representational practices of children in such processes. In contrast, we would want to emphasise that being able to act on the world, for things that matter to people and places, increasingly requires the development of complex forms of *literate* practice. These include being able to formulate and disseminate well-researched and clearly expressed opinions and arguments about spaces and places. In order to do this effectively, and in their own interests, children need to develop competence

in diverse forms of textual, rhetorical image, and print and electronic med literacy curriculum.

URBAN RENEWAL AS A LAN

Where the Study Came From

Ridley Grove R-7 School is located i of the Westwood project.

Westwood is Australia's largest u west of the Adelaide CBD in th Athol Park, Mansfield Park and W

The $600 million project commen international developer Urban Families & Communities (Housir Adelaide Enfield and City of Char

Westwood is transforming this are urban environment that involves r stock with new stock, and better At project completion in 2011 ar have been developed (Urban F Project', paragraphs 1-3).

Westwood is one of the poorest are culturally diverse, and includes ma and Cambodian families. Fifty per speak English as a second language a recognised indicator of poverty. families who have re-located to seel

When urban renewal is undertal the benefits and from having a sa 2001). However, the Ridley Grov with the developers and the local about the ways in which parts of Then school principal, Frank Cai advocates for their school commu previous school, also located in a commitment to contesting the c places that are prevalent in the m curriculum and pedagogy around investigate aspects of the indige young people into the language possible consequences of the cha

neighbourhood
to them, such
In 2003 the
upon:
– Social inclus
– Community
– Critical com
– Problem-bas
– Students' pa
– Designing a
Academics
number of th
documenting te
critical literacy
Janks & Combe
The Urban
internationally
family and you
(Appadurai, 20
ongoing dialog
(Jehl, Blank &
to make some c
between the fee
(in that it incor
and materially
connected the tw
and comfort of
and the conne
community. In a
the children's le
they wanted this
experience diffe
In sum, the s
were to work ov
education and c
design and cons
As literacy educ
undertake this pr
join us, hoping t
and spaces. Tog
(Stephen Loo) an
a framework for
Gardens; in addi
school curriculu
project spanned

university students and many different pedagogical components too numerous to cover here. It involved a cumulative coordinated consideration of place over time, not a once-off thematic unit. Key themes of this curriculum design involved what architect Stephen Loo described as *building stories* and *belonging spaces*. In this chapter, we explore how these themes were instantiated in the teachers' pedagogical practices and, through discussions of children's work, we illustrate how place-making can be an important resource for the development of young people's literate repertoires. Elsewhere, we have reported on this project in terms of children assembling spatial literacies (Comber & Nixon, 2008; Comber, Nixon, Ashmore, Loo & Cook, 2006). Here we explain this place-making project in terms of the pedagogical practices associated with attending to space and place, and designing and representing changing places. We argue that studies of place are uniquely positioned to enhance young people's investments in school learning and literacy. Place-making is important for the long-term psychological health of young people, the environmental well-being of the earth and also for the immediate potential it has to engage youth in complex learning.

ATTENDING TO SPACE AND PLACE

In areas undergoing urban renewal, a great deal of visible material change occurs. This may be ignored by teachers, seen as a problem, or treated as data for analysis and as a stimulus for research. The collaborating teachers, Wells and Trimboli, were interested in urban renewal as providing a landscape for learning, and the design of the school garden was only one part of their wider consideration of the neighbourhood and beyond. Along with architect Loo, the teachers capitalised on the changing nature of the Westwood precinct to make place pedagogical. This involved a range of activities and practices, including for example, tours of the city centre of Adelaide to investigate architectural elements of built environments (pillars, columns, platforms, archways etc), viewing Loo's PowerPoint of unusual buildings, flooding the classroom with architectural magazines, mapping the neighbourhood in terms of the location of student dwellings in relation to the school, studying the design elements of the newly built local parks (Vietnamese garden, Mikkawomma, Settlers' historical garden), conducting a PMI (plus, minus, interesting) analysis of the school grounds, pacing out the Grove Garden space, and responding to surveys about the 'belonging spaces' in their lives. The important principle here was having young people notice the way environments are made and consider how they might have been made differently. Rather than places being seen as static backdrops to everyday life, they were considered as social spaces to which different groups of people connect or belong, differently. Students were inducted into ways of reading the urban and schoolyard landscape, both figuratively and literally. It was a curriculum full of movement in and through places, and ways of thinking about the changing places that they, and people they knew, live in.

Teachers provided opportunities for young people to think and talk about imagined/desired places, 'natural' and built environments, designed and planned spaces as aspects of the changing nature of everyday life. Their curriculum allowed for continuous opportunities for embodied engagement with place through:

- Walking through neighbourhoods; pointing out particular houses and shops that they frequented or lived in
- Touching the pillars; feeling the sculptures and mosaics of urban design in streetscapes
- Researching other playground designs
- Modelling and pegging out possible garden designs
- Retelling memories about, and sharing artefacts from, other places.

Learning ways of attending to place and space arose from several sources. On the one hand, Loo explicitly introduced teachers, researchers and students to selected conceptual resources, design practices and vocabulary from architecture, described as *spatial literacies*. On the other hand, the teachers incorporated relevant literature and scaffolded tasks to have children consider places and spaces from many different perspectives. As researchers who had previously worked on longitudinal studies of students' literacy development in the middle primary years, we were struck by the detail, accurate content and length of the writing of children participating in the Grove Gardens project, in comparison with others we had observed (Comber, Badger, Barnett, Nixon & Pitt, 2002). The affordances of place studies as an inclusive resource for literacy development may be a fruitful area for further research. Knowledge of place and the natural environment can become cultural capital within the classroom when teachers make it the object of study (see also Comber, Nixon & Reid, 2007). The active and embodied researching of places and spaces helped all children assemble significant resources for writing. Here we illustrate this with reference to a text, *My window*, produced by two boys (see Figure 1). The written text was accompanied by two detailed drawings (see Figures 2 & 3).

Grade 3/4 students were invited to choose an image of an interesting building, including depictions of windows, from a variety of sources, and to imagine life from the perspective of a selected window. Based on the children's picture book, *Window* (Baker, 1991), teacher Wells aimed to develop a class picture book, entitled *Windows*. In pairs, students selected and photocopied a picture of a window taken from the outside looking in; chosen images ranged from port-holes to windows in castles, skyscrapers, lighthouses and aeroplanes. Students were asked to imagine themselves *inside* the building, to draw the inside of the window frame, and to write about their imagined space and what they might be doing there. They were also asked to imagine what they could see *outside* the window and to draw and write about that space.

This writing interests us in several respects. It is a highly detailed and evocative piece for nine year old students. The writing about the inside space displays a strong sense of ownership (my bed, my bag, my room, my cat), belonging (warmth, sitting by the fire, talking to my dad), and social history (toys from previous birthdays, my photos, awards; dad and his memories). It represents how the inside space was configured, the boys' feeling of belonging in it, and how it operated as a social space.

126

My Window

In my room I can see the clothes that my mum bought me, my bag and a closet that I put my clothes in. There is a T.V. by the fireplace and my cat is sitting by the fire. My bed is done so I don't have to do it. I can see my poster hanging up on the wall. I am sitting by the fire talking to my dad. He's telling me about the time when he was young. I can see toys that I had for my birthday and I can also see my drawers. On top of my drawers there is a telephone, my photos, awards and a radio.

Outside my room I can see a fancy car. I can see a bus carrying children. I think they're going to swimming because they have got their bathers. Outside I can see my mum waiting for the bus. I hope she doesn't have to wait long out there. I can see a rubbish bin that's very old. I think the workers are going to break that down and build a new one because that bin has been there since we moved in. I can see they have built a new path way because the other one was very hard to walk on and it was old. They also put up a new traffic light. This one is very clean but the old one was old and broken. I can see the Optus building. My dad bought his mobile phone from there. My friend is moving to a different house. I hope our new neighbours are very friendly. I see our new neighbours coming to their new house. I hope they have some kids so I can play with them. I can see my favourite autumn tree. I always go and play on that tree with my friends. I can see some squirrels in that tree. I hope they're not cold over there. Oh, it's five o'clock. It is time for me to go to maths school. I will see you after maths school.

Figure 1. 'My Window': Written Text in Windows Book.

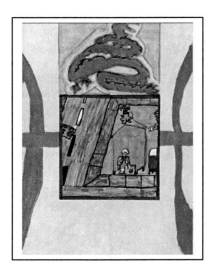

Figure 2. Looking through the window to the view outside.

Figure 3. Full view of activity outside the window.

The writing about the outside space displays a strong sense of their ability to imagine possible socio-spatial scenarios (a fancy car, a bus carrying children, mum waiting for the bus); their awareness of the material nature of neighbourhood places (old rubbish bin, new pathway, new traffic light); their capacities for inventing possible futures and imaginary worlds (potential new neighbours, favourite tree complete with squirrels).

Working in pairs, using the props of the photocopied windows, children were able to draw on their knowledge developed over time to construct complex narratives of people, place and time. They were able to imagine figured social worlds (Holland, Lachicotte, Skinner & Cain, 1998) inhabited by themselves and others and to represent them using a range of semiotic resources, including word, image and layout. The work that children had done materially and intellectually over time had allowed them to develop an attentiveness to place and space, both real and imagined, and this noticing or attending to place had provided rich material for writing and design.

DESIGNING AND REPRESENTING CHANGING PLACES

While the final outcome of the Grove Gardens project was the creation of a re-designed built and planted garden, it took a good deal of pedagogical work on the part of the architect and teachers to reach that goal.[2] In architectural terms, the design of the garden was staged around two main 'projects': *Learning the language [of design]* and *A belonging space*. The concept of *design*, in the architectural sense, was central to both projects, each of which provided the basis for a number of shared and public events (see Comber & Nixon, 2008). The term design, however, is ambiguous; it is both noun and verb, and refers to both structure and process, where the latter involves agency. The design of a building refers to its organisational structure, but also to the agentic *process* in which an architect works creatively with available concepts and design elements to produce that design. Learning to *attend* to spaces and places is a necessary precursor to learning to *design* and *represent* them. In this project, the objective was to involve as many children as possible in all of these processes under the guidance and direction of experienced architects and teachers.

Literacy theorists have also drawn attention to the concept of *design* (Cope & Kalantzis, 2000; Kress, 1995; New London Group, 1996) as part of a broader concept known as a 'pedagogy of multiliteracies'. Central to the multiliteracies argument is the belief that in a globalised knowledge economy, people are required to act as *designers* of new knowledge, as active participants in *creating* and *negotiating* increasingly complex sets of literate practices, which include a critical orientation to representation and communication. In contrast to earlier times, the *active design* of meaning and knowledge in today's world no longer draws predominantly on what Kress calls 'language as writing', but rather on a number of "semiotic modes that are capable of being realised in different materialities" (Kress & van Leeuwen, 2001, p. 6). The involvement of architects in the Grove Gardens project introduced an emphasis on 'design' and 'spatial literacies' as understood in their field, as well as new resources for developing the critical and place-based literacies with which the school had long been engaged.

The work of an architect in designing spaces and structures draws upon highly developed literate practices concerned with space, time, negotiation/consultation and translation. In architecture, *translation* refers to the translation of a client's wishes and ideas into an architect's ideas and concepts, and also to the translation of an architect's preliminary designs into plans in a form that can be operationalised by those who will actually work to change a site. Although we did not expect children to develop the same kinds of spatial literacies that are developed by architects, the pedagogical practices surrounding the design of spaces and places that the architect introduced to teachers, to students and to us, were variations on those he routinely used in architecture workshops. For their part, teachers adapted and extended these activities to suit several learning areas of school curriculum, including technology and design and literacy/English.

Throughout the project, children, teachers and university educators had the opportunity to learn first hand about the complexity of what can be involved in changing a place. This meant learning about not only the kinds of skills involved in producing a vision or 'design concept' that could be realised (taking due account of safety issues and so on), and drawing up plans that could enable the vision to be implemented, but also learning about what changing a place might mean in the lives of people who inhabit and use that place. As noted, several nearby suburbs had already been re-designed and 'renewed' by the developer Westwood. This meant that children did not have to travel very far from the school in order to see tangible evidence of changes to their local landscape that were the outcomes of other people's designs. They knew friends and relatives who had already been affected, many of whom had had to move house and change schools. They also knew full well that, with each passing year, the Westwood redevelopment was coming ever closer towards their street and their house, and that their 'belonging spaces' were places undergoing a process of change.

Over time, teachers' curriculum design spread across modes and media (expressive and reflective writing, drawings, interviews, discussion, modelling, computer imaging), spaces and places (buildings, parks, home, school, neighbourhood) and time (reflections on the past, descriptions of the present, and projections into the future). Children were also engaging in high-end symbolic and semiotic work associated with architectural practice such as the production of preliminary design sketches and annotated to-scale drawings and models. With assistance, some children were also learning how to use a CAD (computer-aided design) program to design a garden that incorporated their preferred design features. In effect, children were assisted to develop skills in *translating* their ideas *from* talk *into* writing, drawing and model-making; that is, from one semiotic medium into another.

During the project, Loo wanted his architecture students to experience consulting with children as 'clients'.[3] At the same time, Loo and the teachers assisted the children to be active participants in processes of design, representation and consultation. As the aim was to make Grove Gardens a 'belonging space' for all the children, as well as for the wider school community, it was important for children involved in our project to consult with other children across the school and preschool, and with parents and other community members who would be regular users of the redesigned space.

A key strategy in this phase of the project was the production of student-produced 'consultation books'. Here we illustrate how the production and circulation of the consultation books assisted children to assemble, display and use the significant resources they had developed for designing, representing and writing about the changes they hoped to bring about in a place that they wanted to change.

In essence, the collectively authored children's texts known as consultation books (see Figure 4) consisted of illustrated writing about what children would like to see and do in the garden area. Children from the two classes participating in the research, represented their key ideas about the garden design on paper – ideas that had been developed over a significant period of time as a result of working with various vocabularies, concepts and media. The task required the children, working in pairs or alone, to produce two complementary texts. The first text was a persuasive written text that explained what they wanted to see in the area and why, and that provided a fulsome description of what it would look like. The second text was a visual text (which could also include some verbal labels), produced in their choice of media, that represented their design plan for the area. These texts were laminated and collated as sets of facing pages in four books (two volumes per class); blank space was left on the written text page to allow for children and other community members to write their responses using marker pens. Finally, the books were taken to every class in the school for discussion and feedback and made available to parents and the local community at a public event.

Figure 4. Front cover of a consultation book.

Figure 5. Facing page drawing from a consultation book.

One example from books produced in the Grade 3/4 class shows what was made possible by a curriculum focus on space and place, combined with the particular pedagogical approach of teacher Marg Wells. The written text on one left hand page reads as follows:

What would I like to see in the area?

A big maze with some switches

Why?

So kids who are waiting can play in it while they are waiting for their mum and dad to pick them up and kids can get tricked because they won't know which is the beginning and which is the end.

What would it look like? Describe.

The walls around the maze are made of cement and are painted in gold. It will be 10 metres high and it will have traps inside it. You have to find a key to get out and you have to take a friend with you.

Here two boys imagine and represent in writing how a desolate school yard space might be transformed into something like 'a maze of switches'. And why? So kids who are waiting can play in it while they are waiting for their mum and dad to pick them up and kids can get tricked because they won't know which is the beginning and which is the end.

That is, the boys have imagined that the redesigned space of the yard could perform a dual social function: both a designated safe place for waiting children, and a place for pleasurable children's play. Their written text combines an awareness of the *social function* that a space designed as a maze might fulfil (kids can play in it while they wait for their parents, friends will enter the maze together), with aspects of their own specific and gendered interests in mazes and other kinds of fantasy and quest games that include 'tricks', puzzles and quests ("you have to find a key to get out").

As in their written text, the boys' *visual* representation on the facing page (see Figure 5) combines elements of realism (grass, pathway, toilet blocks designed for 'big kids only' and some for 'little kids') and elements of fantasy (winged dragon, two kinds of maze). However, drawing on the spatial literacies that had been introduced from architectural practice, the boys' image resembles an architect's plan. For example, it includes an aerial view and a sense of scale; lines depict a pathway that links one side of the area to the other; written labels indicate that a structure is a toilet block or gate; and icons represent seating structures and shelters. But there are also different kinds of visual elements fore-grounded in this image, most notably the vibrant red dragon with yellow wings which seems to be devouring one end of the pathway which is depicted from a lateral view and is comparatively over-sized in scale. Taken together, the boys' written and visual texts convey their desire for Grove Gardens to be redesigned as a place for play and adventure which incorporates elements familiar to them from popular culture and digital play (cf. Burke & Grosvenor, 2003. See also Comber & Nixon, 2008).

Our analysis of the four consultation books produced by children in Grades 3/4 and Grades 5/6 suggests that there were similar positive outcomes for many children. The books enabled children to demonstrate their competence in using a range of semiotic resources (see Comber & Nixon, 2008). For example, by this stage of the project many children were able to represent space using aerial and other perspectives, and to demonstrate an emergent understanding of scale and ratio. They were also able to use drawings to communicate the social nature of space, and to use image and colour in ways that signalled an awareness of the aesthetic dimensions of design. In our view, children were, at the same time, also developing their literate identities, more narrowly conceived. Firstly, they were expanding their *vocabularies* to incorporate architectural terms (e.g. design elements such as wall, pathway and platform) in their design descriptions. Secondly, they were learning to *make a case* for a particular design concept, and to provide *written rationales* for how and why beneficial changes might be made to the appearance and social functions of a designated space. Thirdly, there was evidence that, for some children at least, the curriculum and pedagogy of the project assisted them to *write extended pieces*. What follows is a section of a written page in one book:

What would it look like? Describe

The toilet building will be small and red and inside will be three toilets in boys and girls rooms. The platform will be like stairs that goes very high. The platform will also have rails for safety. The bird house will be small, wooden for birds to go in and out. The bridge will look long and low and the pond will be shallow and clear blue. The court will not take up much space and the tennis court will be light green. The running track will be made out of cement and it will be cream colour. The wall will have holes in it for looking through and the wall is red and it is made out of bricks (Grade 3/4 consultation book).

Once again we note the detailed description which incorporates architectural elements such as platforms and bridges, and the concern for safety, with rails and shallow water. We note also the ambitious nature of the project, including running tracks and a tennis court, sporting facilities often available in more affluent schools. As well there is a concern for the aesthetics of the place with specification of colour for different materials, such as red toilets, cream coloured cement and light green tennis court and clear blue ponds. Unlike other studies of the writing of middle primary aged children, rather than a dearth of detail, here we almost have an over-supply. Yet of course architectural planning and design requires specificity and these children have had considerable time to build their knowledge of the field and the results are evident in their writing.

CONCLUSIONS

My favourite place in the school is Grove Gardens. ... [there] are lots of paintings and things I helped to make. I also helped plant the plants. That's my favourite place.

When Grove Gardens was officially opened, young people from Trimboli's and Wells' classes queued up to have their say. In addition, their writing, including thank you letters to their Principal who was leaving, were full of sentiments such as those expressed by the student above. Wells' and Trimboli's pedagogies, with help from architect Loo, brought together literacy, the arts, and architectural approaches to space and place, in order to offer a place-based curriculum with depth and consequence. It provided students new resources for considering *material*, as well as *imagined*, spaces and places. In summary, we observed students:

– Becoming more attentive to the built environment and aware of how it might be understood and spoken about
– Becoming more motivated to produce a different order of work – incited to write and draw with accuracy and precision; with excitement and imagination
– Developing their affective investments in their *belonging spaces* and in local places that figured significantly in their lives
– Appropriating the semiotic and symbolic means to represent a deeply-felt 'care of place'.

In increasingly globalised times in which who lives where is deeply related to economies, environmental resources (and the lack thereof), labour market needs and escalating political conflicts in and over place, learning to operate with agency and care in specific communities – cultural and geographic – is a daunting, yet urgent pedagogical agenda. The work of teachers in changing places, in sites of urban renewal, is often ignored; likewise young people, safely incarcerated in their schools, are frequently marginalised from place-making projects. To us this seems an incredible waste, not unlike the wastage of resources more broadly, that has brought the planet to state of crisis in terms of climate, water, and so on. Why not harness our education systems, our teachers and our young people into productive and sustainable place-making projects which are simultaneously identity projects for the production of eco-ethical citizens?

NOTES

[1] The project was conducted by Barbara Comber, Helen Nixon & Louise Ashmore from the Centre for Studies in Literacy, Policy and Learning Cultures, Stephen Loo, Louis Laybourne School of Architecture and Design and Jackie Cook, School of Information, Communication and New Media, University of South Australia with teachers, Marg Wells and Ruth Trimboli and young people from Ridley Grove R-7 School, Woodville Gardens, South Australia. The project was funded by the Myer Foundation http://www.myerfoundation.org.au/main.asp: The views expressed in this paper are those of the authors only and do not necessarily represent those of the Myer Foundation.

[2] At the same time, teachers were working within state and school-specific curriculum guidelines and, throughout the project, architecture students were working within different architecture 'workshop' curriculum guidelines as part of undergraduate and honours university programs.

[3] Built into the project design were stages during which the university architecture students consulted the primary school children, and the texts that they had produced, to inform how the children's ideas might be 'translated' into site design concepts. Known as 'the translation team', their job was to first represent and later specify in some detail the design concepts so that the designs could eventually be realised. Further, the garden structures were built by a second team of university students in the 'construction' workshop of their degree program.

REFERENCES

Appadurai, A. (2002, August). *The capacity to aspire: Culture and the terms of recognition.* Presentation at Witwatersrand Institute for Social and Economic Research, Johannesburg.

Arthurson, K. (2001). Achieving social justice in estate regeneration: The impact of physical image construction. *Housing Studies, 16*(6), 807–826.

Baker, J. (1991). *Window*. London: Julia MacRae.

Barton, D. (1994). *Literacy: An introduction to the ecology of the written language*. Cambridge, MA: Blackwell.

Barton, D., & Hamilton, M. (1998). *Local literacies: Reading and writing in one community*. London and New York: Routledge.

Barton, L., Hamilton, M., & Ivanic R. (Eds.). (2002). *Situated literacies: Reading and writing in context*. London and New York: Routledge and Taylor & Francis.

Browne, B., & Jain, S. (2002). *Imagine Chicago: Ten years of imagination in action*. Chicago: Imagine.

Burke, C. (2005). Play in focus. Children researching their own spaces and places for play. *Children, Youth and Environments, 15*(1), 27–53.

Burke, C. (2007). The view of the child: Releasing 'visual voices' in the design of learning environments. *Discourse: Studies in the cultural politics of education, 28*(3), 359–372.

Burke, C., & Grosvenor, I. (2003). *The school I'd like. Children and young people's reflections on an education for the 21st century*. London: RoutledgeFalmer.

Chawla, L. (Ed.). (2002). *Growing up in an urbanising world*. London: UNESCO and Earthscan.

Christensen, P., & O'Brien, M. (Eds.). (2003). *Children in the city: Home, neighbourhood and community*. London and New York: RoutledgeFalmer.

Comber, B. (1998). The problem of 'background' in researching the student subject. *Australian Educational Researcher, 25*(3), 1–21.

Comber, B. (2001). Critical literacies and local action: Teacher knowledge and a 'new' research agenda. In B. Comber & A. Simpson (Eds.), *Negotiating critical literacies in classrooms*. Mahwah, NJ: Lawrence Erlbaum.

Comber, B. (2007). Reading places: Creative and critical literacies for now and the future. In A. Simpson (Ed.), *Future directions in literacy: International conversations*. Sydney, NSW: Sydney University Press.

Comber, B., & Nixon, H. (2005). Children re-read and re-write their neighbourhoods: Critical literacies and identity work. In J. Evans (Ed.), *Literacy moves on: Using popular culture, new technologies and critical literacy in the primary classroom* (pp. 127–148). Portsmouth, NH: Heinemann.

Comber, B., & Nixon, H. (2008). Spatial literacies, design texts and emergent pedagogies in purposeful literacy curriculum. *Pedagogies: An International Journal, 3*(4), 221–240.

Comber, B., Nixon, H., & Reid, J. (Eds.). (2007). *Literacies in place: Teaching environmental communications*. Newtown, NSW: Primary English Teaching Association.

Comber, B., Thomson, P., & Wells, M. (2001). Critical literacy finds a 'place': Writing and social action in a neighborhood school. *Elementary School Journal, 101*(4), 451–464.

Comber, B., Badger, L., Barnett, J., Nixon, H., & Pitt, J. (2002). Literacy after the early years: A longitudinal study. *Australian Journal of Language and Literacy, 25*(2), 9–23.

Comber, B., Nixon, H., Ashmore, L., Loo, S., & Cook, J. (2006). Urban renewal from the inside out: Spatial and critical literacies in a low socioeconomic school community. *Mind, Culture and Activity, 13*(3), 228–246.

Cope, B., & Kalantzis, M. (Eds.). (2000). *Multiliteracies: Literacy learning and the design of social futures*. Melbourne, VIC: Macmillan.

Corsaro, W. (Ed.). (2005). *The sociology of childhood* (2nd ed.). Thousand Oaks, CA: Pine Forge Press.

Derr, T. (2006). 'Sometimes birds sound like fish': Perspectives on children's place experiences. In C. Spencer & M. Blades (Eds.), *Children and their environments: Learning, using and designing spaces* (pp. 108–123). Cambridge, UK: Cambridge University Press.

Fisher, K. (2003, March). Designs for learning in the knowledge age. *SA Architecture Magazine*.

Francis, M., & Lorenzo, R. (2006). Children and city design: Proactive process and the 'renewal' of childhood. In C. Spencer & M. Blades (Eds.), *Children and their environments: Learning, using and designing spaces* (pp. 217–237). Cambridge, UK: Cambridge University Press.

Gruenewald, D. A. (2003a). Foundations of place: A multidisciplinary framework for place-conscious education. *American Educational Research Journal, 40*(3), 619–654.

Gruenewald, D. A. (2003b). The best of both worlds: A critical pedagogy of place. *Educational Researcher, 32*(4), 3–12.

Heft, H., & Chawla, L. (2006). Children as agents in sustainable development: The ecology of competence. In C. Spencer & M. Blades (Eds.), *Children and their environments: Learning, using and designing spaces* (pp. 199–216). Cambridge, UK: Cambridge University Press.

Holland, D., Lachiotte, W., Skinner, D., & Cain. C. (1998). *Identity and agency in cultural and social worlds.* Cambridge, MA: Harvard University Press.

Holloway, S., & Valentine, G. (Eds.). (2000). *Children's geographies: Playing, living learning.* London and New York: Routledge.

Horelli, L. (2006). A learning-based network approach to urban planning with young people. In C. Spencer & M. Blades (Eds.), *Children and their environments: Learning, using and designing spaces* (pp. 238–255). Cambridge, UK: Cambridge University Press.

Janks, H., & Comber, B. (2006). Critical literacy across continents. In K. Pahl, & J. Rowsell (Eds.), *Travel notes from the New Literacy Studies: Instances of Practice* (pp. 95–117). Clevedon, Avon: Multilingual Matters.

Jehl, J., Blank, M., & McCloud, B. (2001). *Education and community building: Connecting two worlds.* Washington, DC: Institute for Educational Leadership.

Jenks, C. (2005). *Childhood* (2nd ed.). Abingdon, Oxon, New York: Routledge.

James, A., Jenks, C., & Prout, A. (1998). *Theorizing childhood.* New York: Teachers College Press.

Kerkham, L., & Comber, B. (2007). Literacy, places and identity: The complexity of teaching environmental communications. *Australian Journal of Language and Literacy, 30*(2), 134–148.

Kress, G. (1995). *Writing the future: English and the making of a culture of innovation.* Sheffield, UK: National Association for the Teaching of English.

Kress, G., & van Leeuwen, T. (1996). *Reading images. The grammar of visual design.* London and New York: Routledge.

Kress, G., & van Leeuwen, T. (2001). *Multimodal discourse: The modes and media of contemporary communication.* London: Arnold.

Leander, K., & McKim, K. (2003). Tracing the everyday 'sitings' of adolescents on the Internet: A strategic adaptation of ethnography across online and offline spaces. *Education, Communication and Information, 3*(2), 211–240.

Leander, K., & Sheehy, M. (2004). *Spatializing literacy research.* New York: Peter Lang.

Leander, K., & Rowe, D. (2006). Mapping literacy spaces in motion: a rhizomatic analysis of a classroom literacy performance. *Reading Research Quarterly, 41*(4), 428–460.

McGregor, J. (2004). Spatiality and the place of the material in schools. *Pedagogy, Culture and Society, 12*(3), 347–372.

Malone, K. (Ed.). (2007). *Child space.* New Delhi: Concept Publishing Company.

Martusewicz, R. A., & Edmundson, J. (2005). Social foundations as pedagogies of responsibility and eco-ethical commitment. In D. W. Butin (Ed.), *Teaching social foundations of education: Contexts, theories and issues* (pp. 71–91). Mahwah, NJ: Lawrence Erlbaum.

New London Group. (1996). A pedagogy of multiliteracies: Designing social futures. *Harvard Educational Review, 66*(1), 60–92.

Nixon, H. (2007). Expanding the semiotic repertoire: Environmental communications in the primary school. *Australian Journal of Language and Literacy, 30*(2), 102–117.

Nixon, H., Comber, B., & Cormack, P. (2007). River literacies: Researching in contradictory spaces of cross-disciplinarity and normativity. *English Teaching: Practice and Critique, 6*(3).

Prinsloo, M., & Breier, M. (Eds.). (1996). *The social uses of literacy: Theory and practice in contemporary South Africa.* Bertsham, South Africa & Amsterdam/Philadelphia: Sached Books and John Benjamins Publishing Company.

Prout, A. (2005). *The future of childhood: Towards the interdisciplinary study of children.* London and New York: RoutledgeFalmer.

Reay, D. (2000). Children's urban landscapes: Configurations of class and place. In S. R. Munt (Ed.), *Cultural studies and the working class* (pp. 151–164). London: Cassell.

Scourfield, J., Dicks, B., Drakeford, M., & Davies, A. (2006). *Children, place and identity.* London: Routledge.

Smith, G. (2002, April). Place-based education: Learning to be where we are. *Phi Delta Kappan,* 584–594.

Somerville, M. (2007, December). _Space and place in education: (Still) speaking from the margins_. Australian Association For Research In Education Conference Proceedings. Retrieved from the AARE Web site: www.aare.edu.au/07pap/som07563.pdf

Spencer, C., & Blades, M. (Eds.). (2006). *Children and their environments: Learning, using and designing spaces.* Cambridge, UK: Cambridge University Press.

Street, B. (2001). *Literacy and development: Ethnographic perspectives.* London: Routledge.

Sutton, S., & Kemp, S. (2006). Young people's participation in constructing a socially just public sphere. In C. Spencer & M. Blades (Eds.), *Children and their environments: Learning, using and designing spaces* (pp. 256–276). Cambridge, UK: Cambridge University Press.

Thomson, P. (2002). *Schooling the rustbelt kids: Making the difference in changing times.* Sydney, NSW: Allen & Unwin.

Urban Pacific Westwood. (2008). The Westwood Project. Retrieved February 2, 2008, from http://www.westwoodsa.com.au/index02.php?id=14

Wells, M., Badger, L., & Kimber, P. (2000). *Social action through literacy.* Adelaide, SA: Department of Education Training and Employment.

Helen Nixon
Barbara Comber
Hawke Research Institute,
University of South Australia

ROSLYN APPLEBY

9. JANE GOES TO TIMOR

How Time, Space and Place Shape English Language Teaching in International Development

This is a travel story - it is specific, particular, and yet situated also in the flows of people, media, languages, disciplines and ideas in a globalised world. It concerns the travel of English language teachers from Australia to work in international aid programs in East Timor; it tells of a teacher's mission, and how that mission was translated into a spatial practice through experiences of embodied engagement in the contact zone (Pratt, 1992). I start the story by outlining the way English language teaching practices are shaped within dominant narratives that privilege time over space, and then take a closer look at how one teacher slipped the temporal bonds to engage with an embodied sense of place.

Although the teacher's journey was neither linear nor without mishap and confusion, inevitably the constraints of this present textual format may render it rather too neatly. Despite its neat appearance, the story does not pretend to offer a universalising solution, but rather seeks an insight into a singular experience that resonates with some collected tales of experiential and pedagogical engagements in the contact zone.[1]

TIME AND SPACE IN DEVELOPMENT AND ENGLISH LANGUAGE TEACHING

The prevailing narrative of overseas aid for international development is one of promoting forward progress towards modernisation, a temporal narrative inscribed with a "simple teleology of the one and only story" (Massey, 1999, p. 281). The story goes like this: through international development aid programs, wealthy countries (like Australia) help poor countries (like East Timor) along the path of economic growth, towards a goal embodied in the "classic image of the West" (Gertzel, 1994, p. 2). The stimulation of market-oriented programs, so the story goes, will propel economic development and bring greater happiness to poorer nations, while fostering the trade and strategic foreign policy interests of donor nations. This story of rational progress is underpinned by a temporal logic that draws together many other disciplines and systems of knowledge and privileges time-as-progress, and time-as-action, over the specificities of space and place.

The problem with this "potent mythology of progress" (Bhabha, 1990, p. 209) lies in the unspoken narrative carried within. Along with a modernist ideal of progress, the international development industry has inherited the systematic

M. Somerville, K. Power and P. de Carteret (eds.),
Landscapes and Learning: Place Studies for a Global World, 139–152

hierarchies of colonialism: donor nations are accorded a superior position, due to their 'developed' status, while recipient nations lag behind in a state of permanent deficit (Escobar, 2004; Rist, 2002). Geographically distant and different places, people and knowledges have been relocated into a chronological scale, measuring their temporal distance from the present, civilised stage of humanity (Mignolo, 2000, p. 283). In the contact zone of interaction between donors and recipients, this inherent hierarchy casts development workers from donor countries in the role of knowledge-bearing international elites, and participants from host countries in the role of knowledge-deficient dependents.

Educational programs, including programs to develop English language skills, fit well into the temporal narrative of development and progress (Kingsbury, Remenyi, & Hunt, 2004). They are seen as investments in human resources development that contribute to economic growth by modernising workforce skills and stimulating economic activity. In the global hierarchy, education for development is associated with the transfer to periphery institutions of knowledge generated in the First World; and educational dependency is linked to the transfer of Western educational forms and models, the preferential use of Western languages, and reliance on Western academic books and journals, thereby rendering 'periphery' universities consumers of knowledge from the 'centre', rather than producers of locally mediated knowledge (Altbach, 1998).

By association, English is presented as *the* language of modernisation and development, a natural, neutral and beneficial technical skill, and an adjunct to progress in any context. As such, improving English language skills has become a central function of the Australian policy for development assistance in education (AusAID, 2007). The notion of English language as a neutral, technical skill tends to preclude scrutiny of the knowledge constructs and hierarchies, linguistic complexities, colonial legacies and geopolitical effects of English language spread within specific contexts (Pennycook, 1994; Phillipson, 1992; Tollefson, 2000). This image of neutrality also underpins an international English language teaching industry that ignores its own situated origins, and presumes to equip teachers from English speaking countries of the 'Centre' with "universally relevant" skills that may be applied in language teaching programs "throughout the Periphery" (Phillipson, 1992, p. 238). Centre-produced methods and materials for English language teaching, have become "synonymous with progress, modernisation, and access to wealth" (Kramsch & Sullivan, 1996, p. 200); however, being 'universally relevant', these pedagogical tools can often be disconnected from the specific local contexts in which they are applied.

Despite these disciplinary and pedagogical conditions, English language teachers have been exhorted to devise language lessons that are relevant to the context of use and engage with students' experience. Just how this is to be achieved in practice, particularly in places where English is a foreign language and seldom used outside the classroom, remains unclear. When working for international aid projects, transient English language teachers may have little understanding of their students' lived context; as foreign 'experts', they are "flown in on sleek jet planes" and expected to perform their role according to a "script and plan" (Toh, 2003, p. 557) that reflects the "best modern methods" of language instruction (Savage, 1997). They are obliged to work towards the achievement of predetermined competencies or outcomes, under time pressures that speak to efficiency but preclude a more exploratory approach to place. The contingencies of place are rendered irrelevant, as context is reduced to a "neutral backdrop" where "androgynous bourgeois agents assert individual choice" (Luke, 1996, p. 311). How, then, can the teacher engage with a deeper sense of place and meaning for language learning? How can we "inhabit the present as if it were a place, a home rather than something we pass in a mad scramble to realise the future?" (May & Thrift, 2001, p. 37).

JANE GOES TO TIMOR

In this section, I relate the experience of Jane[2], who was engaged by a non-government agency to teach in a professional development program aimed at improving the English language skills and language teaching methodologies of East Timorese school teachers. While her account is only one of many in a larger research project, I focus on her story as a singular narrative that illuminates some of the broader issues to do with teachers' estrangements and engagements with place. Jane, a white, monolingual speaker of English in her mid 50s, had many years of experience teaching English language in Australia, but this was her first experience of teaching overseas. Before she applied to teach on the program, Jane's knowledge of Timor was scant:

> Before I applied, I knew nothing about Timor. In '99 when all the [post referendum] trouble was in Dili, my daughter was in India, and I kept thinking, my daughter is involved in this in Delhi [where she was travelling at the time]. You know, that was how little I knew about Timor, much to my shame (Jane, p. 29).

From the outset, Timor was the unknown, out there, strange and exotic, and most certainly dangerous.

Perilous Landscapes

Scouring for information before her travel, she came across the usual representations of Timor, during the period of its transition to independence, as a place of danger. This was a place where various groups were engaged in a violent political struggle to shape the new nation as it emerged from some 450 years of Portuguese colonialism and 25 years of Indonesian occupation and genocide. The 1999 vote for independence had triggered a campaign of violence in which thousands of Timorese were killed or displaced, cities and towns were reduced to rubble, and most of the country's infrastructure was destroyed. An international peacekeeping force, led by Australia, quelled much of the overt violence but had only limited success in producing an air of safety and stability. Australian media carried images of burning buildings, militia insurgents, guns and machetes. Although the peacekeeping forces were followed by an influx of civilian personnel from the

UN and international aid agencies, Jane's family, friends and professional colleagues discouraged her from going because "Oh my goodness it's so dangerous!" (Jane, p. 29). Such fearfulness reinforced an image of Timor as part of Australia's wild northern frontier, a place suitable only for intrepid masculine endeavours and where, as in the colonies, "heroic individual males behave in adventurous ways, exploring undiscovered lands and subduing the inhabitants" (Mills, 1994, p.37).

On the ground in East Timor, Jane was caught up in the endlessly circulating rumours of impending trouble. These sustained the notion of Timor as a perilous place of random, unpredictable violence and resistance to external interference: "there was some conflict ... between the whites and the Timorese ... something is kind of stirring ... stones were being thrown" and rogue groups were felling trees for road blocks, demanding payments from wealthy internationals for safe travel in places that were "quite volatile" (Jane, pp. 15-16). As was the case in earlier incarnations of colonialism, such unruly elements were seen to pose a particular threat to white women, who were then targeted by expatriate authorities as objects of particular concern:

> We were told as females, when we first went there, to make sure we had somebody else with us. It wasn't a good idea to go out at night alone ... I would never have gone to the beach alone ... we were told not to go ... We couldn't go far on our own, we weren't allowed I suppose, to go too far without a [male] driver (Jane, pp. 15-16).

Surrendering to patriarchal control, white women experienced a significant curtailing of their mobility: this was a place for masculine territorial struggle, and women should be fearful, passive and dependent. Development sites are, in this way, emblematic of a modernism that is "profoundly patriarchal" and, in its links to empire, profoundly racist and classist (Massey, 1994). In this gendering of the development story, a second pattern of time and space was realised. Time became aligned with the masculine, knowing subject, with agency and action; space became fixed, subjugated, controllable, and aligned with the feminised object-world (Grosz, 1995). For the female expatriate teachers, one effect of these restrictive, subordinating regimes was to limit their engagements with places and people beyond the boundaries of the expatriate enclaves.

The teachers' sense of isolation in this new place was exacerbated by their restricted knowledge of languages, with most, like Jane, having no proficiency in the languages spoken within Timorese communities. A rich array of national or indigenous languages had survived centuries of colonial interference, traces of Portuguese remained amongst the older generation, and Bahasa Indonesia had a stronghold amongst a younger generation as the language of instruction in schools over recent decades. English language was itself an outsider, representing only the latest wave in a series of colonial languages in Timor. As a common language amongst the recently arrived, relatively wealthy community of international development workers, English appeared to offer the promise of escape from economic deprivation. Although the dreams encouraged by the language have often proved to be illusory, a boom in demand for English as the new language of necessity ensued, and this reinforced the privileged – but separated – status of English language teachers as the expatriate experts.

Pedagogical Scripts

The discourses of isolation and fear in the face of unpredictability had a corollary in Jane's pedagogical performance, where she initially sought safety in the habitual routines and "repertoires of conduct" (Rose, 1996, p. 144) that "mobilise the flesh" (Nespor, 1994, p. 14) and produce the teacher as subject. Such routines are in turn organised through familiar temporal and spatial frames. The broad temporal frame of her teaching practice was established by the drive for modernisation, to be realised through the introduction of improved English language skills and Jane's more 'advanced' teaching methods. Within that broad narrative sweep, a third temporal frame operated, one that has become naturalised and largely invisible in our familiarity with a modernist western education. This is the temporal framework governed by a will to order, where learning is regulated in the form of a stepped curriculum which measures the progress of individual students through developmental stages, and directs them towards a set of predetermined goals to be achieved within a fixed time period. In this way, educational programs are internally structured according to a linear narrative that shapes the classroom as a place dominated by teleological considerations of personal growth and cognitive development towards predictable outcomes (Peters, 1996).

Faced with the unfamiliar context of Timor, Jane drew on the safety of these pedagogical scripts and plans, following the steps and stages of a competency-based syllabus set by the project management and based on an Australian ELT textbook designed for assimilating migrants into an Australian lifestyle. As has been the case for many Western teachers in unfamiliar situations, the textbook became a de facto curriculum for teacher and students, and at first, Jane felt bound to a program that shaped the teaching day as a series of lessons she had to 'get through'. The pages of the textbook provided, in their very fixity, a prescribed pathway through an otherwise fraught and daunting day: "I suppose initially, in a new environment and in teaching something that was new, it was like, this is on the page, okay, I'll get through this today" (Jane, p.11). In a practice similar to her colleagues, Jane's reliance on scripts and plans could be seen in her conscientious habits of planning and organising sequences of work before meeting her students at the commencement of the course, and before each day's work, in a way that 'filled up' what was otherwise represented as the fearfully 'empty' time and space of the classroom. In her determination to focus on and perform the pedagogical script, we see yet again, the conscientious development expert as the active agent of time, working against a background of the world (or, in this case, the 'empty' classroom) as a knowable object; a passive, feminised space (Grosz, 1995).

Looking up from the page and facing this new place, however, Jane's next struggle was to connect her language teaching content, derived from a mandated Australian textbook to the context of Timor:

> I guess we went in with the brief to adapt [the course book and the program] culturally. Okay, I did not *know* the culture, so, how to adapt it culturally, and all I was seeing was, what was happening in that tiny little area where I was living ... so I didn't *have* the experience culturally to change it culturally (Jane, p. 2).

In the case of teaching in development, textbooks provide a mobile form of disciplinary knowledge and also carry within them the representations of supposedly typical situations for English language use. In the most commonly used centre-produced textbooks, such situations are designed to reflect a modern 'international' lifestyle and tend to reduce the complexities of the world by presenting a simplified, sanitised, Western world viewpoint (Gray, 2002, p. 166). This simulacrum of the West then becomes 'universal' disciplinary knowledge, abstracted and severed from its place of origin, to be reterritorialised as norms and ideals in new places (Giddens, 1990; Rose, 1996). For Giddens, this very decontextualisation of knowledge was a necessary condition for its spread from the West around the globe in the processes of imperialism. Yet it is the gap between a deterritorialised textbook world and local conditions that the English language teacher is expected to bridge.

Like many teachers in similar programs, Jane found her own limited experience of the context prevented her from either successfully adapting the spatial representations of the course book to her new surroundings, or drawing some new relation between English as a foreign language and the particular places and histories of Timor.

> [the textbook is based on] a Queensland program ... it's very Australian, so you know. You catch a train, so you'd look at train timetables, but there are no trains in [Timor], Well I could adjust that to bus timetable, but like the microlets (Timorese minibuses) do not have a timetable! So it's all that, culturally so strange and there were a lot of things I left out because at the time I couldn't think of how to change it. And it was so new (Jane, p. 2).

As Jane soon discovered, the typical situations and scripts depicted in the textbook, and forming the basis of lesson plans, like reading timetables, catching trains, even eating breakfast, did not apply to Timor. The scripts and representations of textbooks, being divorced from the world outside the classroom, instead produced an 'English bubble', a disciplinary schema floating detached from the social and historical context of this particular location. For most of the Australian teachers in my study, the disconnection between those imported scripts and plans for teaching, and the particular characteristics of places and people in Timor, led to intense feelings of confusion, disorientation and doubt. Only a few of the teachers clung tenaciously to their 'universal' teaching methods and materials, remaining in the English bubble that hovered above the landscape.

What was not depicted in the anodyne representations of the textbooks were some of the material consequences of western intervention in Timor. For Jane, fragmentary encounters with the outside world began, in small ways, to shake any certainty she might have had about the promise of development to bring progress and modernity to Timor. She saw the spatial boundaries drawn around the development enclaves, the hierarchies of wealth and power that produced a dual economy, and the resultant alienation of development workers from the host community. These discrepancies in wealth were crystallised in a specific place where the detritus of an elite international lifestyle disfigured the landscape. Discarded from expatriate enclaves, mounting waste in the form of toilet paper, water bottles and packaging settled in swelling rubbish dumps: "Now the rubbish tip had only just started and there were people who lived in the rubbish tip and they would go through all that rubbish that had been thrown out" (Jane, p. 9). This despoiling of the landscape and degradation of a host community were problems for which Jane felt a sense of personal responsibility. This was rubbish generated "not only by Westerners, but *this* Westerner", and much of it was waste that was "*never* going to disintegrate" (Jane, p. 9), leaving an ugly scar in the wake of a transient expatriate occupation. Jane's reflections on these discomforting encounters contributed, in turn, to her uncertainties and misgivings about the effects of a pedagogical mission that had similarly promised to bring progress in the form of educational advancement.

LEARNING CONNECTIONS TO PLACE

Destabilising Hierarchies

Jane's moves to make a different sort of connection with the specificities of place in Timor involved subtle spatial and temporal shifts. The first entailed Jane's struggle against the presumptions of status that had constructed a spatial separation between herself and her adult students; a separation that was secured by the hierarchies of progress, development and disciplinary knowledge. Within these hierarchies, local colleagues and students were positioned as subordinate to foreign teachers, who flew in as knowledgeable expatriate experts, and were expected to maintain professional standards by approaching their task, their students, and the social, economic and political context, with an objective detachment. The implied "superiority of being us" (D'Cruz & Steele, 2003, p. 37), so evident in interactions between donor and host communities in development, reproduced relationships between coloniser and colonised, and created a discomforting position that Jane struggled to resist.

> I felt a lot of the Timorese, because I was white, it was this kind of thing [bowing] like especially one of the fellows who worked at the college, and [I'd say] "Domingos, please don't", and he'd be like this [bowing], and that was just [cringes] that was just, I didn't like that (Jane, p.15)

She was concerned that the respect her local colleagues and students gave her created a hierarchy of "I am here [gesturing a hand placed high] and you are there [a hand placed low]", producing a wariness and "this distance" between them that she attempted to break down (Jane, p.17). Jane's struggle was one towards disrupting the boundaries between self and other, between self and the environment, in the contact zone. In this process, the separated, ordered spatiality of neo-imperial culture could be reconceived in terms of porousness and fluidity that allow for an engagement with the 'other' (Pratt, 1992, p. 222).

Despite these moves to break down boundaries, Jane was cautious to avoid any claims to belong to East Timor in a way that might replicate (neo)colonial possession. Expressions of affirmation and connection thus left her in an in-between space, neither part of the local community, nor completely identified with the expatriate community.

> With the East Timorese that I worked with, I was made to feel very welcome, but I'm *not* East Timorese, I didn't have the language, and I think the first step in any culture is to learn the language. And so yes, I didn't feel like an outsider, that it was lonely being an outsider, but I felt, I certainly wasn't an East Timorese (Jane, p. 17).

Language, then, was seen as central to the production of belonging. Whereas development discourses envisage English language as building global communities and bringing recipient communities forward into a globalised world, Jane became aware that her own deficiencies and failings in other languages and ways of understanding, had left her out of place. Far from being disabling, however, the uncertainty of this liminal location eventually opened up new spatial and temporal possibilities. Over time, Jane recalled a particularly strong sense of being in a new place in terms of a gradual shift in both space and time that flowed into her classroom work. Being in a new place was not a matter of bringing change to an impoverished recipient community: rather, "being there *changed me*" (Jane, p. 24).

Jane's attempt to shift from a position of teacher-as-expert was evident in an acknowledgement that the foreign teacher was not necessarily the one who 'knew' what was going on, either inside or outside the classroom. Resisting the position of the knower, Jane sensed that, as an 'outsider', she "*never* knew what was going on"; however, this "wasn't bewildering' or a cause of anxiety. "In the end you don't know what was going on anyway ... but it really, it doesn't matter that you don't know, and probably you'll never know" (Jane, p. 17). In this move, rather than positing a transcendent, knowing subject, a detached "monarch-of-all-I-survey" (Pratt, 1992, p. 213), Jane sought to relinquish the a priori position of authority granted her as the teacher, and through contextual experiences of "disorientation, incomprehension, self-dissolution" (p. 222) became open to a different sort of engagement with place.

Moving Outside the Classroom

A further shift involved a move outside the boundaries of the classroom, a move that also saw a further reversal in the balance between teacher and students' expertise. The conventional asymmetry of power between teacher and student is enabled, in part, by the enclosure of the modernist classroom within firm boundaries. Such enclosure can be seen as an attempt "to stabilise the meaning of particular envelopes of space-time" (Massey, 1994, p. 5), and subjects those within to the gaze of disciplinary authority. In an early attempt to disrupt this pattern and to make connections with her students, Jane drew a time-line of her own life experiences, and used this as a model in the hope of eliciting students' own life stories. But students were reluctant, resistant. When inside the space of the classroom they were "very non-committal about their personal stories and about the war" (Jane, p. 10), eluding the spatial schema of the panopticon and the disciplinary gaze.

However, a move beyond the institutional envelope opened up possibilities for different, destabilising "spatial practices" (de Certeau, 1984, p. 96). And although Jane had insufficient knowledge of the culture of East Timor to adapt the content of the textbook to that context, moving outside the classroom allowed a more subtle, spatially nuanced, contextualisation of language and meaning. It also enabled a different connection between the teacher, the student and the production of "spatial history" (Carter, 1987). When outside the classroom, students' stories about the meanings of various places were more readily shared. Walking down the street, she would be shown where "this place was bombed, the bombs came over here, this happened here, and that sort of thing" (Jane, p. 10). In this spatial practice, the students had become the experts, narrating the stories-in-walking that "weave places together" (de Certeau, 1984, p. 97).

Nevertheless, engagement with the students' stories was not without its difficulties. These were also places "haunted by many different spirits hidden there in silence, spirits one can invoke or not" (de Certeau, 1984, p. 108). Here, de Certeau recognises that the verbal relics and debris, the shy, silenced memories that emerge from places, do so in resistance to the 'proper', disciplinary organisations of space and place. One such resistant engagement arose when Jane visited a Timorese beach with her students after studying textbook stories and information about Australian beaches. While beaches in Australian textbooks are often represented as jolly scenes of outdoor living, these beaches had a different meaning to tell. On the beach together, other stories surfaced, fragments and memories of other times in this place. The students told her that:

> going down to the water and swimming is not something that they did ... swimming or being in the water was avoided because, when the Indonesians were there that was part of the torture, they'd take them down to the beach and put their head down underneath and that kind of thing ... it takes a bit of courage to [go there], because this is what happened. (Jane, p. 3)

Outside the classroom there were communal practices of remembrance, recalling into the present personal memories of violence and trauma: "things *extra* and *other* [that] ... insert themselves into the accepted framework, the imposed order" (de Certeau, 1984, p. 107). In these events, the imposed order showed its instability; the beach was constructed through different experiences of different groups and individuals, as a liminal space of contested meanings. Through these narratives, the talk between teacher and students turned from the routine functions set out in the textbook to talk emerging from the contingencies of place, not only alluding to past trauma, but also discussing the construction of a new nation built on old ties and allegiances, the writing of a new constitution, the role of the church in the new state, the impassioned speeches of Xanana on his election rounds.

Shifts in Time

In Jane's experience, there was evidence not only of the development of a different sense of space and place, but also of a different sense of time, as personal and community histories, and possible futures, were brought into the space of the language classroom. These were times uncontained by the causality and predictability of historicism, or the strictures of clock time that govern the modernist mission of education. The most pressing articulation of time appeared in almost every teacher's perception that there was never enough of it: their foreign presence, in a place of long historical struggle, was transient and fleeting. This was particularly true for teachers on short term contracts where the measurement of progress was tied to unrealistic objectives and time constraints. Such were the hopes and desires resting on the promises of English language that any amount of time was felt by the teachers to be insufficient to achieve what was expected of them.

Taking a different approach to time, Jane's observations help to put the notion of teaching into a longer and more complex perspective of local time. Her shifting sense of time appeared in accounts of a different tempo or pace, more in line with the exigencies of events outside the classroom walls, taking precedence over the regulated time imposed by institutional and disciplinary requirements. Holy days, family obligations, anniversaries and political involvements were, for some, primary commitments around which time was organised. Although some of Jane's expatriate colleagues became frustrated when other priorities interrupted their 'normal' temporal expectations of timetabled classes, others enjoyed the sensation of a merging with experiences of time evolved within this context. Jane's easing into a different way of organising and experiencing time was evident in her changing relationship with the teaching plan that structured her pedagogical practice. This change of pace was realised in a release from the boundaries of the textbook: "I mean I didn't have to open the book and think oh, my god what am I doing today?" (Jane, p. 24). In her pedagogical practice, this meant she could be more flexible, to "risk", and "begin to be creative, which I wasn't, I wasn't there in that space when I first started" (Jane, p. 25).

Jane's earlier idea of professionalism had suggested a valorisation of productive time also typical of an industrial, industrious modernity (Adam, 2003). Rushing around, "still working at Australian pace" (Jane, p.11), her embodied, pedagogical performance had reflected a regulatory politics of time that underpins development and strives for progress and productivity. As Adam points out, such notions of "time thrift", aimed at maximising labour force efficiency, have been ingrained in the West since the industrial revolution and have been central to the neo-colonialist agenda of globalisation and development:

to be 'modern', 'progressive', even 'civilised' means to "embrace the industrial approach to time" (Adam, 2003, p.71). But these habits were gradually challenged and then changed by a new, phenomenal sense of being in place and time:

> Once I could slow down to East Timor, it was difficult to keep, I suppose the professionalism, my expectations of teaching, and to be able to slow down to the pace that one has to slow down to, you know with the heat and things, and that was, I think I managed it towards the end … I was able to sort of slow down, I didn't have to go [gestures of speedy, robotic talking and moving] (Jane, p. 11).

She had moved from a place of having "conflict going on, rushing here, rushing there", to "slowing down", and learning just to "be there" (Jane, p. 24). Both inside and outside the classroom, the temporal bonds that had regulated her way of being slipped away:

> I had never experienced that continual sense of being in the moment that I did towards the end there … I thought, my joy is being here, that's how I felt … it was so sharp and so beautiful, but that experience I've only ever had like for seconds or for minutes or for a day, but I'd get up in the morning and it would be there, and you know, it would be there, the wonderment I think.

> To be aware, to be conscious, to be content, to be happy, um, to be there. To not have conflict going on, um, as to, I suppose I had learnt to live in 'Timor time' and not have that conflict of rushing here, rushing there, and knowing things will get done. Yeah, so that slowing down to be in 'Timor time' and to 'be there' … I was very content, and everywhere I looked I thought, 'this is great, I am happy to be here' (Jane, p. 24).

This embodied expression of pleasure in 'being there', de Certeau describes as another 'spatial practice', "under-expressed in the language it appears in like a fleeting glimmer" (de Certeau, 1984, p. 108). If a regimented, commodified ordering of time and space, 'rushing here, rushing there', signalled a detachment from or conflict with the phenomenal world, Jane's changing experience of time seemed to indicate a closer sensate engagement with being in place that, in turn, infused her pedagogical practice.

Being There

At the beginning, Jane's story of Timor was one of fearfulness and trepidation; everywhere she went, she was chaperoned to avoid the unwelcome confrontations of the contact zone. On her teaching assignments in different locations, she had been instructed to travel in the institutional four-wheel drive that signifies the western aid worker as privileged foreigner: large, white, and air-conditioned, they stand out from the Timorese landscape as the expat cocoon, just passing through. By the end of her journey, however, these detached, anxious ways of relating to place had been transformed: "any fears that I had, had dropped away" (Jane, p. 24). After her teaching day at a village some distance from her base, rather than waiting as usual to be collected by the vehicle, she walked.

[At the beginning] I used to just sit and wait for the car, and towards the end of my time there, the time when I felt that I'd settled in, I started walking … I felt so comfortable, it was at sunset, everybody spoke to me: "where are you going?" uh, what was it, "bapasa Baucau", and they looked at me like: "you're walking to Baucau?! Is she off her head?!" *They* do it every day, but you know, and I had the pack full of books and stuff, and everybody was really friendly, and I felt very comfortable. I certainly didn't feel threatened at all … it was lovely, that time when I walked back … just talking to everyone at that time of night when they were outside and, yeah …(Jane, p. 15).

The 'pack full of books' had not been abandoned, but Jane was no longer so tied to their scripts and plans, instead experiencing a different sort of relationship between language, pedagogy and the possibilities of place. Walking here has become the "spatial acting-out of the place" and "a space of enunciation" (de Certeau, 1984, p. 98). Rather than being the passive object of development discourses, and of masculine surveillance and control, viewing the landscape from the impersonal safety of the four-wheel drive, Jane encountered a more practical, nocturnal, sensual knowledge of place, made up from fragments of conversation, and the rhythm of walking in the contact zone.

RE-READING LANGUAGE AND DEVELOPMENT

Jane's story demonstrates some of the ways in which English language teaching relates to the development context, and the ways in which this relationship is shaped by naturalised, modernist regimes of time and space. Through these regimes, underlying temporal narratives propel development pedagogies in a 'mad scramble' to realise a future while, at the same time, spatial separations sustain the gendered and racialised legacies of a colonial past. Jane's fears of being in a new place were heightened by circulating rumours of impending violence and corresponding discourses of hypermasculinity that encouraged a shrinking detachment from a wild world beyond the boundaries of a closed, expatriate society. A sense of alienation from place was then reiterated through Jane's initial compliance with routines that organised her pedagogical performance in accordance with norms and expectations from elsewhere. However, as Toh (2003) has observed, a focus on scripted performance and dissemination of modern methods leaves little room for a critical orientation towards English language teaching, or the complicity of English in the patterns of social, economic and political hierarchies of development. For an insight into those ways of being that defy or undermine the conventional discourses of English language teaching and development, I have focused more closely on how other manifestations of space and place emerge in Jane's narrative, in the "microbe-like, singular and plural practices" and "surreptitious creativities" which a totalising system is designed to domesticate or suppress (de Certeau, 1984, p. 96).

For Jane, it was the mismatch between conventional pedagogical routines, and the contradictory fragments of lived experience encountered in the world outside the classroom, that led to doubts about the viability of a mission for development styled by external goals. Resisting the transcendent subject position accorded her as the expatriate expert, Jane found another way of being-in-the-world, of connecting to local places and people, unfolding some small particles of the stories accumulated in places, and reconstructing spatial histories. This experience was more than something she could read in a book or watch in a film, it was something to do with the embodied experience of being there, an embodied engagement with landscape, with learning, with place. Walking, listening and memory led her to an engagement with spatiality, and produced an embodied, situated, partial knowledge of place that informed her pedagogy. These involvements allowed Jane to be present in the contact zone, outside and inside the classroom, in ways that resisted the most overt expressions of power, distance and detachment that can too easily characterise the pedagogical practices of disciplinary knowledge, and the world of international development. Her spatial practices allowed a more flexible interaction between teacher and student, and between English language teaching and the cultural and political dimensions of local places and contexts of learning in development.

Using a framework of time, space and place to reflect on Jane's narratives has enabled a different reading of English language teaching and development. This new reading points to the importance of interrogating the ways and the extent to which performing English language teaching is colonised by notions of time and space that tie the discipline into global institutional, economic and social systems, and into the stratification of cultural politics in local places. It offers a means of questioning the way spaces, places and people are connected or disconnected through language and language teaching, and attempts to open the classroom space to the phenomenal, cultural and political influences and knowledges of local places. This is a process that, for the teacher, signals time and space as dimensions with which to critically rethink the textual and political relation between global and local space, and implies learning new ways of being in a postcolonial world. In some small ways, Jane's experiences help us imagine what a place-based English language teaching might look like.

NOTES

[1] The teacher's narrative draws on interview data collected in a larger research project that investigated the role of English language teaching in international development. A full account of the project will be published in Appleby (forthcoming) *Experiencing Time, Space and Gender: English Language Teaching and International Development*. Clevedon: Multilingual Matters.

[2] Jane is a pseudonym for one of the teachers interviewed in the research project.

REFERENCES

Adam, B. (2003). Reflexive modernisation temporalised. *Theory, Culture and Society, 20*(2), 59–78.

Altbach, P. G. (1998). *Comparative Education: Knowledge, the university, and development.* Greenwich, CN: Ablex.

AusAID. (2007). *Better Education: A policy for Australian development assistance in education.* Canberra, ACT: Commonwealth of Australia.

Bhabha, H. K. (1990). DissemiNation: Time, narrative, and the margins of the modern nation. In H. K. Bhabha (Ed.), *Nation and narration* (pp. 207–221). London and New York: Routledge.

Carter, P. (1987). *The road to Botany Bay*. London: Faber & Faber.

D'Cruz, J. V. D., & Steele, W. (2003). *Australia's ambivalence towards Asia: Politics, neo/post-colonialism, and fact/fiction* (2nd ed.). Monash University, Australia: Monash University Press.

De Certeau, M. (1984). *The practice of everyday life* (S. Rendall, Trans.) Berkeley: California University Press.

Downer, A. (1996). *Education and training in Australia's aid program (Policy Statement by the Minister for Foreign Affairs)*. Canberra, ACT: Australian Agency for International Development.

Escobar, A. (2004). Development, violence and the New Imperial Order, *Development, 47*(1), 15–21.

Gertzel, C. (1994). The New World Order: Implications for development. *Development Bulletin, The Australian Development Studies Network, ANU, 32*(Briefing Paper 35), 1–8.

Giddens, A. (1990). *The consequences of modernity*. United Kingdom: Polity.

Gray, J. (2002). The global coursebook in English Language Teaching. In D. Block & D. Cameron (Eds.), *Globalization and language teaching* (pp. 152–167). London: Routledge.

Grosz, E. (1995). *Space, time and perversion: The politics of bodies*. St Leonards: Allen & Unwin.

Kingsbury, D., Remenyi, J., & Hunt, J. (2004). *Key issues in development*. Basingstoke and New York: Palgrave Macmillan.

Kramsch, C., & Sullivan, P. (1996). Appropriate pedagogy. *ELT Journal, 50*(3), 199–212.

Luke, A. (1996). Genres of power? Literacy education and the production of capital. In R. Hasan & G. Williams (Eds.), *Literacy in society* (pp. 308–338). London: Longman.

Massey, D. (1994). *Space, place and gender*. Cambridge, UK: Polity Press.

Massey, D. (1999). Spaces of politics. In D. Massey, J. Allen, & P. Sarre (Eds.), *Human geography today* (pp. 279–294). Cambridge, UK: Polity Press.

May, J., & Thrift, N. (2001). Introduction. In T. Skelton & G. Vallentine (Eds.), *TimeSpace: Geographies of temporality* (pp. 1–46). London: Routledge.

Mignolo, W. D. (2000). *Local histories/Global designs: Coloniality, subaltern knowledges, and border thinking*. Princeton, NJ: Princeton University Press.

Mills, S. (1994). Knowledge, gender, and empire. In A. Blunt & G. Rose (Eds.), *Writing women and space: Colonial and postcolonial geographies* (pp. 29–50). New York: The Guilford Press.

Nespor, J. (1994). *Knowledge in motion: Space, time and curriculum in undergraduate physics and management*. London: The Falmer Press.

Pennycook, A. (1994). *The cultural politics of English as an international language*. London: Longman.

Peters, M. (1996). *Poststructuralism, politics and education*. Westport, CT: Bergin & Garvey.

Phillipson, R. (1992). *Linguistic imperialism*. Oxford, UK: Oxford University Press.

Pratt, M. L. (1992). *Imperial eyes: Travel writing and transculturation*. London: Routledge.

Rist, G. (2002). *The history of development: From western origins to global faith* (P. Camiller, Trans. 2nd ed.). London: Zed Books.

Rose, N. (1996). Identity, genealogy, history. In S. Hall & P. du Gay (Eds.), *Questions of cultural identity* (pp. 128–150). London: SAGE.

Savage, W. (1997). Language and development. In B. Kenny & W. Savage (Eds.), *Language and development: Teachers in a changing world* (pp. 283–337). London: Longman.

Toh, G. (2003). Toward a more critical orientation to ELT in South East Asia. *World Englishes, 22*(4), 551–558.

Tollefson, J. W. (2000). Policy and ideology in the spread of English. In J. K. Hall & W. G. Eggington (Eds.), *The sociopolitics of English language teaching* (pp. 7–21). Clevedon, Avon: Multilingual Matters.

Roslyn Appleby
University of Technology Sydney

SECTION III: THEORISING PLACE DIFFERENTLY

NOEL GOUGH

10. HOW DO PLACES *BECOME* 'PEDAGOGICAL'?

> We live ... lives based on selected fictions. Our view of reality is conditioned
> by our position in space and time – not by our personalities as we like to
> think. Thus every interpretation of reality is based on a unique position. Two
> paces east or west and the whole picture is changed (Lawrence Durrell, 1963,
> pp. 14-15).

I did not begin to think of my research as 'place studies' until 4 April 2007, when
I received the following email message from one of the editors of this volume,
Margaret Somerville – a rhizomatic shoot popping up in my inbox:

> Hi Noel,
>
> I met you a long time ago through a seminar ... at UNE [University of New
> England]. I am now at Monash [University] Gippsland and I am organising a
> symposium with David Gruenewald as a leader about place pedagogies
> research on 14 August [2007] and we would love you to come along to speak.
> We are planning a lecture by David and then a series of three panels in which
> 4 speakers address issues of space and place from their particular theoretical
> perspective...
>
> Can you please let me know if you are interested?
>
> Thanks, Margaret

Up to this time, I doubt that I would have nominated 'issues of space and place' as
being among the chief objects of my inquiries in education, although a moment's
reflection was enough for me to realise that this was a very reasonable
interpretation.[1] Moreover, I was sufficiently familiar with Gruenewald's work in
environmental education (e.g. Gruenewald, 2004) – a field with which I identify
strongly – to accept Somerville's invitation with no hesitation. However, the
draft flyer for the *Landscapes and Learning* symposium that accompanied the
invitation provided a further impetus for my engagement with place pedagogies
research. The flyer included a prominent epigraph, "*place is profoundly
pedagogical*" (attributed to Gruenewald, 2003; emphasis in original), that
immediately prompted me to question – and to anticipate dissenting from – its
implicit assumptions. To simply *assert* an essential relationship between place and
pedagogy is too totalising for my taste.[2] Thinking about the inadequacy of this
essentialist (and static) assertion generated the working title for my contribution to
the symposium, which I have retained as the title for this chapter. I cannot imagine
'place' (as a generic abstraction) or 'a place' (as a specific location) *being*

M. Somerville, K. Power and P. de Carteret (eds.),
Landscapes and Learning: Place Studies for a Global World, 155–173

"profoundly pedagogical"; but I can imagine 'places' (as specific locations) *becoming* 'pedagogical' through cultural practices that enable or encourage us to attend closely to their multifarious qualities, including not only those that we might consider to be 'profound' (such as the deep, pervasive or intense qualities that we sometimes call the 'spirit' of a place), but also their more superficial, ephemeral or obvious characteristics.

As an environmental educator, my particular interest is in the relations of 'natural'[3] places to pedagogies. In the remainder of this chapter, I explore some of the ways in which places 'becoming-pedagogical' might be related to the ways that nature is envisioned, named, traversed and transformed. However, I first need to say a little more about how my work has changed in recent years, with particular reference to the material places in which it has been situated and to which it refers.

CHANGING PLACES

Prior to the *Landscapes and Learning* symposium, Somerville circulated a paper that she described as a 'provocation' for the conversations that the symposium was intended to stimulate (Somerville, 2008). I was pleasantly surprised to find that her paper begins by referring to some of the ways of theorising place that have been generative for me – and I am delighted that she finds them to be generative too. The title of the particular work to which she refers, 'Shaking the tree, making a rhizome: towards a nomadic geophilosophy of science education' (Gough, 2006), clearly signals my theoretical debt to Deleuze and Guattari (1987/1980), but I am now also indebted to Somerville for her generous and insightful reading of my essay – a reading that generates further interpretations and understandings of the deconstructive strategies I deployed in it.

I wrote 'Shaking the tree' for a special issue of *Educational Philosophy and Theory* on the philosophy of science education. My article builds upon Sandra Harding's (1993) critique of the Eurocentrism and androcentrism of scientific knowledge. I argue that both popular media culture and non-Western knowings tend to be ignored or devalued within many forms of Western science education and that these exclusions contribute to what Harding calls an increasingly visible form of scientific illiteracy. Somerville elaborates on the nomadic geophilosophy of science education that I attempt to demonstrate in my article, and draws particular attention to a passage in which I explain how a song, 'Shaking the Tree' (Peter Gabriel & Youssou N'Dour, 1989), inspired my essay:

> Peter Gabriel and Youssou N'Dour's song, 'Shaking the Tree', is in several ways emblematic of my project. It is a call to change and enhance lives composed in a spirit which complements Deleuze and Guattari's (1994) practical 'geophilosophy' (p. 95), which seeks to describe the relations between particular spatial configurations and locations and the philosophical formations that arise therein. Both Gabriel and N'Dour compose and perform songs about taking action to solve particular problems in the world, and Deleuze (1994) believes that concepts 'should intervene to resolve local situations' (p. xx) (Gough, 2006, p. 625).

Somerville (2008) offers an interpretation of my words for which I am deeply grateful, because she makes explicit some aspects of my method that I struggled to articulate:

> This richly layered metaphorical passage works on several levels and I would like to briefly reflect on these. 'Shaking the Tree' is a song, so we begin with a metaphor of singing, sound and the human voice, of creative expression in song, a move between a metaphysics of logics and of poetics. Then we have the subject of the song, the tree, as an image of nature, being shaken, a vigorous physical action related to radical social critique. This action has both practical and metaphysical implications. The image of 'shaking the tree' is connected with Deleuzian notions of the problematic of the tree as opposed to the rhizome as a metaphor of thought. In this paper the tree stands for the certainties and hierarchies of western science and the paper is Gough's song, a song that is both practical and located, metaphysical and transformational. He names the variety of assemblages available to shake the tree of modern Western science: 'arts, artefacts, disciplines, technologies, projects, practices, theories and social strategies' (Gough, 2006, p. 626). In his paper he deploys many of these to disrupt the certainties of modern Western science (education).

I have for many years tried to heed Donna Haraway's (1991) advice that "the only way to find a larger vision is to be somewhere in particular" (p. 196), that is, to work towards situated and embodied knowledge claims. In 1998 I began to work in an Australia-South Africa institutional links program and, between then and 2004, made over a dozen visits to various sites in southern Africa to work for periods of between two and six weeks at a time with colleagues and doctoral students on various 'capacity-building' activities around issues of research methodology and supervision, with particular reference to environmental education and science education. In the course of this work I quickly became aware of the many material and theoretical difficulties and complexities of being "somewhere in particular", especially when I was expected (or assumed) to be situated in several places at once. Like Haraway (1991), I aspired to put "a premium on establishing the capacity to see from the peripheries and the depths", but I was also aware of the "serious danger of romanticising and/or appropriating the visions of the less powerful while claiming to see from their positions" (p. 191). To 'see' from marginalised or subjugated locations is neither easily learned nor unproblematic. By 1999 I had begun, with tongue only partly in cheek, to characterise myself as a "travelling textworker" (Gough, 1999), an identity through which I could collaborate with co-workers on very site-specific tasks *in* particular places without ever pretending to be *of* those places. Like Somerville (2008), my practice drew on poststructuralist and postcolonialist theorising, and the more productive collaborations tended to be consistent with the three key principles of the place-responsive pedagogy that she describes, namely: (i) our relationship to place is constituted in stories and other representations; (ii) place learning is local and embodied; and (iii) deep place learning occurs in a contact zone of contestation.

My "travelling textworker" disposition has clearly informed my performance of the strategies I describe in 'Shaking the tree' as a "nomadic geophilosophy" (more recently I have characterised these strategies as "rhizosemiotic play" – see Gough, 2007a, 2007b). However, I doubt that I would ever have written 'Shaking the tree' without my extended experiences of working in southern Africa. The song itself celebrates and affirms the women's movement in Africa, and took on new meanings for me when I personally witnessed the many materialisations of patriarchal traditions and gender discrimination that remain pervasive across the continent. In addition, a key section of the paper, "mosquito rhizomatics", began to take shape as a direct result of seeing how *particular* assemblages of parasites, mosquitoes, humans, technologies and socio-technical relations produce *particular* manifestations of malaria in different places. Malaria kills around 3 million people per year in sub-Saharan Africa, most of them under the age of five, and it is no coincidence that the localities hit hardest by the most severe forms of malaria have economic growth rates significantly lower than those in which it is rarely fatal.

In one sense, it is tempting to see my southern African experiences as evidence of Gruenewald's (2003) assertions that "places are profoundly pedagogical" (p. 621), that "places teach us about how the world works" and that "places make us" (p. 621). But in those same experiences I can also find evidence of his alternative formulation: "that places are what people make them – that people are place makers and places are a primary artifact of human culture" (p. 627). Indeed, much of the work in which I participated in southern Africa was explicitly directed towards changing the places in which we worked, to make them places that would no longer 'teach' the determinisms of apartheid and the patriarchy, sexism, homophobia, class and language bias, ethnic nationalism, and other social and spatial arrangements that supported its ideological machinery.

Since June 2006 the focus of much of my everyday practice has shifted from the international to the local. Although my interests in transnational curriculum inquiry and the globalisation of higher education are in no way diminished, my institutional responsibilities demand that I attend closely to practices of environmental education that are, in every sense, much closer to home. As the first full professor of outdoor and environmental education to be appointed in my university (and, indeed, in Australia), I have a responsibility to walk my ecocritical talk.

EDUCATING FOR ECOCRITICAL LITERACY

The use of the term *ecocriticism* to name a relatively new movement in literary criticism (especially in North America) emerged in the early 1990s, although the word itself had appeared some years earlier (see, e.g., William Rueckert, 1978). For example, a session at the 1991 Modern Language Association conference, 'Ecocriticism: the greening of literary studies', became the working title of an anthology eventually published as *The Ecocriticism Reader: Landmarks in Literary Ecology* (Cheryll Glotfelty & Harold Fromm, 1996). Other initiatives around this time include the launchings of the Association for the Study of Literature and Environment (ASLE) in 1992, and the journal *Interdisciplinary Studies in Literature and Environment* in 1993.

As a university teacher and researcher with particular interests in environmental education, I could readily identify with this emerging field. For example, I could see a number of my own dispositions reflected in William Howarth's (1996) description of an *ecocritic* as "a person who judges the merits and faults of writings that depict the effects of culture upon nature, with a view toward celebrating nature, berating its despoilers, and reversing their harm through political action" (p. 69). However, the objects of my ecocritical attention are not only those that members of the ASLE might call 'literature'. Environmental educators in schools, educational bureaucracies, and universities produce textbooks, syllabuses, curriculum materials, and journal articles that also constitute "writings that depict the effects of culture upon nature" (where 'writings' are understood to include any medium for representing environments and/or environmental issues). My concern is that many environmental educators, through activities that they believe to be 'celebrating nature' (or even to be describing it dispassionately and objectively), might actually be despoiling and harming nature, albeit unintentionally. Thus, although I have dabbled in literary ecocriticism (Gough, 1998), I am more interested in applying its principles and theoretical frames to advance environmental education as *educating for ecocritical literacy*.

I use the term 'ecocritical literacy' hesitantly and cautiously. Education is now so littered with literacies – 'computer literacy', 'environmental literacy', 'media literacy', 'scientific literacy', 'technological literacy' and so on – that the term is in danger of becoming an empty signifier. I agree with Andrew Stables and Keith Bishop (2001) that most references to environmental literacy in the literature of environmental education exhibit a 'weak' conception of literacy that ignores many contemporary debates about language and literature, such as the limits of representation, referentiality and textuality. I therefore use the term 'ecocritical literacy' to tactically distance my project from naïve or shallow versions of environmental literacy, and to emphasise the need for environmental educators to embrace a 'stronger' conception of literacy that takes account of the broader ramifications of understanding environmental education as a textual practice – a practice that is susceptible to improvement through inquiries in disciplines of the arts and humanities that have previously been undervalued in environmental education, including language arts, semiotics, literary criticism and cultural studies. In the remainder of this chapter, I will first demonstrate the relevance of such studies to environmental education by critiquing two commonplace signifying practices that restrict the becoming-pedagogical possibilities of places: *defining* and *naming*. I will then describe three examples of place-focussed pedagogical practices.

AGAINST DEFINITION

Questions of definition often seem to loom large for environmental educators and I would venture the view that an obsession with defining terms is one manifestation of a weak conception of literacy. Consider, for example, the following extract from

Mitiku Adisu's (2005) review of William Scott and Stephen Gough's (2004) *Sustainable Development and Learning: Framing the Issues*, in which he historicises the concept of *sustainable development*.

> Twenty years ago 'sustainable development' was a newly-minted notion. Unlike theorists of modernisation and economic growth, the proponents of sustainable development promised that growth and environmental protection are not mutually exclusive and that one can have the cake and eat it too. Therein lay the charm – and the risk. The risk is in overlooking the fact that humans had, from time immemorial, a sense of the benefits of coexisting with the natural world and with each other. The charm is in that the new term engendered great optimism and created space for multiplicity of voices. Twenty years later, however, the promise remains as ambiguous and elusive as ever. Today, the respectability of the phrase is being contested by emerging definitions and by variant terms. Then as now, the focus of such inventiveness was decidedly to create awareness and improve the quality of life in a world of disparities and limited resources. Unfortunately, the minting of new phrases also favored those better disposed to set the global agenda (n.p).

Adisu rightly reminds us that we have already had two decades of sustainable development and that, as a concept, it remains "as ambiguous and elusive as ever". But I am a little puzzled by his implicit positioning of the ambiguity and elusiveness of sustainable development as a matter of troubling concern. Why should the 'respectability' (a curious term to invoke here) of sustainable development be anything but 'contested'? Although Scott and Gough (2004) begin by treating sustainable development "*at least initially*, as a set of contested ideas rather than a settled issue" (p. 2, my emphasis) and "set precision aside and begin with working definitions which are as *inclusive* as possible" (p. 1, authors' original), they nevertheless "see definition [of both (lifelong) learning and sustainable development] as a core process of the book" (p. 1). In other words, these writers (authors and reviewer alike) appear to be saying that contestation, ambiguity and multiplicity are conditions to be tolerated as we struggle to overcome them and eventually reach authoritative, stable and settled definitions. I agree with Adisu that Scott and Gough succeed, to a commendable degree, in bringing together many diverse perspectives on both learning and sustainable development "in an effort to make sense of the contradictory, the inconspicuous, and the time-constrained features of our individual and collective lives" (n.p.), but I also fear that they succumb to universalising ambitions by regarding contestation, ambiguity and multiplicity as problems to be solved (and which are, in principle, solvable) rather than as qualities that signal marvellous potentials for an on-going, open-ended fabrication of the world.

Thus I was not particularly surprised to find that poststructuralist thought is something of a 'blind spot' (see Gough, 2002; Jon Wagner, 1993) for Scott and Gough and that they very largely ignore the possibilities and potentials afforded by poststructuralism and deconstruction for thinking imaginatively and creatively about socio-environmental problems. Indeed, they completely ignore deconstruction and make only two cursory references to poststructuralism, firstly in a section on "Language and understanding; language and action" in which they conflate 'post-modern' and 'post-structuralist' (p. 26), and secondly in a section titled "Literacies: the environment as text" in which they assert: "As structuralists and post-structuralists have pointed out, one way of looking at the world is to say that *everything* is a text" (p. 29; authors' emphasis).[4] This appears to be an extension (and, I would argue, a misinterpretation) of Jacques Derrida's much-quoted assertion that "there is nothing outside the text", which is in turn a somewhat misleading translation of *"Il n'y a pas de hors-texte"* (literally, "there is no outside-text"). But Derrida is not, as some of his critics insist, denying the existence of anything outside of what they (the critics) understand as texts; his claim is not that *"il n'y a rien hors du texte"* – that the only reality is that of things that are inside of texts. Rather, his point is that texts are not the sorts of things that are bounded by an inside and an outside, or *'hors-texte'* (Whitson 2006, p. 2): nothing is ever outside text since nothing is ever outside language, and hence incapable of being represented in a text (Derrida, 1976)[5].

NAMING NATURE

Poststructuralism invites us to approach questions of definition differently from those who take its importance for granted. Criminologist Mark Halsey (2006) exemplifies this different approach in *Deleuze and Environmental Damage: Violence of the Text,* a monograph on environmental law, which he introduces as follows:

> [O]ne of the key purposes of this book is to offer a micropolitical account of the evolution of such taken-for-granted concepts as 'Nature', 'sustainability', and 'environmental harm'. For what law prescribes as permissible in respect of Nature, and *ipso facto*, what it deems to be ecologically criminal, is intimately linked to how such terms have been spoken of, imagined, and otherwise deployed over time. To believe other than this is to turn away from the ethical, and at times violent, dimensions that go along with speaking and writing the world (p. 2).

Halsey critically examines the process, impact, and ethics of naming nature, focussing specifically on the categories and thresholds used over time to map and transform a particular area of forested terrain, namely, the Goolengook forest block in far eastern Victoria, and the socio-ecological costs arising from these thresholds and transformations and ensuing conflicts. Although Halsey is a criminologist, his study is not specifically about 'crime' or even 'environmental crime':

> It is instead about the ways such terms as 'harm', 'sustainability', 'ecological significance', 'value', and 'right', have been coded, decoded, and recoded by various means, at various times, with particular results. Further, this is not a study about 'justice' – at least, not in the transcendental sense of the term. But it is most certainly about the ways law marks the earth. More particularly, it is about the composition of the various knowledges law calls

upon to justify its 'justness', its 'rightness', and its 'comprehensivity' when it permits, for instance, the conversion of a 10,000 year old ecosystem into scantling for houses or paper for copying machines (pp. 2-3).

Halsey provides a detailed account of the modes of envisaging, enunciating and inscribing the particular geopolitical space now known as Goolengook forest block over time and the 'violence' that makes these visions, enunciations and inscriptions possible – the *'violence borne by way of the slow and largely inaudible march of the categories and thresholds associated with using and abusing Nature'* (p. 3, author's emphasis).

Typically, accounts of the conflict over Goolengook (and other forest conflicts) are rendered as variants on David and Goliath narratives: greenies versus loggers, or greenies versus government, or sometimes loggers versus government. Halsey contends that stories based on such dichotomies fail to articulate sufficiently the subtleties and nuances contributing to forest conflict as *event* – as "something which is both a discursive invention (i.e. an object of our policies, laws, imaginings) *and* a body consistently eluding efforts to frame, categorise, think, speak – in short, *represent*, 'its' aspects" (p. 3).

Halsey applies poststructuralist concepts, especially the work of Deleuze and Guattari, to demonstrate that the conflicts at Goolengook are about something much more than 'forests' (Australian or otherwise) – they also raise critical questions about subjectivity (who we are), power (what we can do) and desire (who we might become). For example, the struggles at Goolengook raise questions about the ontological consistency and ecopolitical utility of categories such as 'we', 'society', 'global', 'environment', 'forest block', 'old-growth', 'truth', 'harm', 'right', 'crime' and so on. Halsey shows clearly how the geopolitical terrain of Goolengook has been textually configured over time – by Indigenous knowledges, legislation, management plans, mining leases, etc. – and how, why and for whom each textual configuration 'works'.

Halsey draws on Deleuze and Guattari to argue that places such as Goolengook *become* – that they are always already invented and fabricated, although they are no less 'real' for being so. He suggests that the process of 'becoming-known', 'becoming-forest' (or, for that matter, becoming-uranium mine, becoming-housing estate, becoming-hydro-electric dam, etc.), and thus of 'becoming-contested', is intimately related to what he calls four 'modalities' of nature involving the way nature is *envisioned*, the way nature is *named*, the *speed* at which nature is traversed and transformed, and the *affect* (image, concept, sense) of nature that is subsequently produced (p. 229). These modalities always already harbour an ethic linked to the production of a life (or lives) and/or a death (or deaths). For example, the Australian Federal Government envisions 'forest' to mean "an area... dominated by trees having usually a single stem and a mature stand height exceeding 5 metres" (Commonwealth of Australia, 1992, p. 47). Envisioning 'forest' in terms of trees exceeding 5 metres – rather than, say, 20 metres – has significant consequences for biodiversity, employment, resource security, research and development, and so on.

Following Halsey, I argue that we can usefully explore possibilities for places 'becoming-pedagogical' by reference to the modalities of nature he identifies. In the following sections, I present three pedagogical vignettes that involve aspects of three of these modalities: these focus, respectively, on unnaming nature, envisioning nature in a video game, and choosing a speed for traversing a forest.

UNNAMING NATURE

Ursula Le Guin (1987) demonstrates how we might use words to subvert the contemporary politics of naming nature. In one of her short stories, aptly titled 'She Unnames Them', Le Guin mocks the biblical assertion that Adam determined the names of every living creature. In this story Eve collaborates with the animals in undoing Adam's work: "Most of them accepted namelessness with the perfect indifference with which they had so long accepted and ignored their names" (p. 195). In 'She Unnames Them' Le Guin demonstrates the practicality of some insights that we can draw from relating deep ecology to semiotics. Modern science maintains clear distinctions between subject and object and, thus, between humans and other beings, plant and animal, living and non-living, and so on. These distinctions are sustained by the deliberate act of *naming*, which divides the world into that which is named and everything else. Naming is not just a matter of labelling distinctions that are already thought to exist. Assigning a name to something constructs the illusion that what has been named is genuinely distinguishable from all else. In creating these distinctions, humans can all too easily lose sight of the seamlessness of that which is signified by their words and abstractions. So, in Le Guin's (1987) story, Eve says:

> None were left now to unname, and yet how close I felt to them when I saw one of them swim or fly or trot or crawl across my way or over my skin, or stalk me in the night, or go along beside me for a while in the day. They seemed far closer than when their names had stood between myself and them like a clear barrier ... (p. 196).

We could do with some creative unnaming in our work. We could start with some of the common names of animals and plants that signify their instrumental value to us rather than their kinship. There is a vast difference between naming a bird of the Bass Strait islands an 'ocean going petrel' or a 'short-tailed shearwater' and naming it a 'mutton bird'. Only one of these names identifies a living thing in terms of its worth to us as dead meat.

Names are not inherent in nature; they are an imposition of human minds. It is as if we wish to own the earth by naming it. We corrupt education by naming parts – by constructing illusions that suggest that meaningful distinctions can be made between 'facts' and 'values', or between 'perception' and 'cognition', or that 'arts', 'humanities' and 'sciences' are separate 'subjects' (when we treat them as *objects* anyway). Furthermore, we cannot reconstitute the whole by 'integrating' the names. Integration in education is a desperate attempt to recapture the wholeness that has been lost through naming. Unnaming our professional identities as 'environmental' or 'outdoor' or 'science' educators is one way in which we might establish closer connections and continuities with one another and with the earth. Unnaming makes it harder to explain ourselves – we cannot chatter away as we are so accustomed to doing, hearing only our own words making up the world, taking our names and what they signify all for granted.

In *Always Coming Home*, Le Guin (1986) offers a meditation on a particular patch of scrub oak that suggests another critical perspective – I am tempted to call it 'uncounting nature' – on modern scientific techniques of observing and interpreting nature:

> Look how messy this wilderness is. Look at this scrub oak, *chaparro*, the chaparral was named for it … there are at least a hundred very much like it in sight from this rock I am sitting on, and there are hundreds and thousands and hundreds of thousands more on this ridge and the next ridge, but numbers are wrong. They are in error. You don't count scrub oaks. When you count them, something has gone wrong. You can count how many in a hundred square yards and multiply, if you're a botanist, and so make a good estimate, a fair guess, but you cannot count the scrub oaks on this ridge, let alone the ceanothus, buckbrush, or wild lilac, which I have not mentioned, and the other variously messy and humble components of the chaparral. The chaparral is like atoms and the components of atoms: it evades. It is innumerable. It is not accidentally but essentially messy … This thing is nothing to do with us. This thing is wilderness. The civilised human mind's relation to it is imprecise, fortuitous, and full of risk. There are no shortcuts. All the analogies run one direction, our direction … Analogies are easy: the live oak, the humble evergreen, can certainly be made into a sermon, just as it can be made into firewood. Read or burnt. *Sermo*, I read; I read scrub oak. But I don't, and it isn't here to be read, or burnt.

> It is casting a shadow across the page of this notebook in the weak sunshine of three-thirty of a February afternoon in Northern California. When I close the book and go, the shadow will not be on the page, though I have drawn a line around it; only the pencil line will be on the page. The shadow will then be on the dead-leaf-thick messy ground or on the mossy rock … and the shadow will move lawfully and with great majesty as the earth turns. The mind can imagine that shadow of a few leaves falling in the wilderness; the mind is a wonderful thing. But what about all the shadows of all the other leaves on all the other branches on all the other scrub oaks on all the other ridges of all the wilderness? If you could imagine those even for a moment, what good would it do? Infinite good (pp. 239-41).

ENVISIONING NATURE IN A VIDEO GAME

At the time of writing, John Martin is a doctoral student in educational communications and technology at the University of Wisconsin-Madison. Since 1993 he has also helped to run Flying Moose Lodge, a deep woods summer camp for boys in Maine, USA. He brings these interests together in his research on experiential learning, educational design, and what he calls "the importance of situating learning in culturally significant places".[6] In a paper titled 'Making video games in the woods: an unlikely partnership connects kids to their environment', Martin (2008) examines some of the successes and failures of his three-year study of incorporating place-based Augmented Reality games in outdoor activities:

> Video games and computers have been derided as 'inside' technologies that pull kids away from the outdoors. They connect less with, and value less, their outdoor environments. Rather than fight the pull of these inside technologies and their attraction to kids, we have developed a handheld outdoor GPS-enabled video game platform that attempts to build in the lure of video games and online social spaces, and connect them with real places. Kids play a place-based hiking video game, and then help redesign it for their peers (p. 1).

Martin's study encompasses six trips of 11-15 year old boys, and counsellors, over the course of three summers. The first was a fact-finding trip to come up with ideas for a game. The boys carried a handheld GPS, notebook and video camera, and documented their progress as they explored the landscape with an eye toward designing a game. They created a rudimentary game narrative involving five characters (including Axeman Sam, Pat the Pirate, and Harry the Hiker), and a few quests. The second group played, critiqued, and redesigned the game based on John Marsden's (1993) young adult novel, *Tomorrow When the War Began*, and John Milius's (1984) film, *Red Dawn*. In this narrative, woven together by Martin from the boys' ideas, a rival (rich) camp attacks and takes over the boys' camp while they are hiking in the area. The group is 'contacted by videophone' (that is, their location triggers a video on the handheld computer) by a survivor and has to perform a number of quests in order to foil the rich camp's evil plan to construct a Grey Poupon mustard factory on the pristine shores of the lake. Quests include spy-like activities designed by the boys to appeal to their peers, such as surreptitiously topping three nearby mountain peaks to triangulate and decode messages sent out by invading campers, setting up a low-impact campsite to avoid detection by the invading camp's scouts and canoeing under cover of darkness to the centre of the lake to broadcast a counter-message. The following groups test-played the game and developed it further.

Martin's particular study connects to a broader issue for place-conscious educators. If we are to have meaningful place-based pedagogical encounters with young people, we need to understand the new literacies and learning styles that today's 'screenagers' develop through playing video games.[7] James Paul Gee (2007b) explores this issue very thoroughly in *What Video Games Have to Teach Us About Learning and Literacy* (see also James Paul Gee, 2007a). Gee argues that schools, workplaces, families, and academic researchers have much to learn about learning from good video games and also that they can use games and game technologies to enhance learning. Many video games incorporate learning principles that are strongly supported by contemporary research in cognitive science.

For example, Gee notes that video games are long, complex and hard – yet people (especially but not only young people) spend many hours playing them, involving themselves in complex learning, and even paying for the privilege. He argues that the way to make complex tasks easier to learn is *not* to make them simpler: game designers understand that although games must be easy to learn, game players demand that the games themselves be difficult.

According to Gee, human minds and video games work in similar ways. At one time we assumed that the human mind functions like a big inference engine, manipulating symbols and rules. But humans do not follow rules – they act on experiences from which they construct simulations in their minds. The brain is a neural network and experience forms a pattern of neural activation in the mind; cognition is a process of reflecting and manipulating these patterns of perception. Conventional schooling in Western nations is based on a 'content fetish' – that if a learner understands 100 facts about biology then he or she has 'mastered' biology. Gee argues that learning biology, like learning a video game, should be about asking of this learning, "what experiences did it give you?"

Gee (2007b) derives a set of thirty-six learning principles from his study of the complex, self-directed learning each game player undertakes as s/he encounters and masters a new game. He suggests that adherence to these principles could transform learning in schools, colleges and universities, both for teachers and, most importantly, for students. Many of these principles are consistent with experiential learning, and suggest many generative possibilities for outdoor and environmental education.

TRAVERSING LYELL FOREST: CHOOSING A SPEED

A number of my colleagues in outdoor and environmental education at La Trobe University are developing place-based pedagogies that converge with and complement those articulated by Gruenewald and Somerville and that I see as being implied by Halsey and Le Guin. For example, Alistair Stewart (2003, 2004a, 2004b, 2006) is investigating place-conscious natural history with particular reference to the Murray River (Australia) and its environs. Similarly, Andrew Brookes (2000, 2002a, 2002b, 2004, 2005) focuses on 'situationist' outdoor education practices that develop deep consciousness of particular places. Here I borrow extensively from his account of developing an appropriate pedagogy for the Lyell Forest (near Bendigo, Victoria) that demonstrates how different modalities of nature may be enacted through different pedagogical choices.

Brookes (2005) examines relationships between outdoor activities and environmental learning by considering bushwalking as a cultural practice in Victoria. From the early 1900s, small numbers of city-dwellers sought to understand the Australian environment by bushwalking in their leisure time, often as members of a club. Accounts by bushwalkers published in the early post-war period indicate that they understood bushwalking to be a knowledge-based activity, which the clubs assisted by providing a social milieu for telling stories of past experiences and for planning future visits. Tales of exploration and discovery permeate many accounts, but the dominant theme was of individually and collectively building experience of the bush regions around Melbourne. Bushwalking maintained and transmitted experiential knowledge through programs of walks that formed loose patterns of repetition and geographical coverage (see Brookes, 2002b, pp. 410-411).

The development of more formalised outdoor education courses during the 1970s inflected bushwalking towards becoming either an activity for its own sake or a technical exercise. This change was particularly evident in approaches to navigation:

> At least in the early years, the bushwalker was someone who 'knew the bush'. Accurate topographic maps were not available, and bushwalking clubs allowed knowledge to be shared, through written accounts of trips, contacts with local stockmen who grazed cattle in the bush under licence, sketch maps made on previous trips, and above all through providing relationships with experienced and trusted individuals...

> In contrast, when bushwalking became part of formal education there was more emphasis on technical navigation... Topographic map-reading and navigation using a compass became central to bushwalking instruction. Maps originally developed for the military provided information that enabled the technically competent to plan a bushwalk as a strategic exercise in unknown terrain...

> At two extremes, navigation can be approached using the knowledge and worldview of an invading military force with no local knowledge but advanced technology, or from the perspective of a local defending force with little technology but who know the country. The sport of orienteering – competitive cross country navigation, based on maps using standardised information similar to military maps, and with very little if any local cultural information, contains within it an invader's perspective of the land as a strange place, offering strategic challenges than can be overcome with strength and skill. This might be contrasted with older traditions of mountain guiding, earlier forms of bushwalking, and Aboriginal ways of knowing, in which local experience was essential (Brookes, 2002b, p. 418).

Making pedagogical choices among different ways of knowing the Victorian bush requires detailed site-specific knowledge. The Victorian bush is not singular – it is a multitude. Brookes (2005) draws on his experience of using Lyell Forest as a site for learning to demonstrate the importance of situation-specific details in understanding how outdoor activities shape and distribute knowledge in communities, and why we might choose one activity rather than another in locally-based environmental education.

The Lyell Forest is well suited to technical navigation training and is a popular place for orienteering. The vegetation is not too thick to prevent running, the topography is a mixture of complexity and subtlety, and there are boundaries that prevent anyone from becoming really lost. But the Lyell Forest does not attract bushwalkers. It is small, has no water, and may seem drab and uninteresting in comparison to the landscapes favoured by many bushwalkers. The forest also bears the scars of many different uses and abuses since the 1850s, and thus does not fit the imported American ideal of pristine wilderness (which has recently found favour in Australia despite the inconvenient truth of Aboriginal occupation of the land).

The Lyell Forest is part of the Box-Ironbark group of forest types found mostly inland of the mountain range along the east coast of Australia. Between 3% and 45% of the different types of Box-Ironbark vegetation that existed at the time of European settlement now remain, and these remnants have in turn been altered since then, through a series of interrelated 'ripple effects' which continue to spread. For example: very little forest remains along streams or rivers – it is almost all along ridges, which has had consequences for the rivers, and also for the wildlife that lives in the forest; trees have been cut down faster than they can grow back and there are few large old trees in the forests; the forests are mainly in small fragments, so although they are mostly government owned, they are difficult to manage compared to the large blocks of land that can be managed as a national park.

As a group, the Box-Ironbark forests have wider environmental significance. Almost all of them are within the Murray-Darling catchment, which supports 60% of Australian agriculture and faces many difficulties, some of which depend in practical ways on how those living in Box-Ironbark areas understand and treat the land. None of these facts determine what people should or should not do in the Box-Ironbark forests, but they indicate what might be at stake in the relationship between a human community and a forest.

Different outdoor activities provide lenses through which to 'see' forests. Orienteers prefer an area that is not familiar to them, mapped according to desired topographical features (rather than cultural features), and terrain where running is possible. Once an area has been mapped the map may be used many times but, symbolically at least, orienteering resembles the search for new land 'beyond the frontier'. Fossickers see a historical landscape, focussing in particular on the sites of the nineteenth century gold rushes. But they also look for 'new ground', because they hope to find places where other contemporary fossickers have not used their metal detectors. Beekeepers develop particular local knowledge, especially about the trees; different species produce different honey, at different times, and older trees produce more nectar. A fox-shooter might sometimes be an orienteer. An apiarist might be a naturalist, or collect firewood. These examples should suffice to demonstrate that outdoor activities can create complex maps of knowledge of a forest within a human community.

Each of these ways of knowing produces tensions between technical skills and personal experience, and between taking some benefit from the forest and becoming familiar with it. Individuals will learn different things about the forest from the particular activity they have chosen, but the meaning of that knowledge will also be shaped by the activity. A practical problem for outdoor environmental educators is judging whether an activity can be shaped to develop particular knowledges or to create particular meanings.

For example, the Lyell Forest has a relatively small number of old trees. Boxes and Ironbarks grow slowly and may require centuries to reach large sizes in some locations. Hollows, which are essential for much of the wildlife – particularly some of the mammals, but also some birds and goannas – form slowly in these trees. Much of the wildlife is nocturnal, and local people may be unaware of what lives in the forest or of the importance of hollow trees. The activity that Brookes introduces to outdoor education students has a simple premise. Students take a small area of forest and get to know the hollow trees in the area. The process begins in the first year of their course, requires that they spend several nights in the forest and encourages them to spend more. They must learn what lives in the trees in a respectful, unobtrusive way. They may observe, but are allowed no trapping, spotlighting, banging on trees, playing recorded mating calls, feeding or intrusive viewing (such as climbing trees to inspect holes in daylight). They must learn to see signs of wildlife, and wait until the creatures show themselves. The purpose of this activity is to teach students how an activity can be designed which, in a small way, weaves some important but neglected aspects of the forest into the lives of local people.

The activity has a very different structure and pace from bushwalking – students walk from tree to tree, looking for scratches on the bark and signs of hollow branches. They arrange their day so that in the evening they can quietly watch a tree to see what creatures emerge. Many of the animals that live in the trees only come out at night, which, combined with the fact they hide in hollows, means that for many local people they barely exist. For the students, the activity makes the forest come to life in a particular way.

A single activity may teach some facts, but it is important that students understand how an on-going relationship changes the meaning of an activity. Students who have visited an area more than once recognise things that they have seen before, and notice changes. They not only learn about wildlife and its relationship to the trees, but they connect what they have seen with personal stories. Students who expect to visit again have a reason to remember what they learn. Brookes uses a simple device to introduce this social aspect of learning. Students in the final year of their course introduce first year students to a small area of forest over three days and nights. The first year students visit the forest on several more occasions over the next two years. Then, in their final year, they in turn introduce a group of first year students to 'their' piece of forest.

A map of students' movements through the forest would show a very different pattern and pace from that of an orienteer visiting checkpoints, or a bushwalker passing through. The rhythm of activity is also different, because it has to take into account the schedule the wildlife sets. Instead of all meeting for an evening meal, students disperse to watch different trees at dusk. The activity also has some clearly evident social signatures. Students walk without maps, and speak of places in colloquial and idiosyncratic ways: 'the goanna tree'; 'the Red Box tree where we saw the sugar gliders'; 'the echidna stump', and so on. When groups meet in the forest at least some of their conversation involves an exchange of stories about what they have seen. Thus wildlife becomes part of their social networking, in a similar way to which stories about sporting events on the weekend have a social function in the workplace.

The interweaving of knowledge about wildlife with personal stories and social relationships makes this activity a little more like an indigenous way of knowing, and a little less like a field trip for a science class or walking for sport. Brookes calls the activity a recreation activity because for some students at least it provides the same interest and motivation as recreation; some have returned many times to watch 'their' trees. However, it is also a modest program, and it is important to note that it is more successful on some occasions than others. Which groups should undertake what activities where, if Australians are to learn how to live sustainably in Australia, is a much bigger question.

INCONCLUSION

Deleuze and Guattari (1987) explain that rhizomes have no beginnings or ends but are always in the middle: beginnings and ends – like introductions and conclusions – imply a linear movement, whereas working in the middle is about "coming and going rather than starting and finishing" (p. 25). Thus, I have no desire to provide a 'conclusion' to this essay but will simply pause with this 'inconclusion' – a brief reflection in the middle of the comings and goings it performs.

I do not intend the stories, vignettes, arguments and meditations that I have assembled here to be interpreted as constituting a 'case' for any particular approach to theorising place in education. Nor have I attempted to answer the question posed in this chapter's title. Rather, I have explored a number of positions, dispositions and tactics that offer ways to think and act that have moved me in the direction of new or renewed possibilities for representing and performing place-informed pedagogies. These ways of thinking and acting have been generative for me, and I offer them to readers for their own appraisal of their usefulness.

ACKNOWLEDGEMENT

The section on traversing Lyell Forest draws extensively on Andrew Brookes' invited keynote address to the Annual Meeting of the Japan Society of Sports Sociology, Hokkaido University of Education, Asahikawa, Japan, 2004. The only published version of this address (Brookes, 2005) is a Japanese translation. With Dr Brookes' kind permission, I have abridged and adapted significant portions of his address for inclusion in this chapter. Although I take responsibility for the final form of the wording in this section, I gratefully acknowledge Dr Brookes as the author of its substantial content.

NOTES

[1] By way of illustration, I used the Lawrence Durrell epigraph with which I began this chapter in my first essay on the generativity of poststructuralism for environmental education (Gough, 1991). However, my emphasis then was on the positionings provided by 'selected fictions' rather than spatial positionings.

[2] As it happens, the flyer's epigraph is a slight misquotation. Gruenewald (2003) actually asserts that 'places are profoundly pedagogical' (p. 621), which is a less totalising formulation because 'places' imply specific locations rather than the generic abstraction of 'place'.

³   The 'scare' quotation marks here signify that I read terms such as 'natural' and 'nature' *sous rature* (under erasure), following Jacques Derrida's approach to reading deconstructed signifiers as if their meanings were clear and undeconstructable, but with the understanding that this is only a strategy (see, for example, Derrida, 1985).

⁴   Scott and Gough attribute this assertion to Stables (1996).

⁵   I am grateful to Tony Whitson (2006) for clarifying the implications of misleading translations of Derrida's (in)famous aphorism.

⁶   http://regardingjohn.com/learn/ (accessed 21 July 2009)

⁷   The term 'video games' encompasses all games played using digital visual interfaces, including computer games, web-based role-playing games and simulations, and platform games played with digital consoles or hand held devices.

REFERENCES

Adisu, M. (2005). Sustainable development and learning: Framing the issues. *Education Review: A Journal of Book Reviews*.

Brookes, A. (2000). Nature-based tourism as education for sustainability: Possibilities, limitations, contradictions. *Australian Journal of Environmental Education, 15/16*, 25–32.

Brookes, A. (2002a). Gilbert White never came this far south. Naturalist knowledge and the limits of universalist environmental education. *Canadian Journal of Environmental Education, 7*(2), 73–87.

Brookes, A. (2002b). Lost in the Australian bush: Outdoor education as curriculum. *Journal of Curriculum Studies, 34*(4), 405–425.

Brookes, A. (2004). Astride a long-dead horse. Mainstream outdoor education theory and the central curriculum problem. *Australian Journal of Outdoor Education, 8*(2), 122–133.

Brookes, A. (2005). Outdoor activity in the context of nature and society. *Japan Journal of Sport Sociology, 13*, 12–22.

Commonwealth of Australia. (1992). *National forest policy statement*. Canberra, ACT: Commonwealth of Australia.

Deleuze, G. (1994). *Difference and repetition* (P. Patton, Trans.). New York: Columbia University Press.

Deleuze, G., & Guattari, F. (1987/1980). *A thousand plateaus: Capitalism and schizophrenia* (B. Massumi, Trans.). Minneapolis, MN: University of Minnesota Press.

Deleuze, G., & Guattari, F. (1994). *What is philosophy?* (G. Burchell & H. Tomlinson, Trans.). London: Verso.

Derrida, J. (1985). Letter to a Japanese friend (M. Ann Caws, & I. Lorenz, Trans.). In D. Wood & R. Bernasconi (Eds.), *Derrida and différance* (pp. 1–5). Warwick: Parousia Press.

Derrida, J. (1976). *Of grammatology* (G. Chakrovorty Spivak, Trans.). Baltimore: The Johns Hopkins University Press.

Durrell, L. (1963). *Balthazar*. London: Faber and Faber.

Gabriel, P., & N'Dour, Y. (1989). *Shaking the tree* [Song]. London/Paris: Peter Gabriel Ltd/Editions Virgin Musique.

Gee, J. P. (2007a). *Good video games and good learning: Collected essays on video games, learning and literacy*. New York: Peter Lang.

Gee, J. P. (2007b). *What video games have to teach us about learning and literacy* (2nd ed.). New York: Palgrave Macmillan.

Glotfelty, C., & Fromm, H. (Eds.). (1996). *The ecocriticism reader: Landmarks in literary ecology*. Athens GA and London: The University of Georgia Press.

Gough, N. (1991). Narrative and nature: unsustainable fictions in environmental education. *Australian Journal of Environmental Education, 7*, 31–42.

Gough, N. (1998). Playing with wor(l)ds: science fiction as environmental literature. In P. D. Murphy (Ed.), *Literature of nature: An international sourcebook* (pp. 409–414). Chicago and London: Fitzroy Dearborn.

Gough, N. (1999). *Tales of a travelling textworker: Troubling 'freedom' in post-apartheid environmental education*. Paper presented at the 17th Annual Conference of the Environmental Education Association of Southern Africa.

Gough, N. (2002). Ignorance in environmental education research. *Australian Journal of Environmental Education, 18*, 19–26.

Gough, N. (2006). Shaking the tree, making a rhizome: Towards a nomadic geophilosophy of science education. *Educational Philosophy and Theory, 38*(5), 625–645.

Gough, N. (2007a). Changing planes: Rhizosemiotic play in transnational curriculum inquiry. *Studies in Philosophy and Education, 26*(3), 279–294.

Gough, N. (2007b). Rhizosemiotic play and the generativity of fiction. *Complicity: An International Journal of Complexity and Education, 4*(1), 119–124.

Gruenewald, D. A. (2003). Foundations of place: A multidisciplinary framework for place-conscious education. *American Educational Research Journal, 40*(3), 619–654.

Gruenewald, D. A. (2004). A Foucauldian analysis of environmental education: Toward the socioecological challenge of the Earth Charter. *Curriculum Inquiry, 34*(1), 71–107.

Halsey, M. (2006). *Deleuze and environmental damage: Violence of the text*. Aldershot, Hampshire: Ashgate.

Haraway, D. J. (1991). *Simians, cyborgs, and women: The reinvention of nature*. New York: Routledge.

Harding, S. (1993). Introduction: Eurocentric scientific illiteracy – a challenge for the world community. In S. Harding (Ed.), *The 'Racial' economy of science: Toward a democratic future* (pp. 1–22). Bloomington and Indianapolis: Indiana University Press.

Howarth, W. (1996). Some principles of ecocriticism. In C. Glotfelty & H. Fromm (Eds.), *The ecocriticism reader: Landmarks in literary ecology* (pp. 69–91). Athens GA and London: The University of Georgia Press.

Le Guin, U. K. (1986). *Always coming home*. London: Victor Gollancz.

Le Guin, U. K. (1987). *Buffalo gals and other animal presences.*. Santa Barbara, CA: Capra.

Marsden, J. (1993). *Tomorrow, when the war began*. Sydney, NSW: Pan Macmillan.

Martin, J. (2008, 24-28 March). *Making video games in the woods: An unlikely partnership connects kids to their environment*. Paper presented at the Annual Meeting of the American Educational Research Association, New York, USA. Retrieved July 21, 2009, from http://regardingjohn.com/papers.

Milius, J. (Director). (1984). *Red Dawn* [Film]. USA: MGM/UA Entertainment Co.

Rueckert, W. (1978). Literature and ecology: An experiment in ecocriticism. *Iowa Review, 9*(1), 71–86.

Scott, W. A. H., & Gough, S. R. (2004). *Sustainable development and learning: Framing the issues*. London and New York: RoutledgeFalmer.

Somerville, M. (2008). A place pedagogy for 'global contemporaneity'. *Educational Philosophy and Theory* (Online Early). Retrieved January 21, 2008, from www.blackwell-synergy.com/doi/pdf/10.1111/j.1469-5812.2008.00423.x

Stables, A. (1996). Reading the environment as text: Literary theory and environmental education. *Environmental Education Research, 2*(2), 189–195.

Stables, A., & Bishop, K. (2001). Weak and strong conceptions of environmental literacy: Implications for environmental education. *Environmental Education Research, 7*(1), 89–97.

Stewart, A. (2003). Reinvigorating our love of our home range: Exploring the connections between sense of place and outdoor education. *Australian Journal of Outdoor Education, 7*(2), 17–24.

Stewart, A. (2004a). Canoeing the Murray River (Australia) as environmental education: A tale of tale of two rivers. *Canadian Journal of Environmental Education, 9*, 136–147.

Stewart, A. (2004b). Decolonising encounters with the Murray River: Building place responsive outdoor education. *Australian Journal of Outdoor Education, 8*(2), 46–55.

Stewart, A. (2006). Seeing the trees and the forest: Attending to Australian natural history as if it mattered. *Australian Journal of Environmental Education, 22*(2), 85–97.

Wagner, J. (1993). Ignorance in educational research: Or, how can you not know that? *Educational Researcher, 22*(5), 15–23.

Whitson, J. A. (Tony). (2006). *Est-ce qu'il n'ya pas de hors-curriculum.* Paper presented at the Second World Curriculum Studies Conference. Retrieved May 18, 2006, from www.udel.edu/soe/whitson/curriculum/files/wcsc2_whitson.pdf

Noel Gough
La Trobe University

ALAN MAYNE

11. STRANGE ENTANGLEMENTS

Landscapes and Historical Imagination

In conventional epistemology those disciplines at the cusp of the humanities and social sciences – such as history, geography, archaeology, and anthropology – have largely disregarded landscape as a platform for learning. Space was considered to be "an abstract dimension or container in which human activities took place" (Tilley, 1994, p. 9). Place was regarded unproblematically as a passive stage or a backdrop for the dramas of social life. Place and space were assigned an ahistorical universality; they were disconnected from the entanglements and particularities of social life and action. Henri Lefebvre writes that "Not so many years ago, the word 'space' had a strictly geometrical meaning: the idea it evoked was simply that of an empty area... To speak of 'social space', therefore, would have sounded strange" (Lefebvre, 1991, p. 1). That thinking has changed, and human space is now widely acknowledged to reflect the historical operation of socio-economic processes. By the 1980s, for example, social historians who studied the industrial and urban transformation of Britain during the nineteenth century argued that "The townscape reflected the play of unbridled market forces" (Englander, 1983, p. x). But such conceptualisations of space, as Manuel Castells complained, still separate structures from actors and treat social space impersonally as though it was "created by an economically determined structural logic" rather than directly by human interaction (Castells, 1983, p. xvi). Space remains "nothing more than the passive locus of social relations" (Lefebvre, 1991, p. 11).

Historical understanding of the modern world is correctly preoccupied with tracing the globalising effects of capitalism and colonialism, and with the impacts upon particular places of the urbanising and diasporic consequences of those processes. But the vernacular social landscapes that were formed by those impacts (and which in turn impacted upon those processes) have been inadequately studied. People are analysed at a remove from the places they shaped and which shaped their lives and identities. Although some of the material shells of past social life, such as encampments, buildings, townscapes, have been examined by architects, archaeologists and geographers, the broader phenomenology of landscape as an enveloping social milieu has not. It is an odd disjunction because, as Simon Sharma points out, "it is our shaping perception that makes the difference between raw matter and landscape" (Sharma, 1995, p. 10). Henry Glassie – ethnographer,

M. Somerville, K. Power and P. de Carteret (eds.),
Landscapes and Learning: Place Studies for a Global World, 175–193

folklorist, interpreter of vernacular architecture and material culture – has complained that historians in particular:

> feel the land, its fields, houses, and buried broken crockery, cannot serve truly as documents [that elucidate the past]. Only the written word is meaningful and useful, and the historian's story retains its dreary elitist bias, since few of the past's people wrote and most of them were tied to an upper-class minority ... Yet beyond, around us, spreads the vast and democratic handmade history book of landscape (Glassie, 1982, p. 603).

W. G. Hoskins was a lone voice when, in 1955, he argued that one "cannot understand the English landscape ... without going back to the history that lies behind it", and urged historians to study the "cultural humus of sixty generations or more [that] lies upon it" (Hoskins, 1955, pp. 13, 235). Increasingly since the 1980s, however, pedagogies of place in history and cognate disciplines have been built upon the realisation that human territories and settlements are socially produced, and that historical landscapes thus constitute a pastiche of elements – often contradictory and conflict-ridden – that embody the lives, practices, identities, aspirations, and memories of the diversity of people who have been associated with them. This changing emphasis can be seen in 1982, for example, in Glassie's remarkable ethnography of "four square miles of undramatic landscape" in Ireland, *Passing the Time in Ballymenone*, and in Rhys Isaac's Pulitzer Prize winning history of the shaping of a colonial landscape, *The Transformation of Virginia 1740-1790* (Glassie, 1982, p. xiii; Isaac, 1982). It can be seen several years later in Richard Dennis' insertion of an "ecological emphasis" into the social geography of nineteenth-century English industrial cities (Dennis, 1984, p. 10). And it is evident in Anne Yentsch's trail-blazing *A Chesapeake Family and their Slaves*, an archaeological study of the aristocratic Calvert family in eighteenth-century Maryland, the central motif of which is the transforming of space into place (Yentsch, 1994, p. 3). As Stephen Kern says of such studies, "The traditional view that space was an inert void in which objects existed gave way to a new view of it as active and full" (Kern, 2003, p. 152). Space, then, is not simply an essence nor even a fixed result. Even to call it a medium is deemed by Lefebvre to be "woefully inadequate" (Lefebvre, 1991, p. 411). It is a milieu inseparable from human imagination and interaction. This viewpoint offers exciting opportunities for innovative pedagogies of landscape. But until the conceptual intricacies and methodologies that underpin this "new view" are fully described and applied, traditional viewpoints will persist.

In this chapter, space is considered as the milieu within and through which interactions take place, and that on earth is ecologically connected with all interacting agents. Human social interaction defines it in general terms as territories, regions, nations, and as the intersecting zones between discrete groups, activities and constructs. Space is distinguished from place by the specificity and intensity of human interaction. Place is considered here as a particular spatial or imaginary location – a landscape, a room, a camping spot, or a neighbourhood – which is delineated by, and endures because of, human association. It is, in Gaston Bachelard's terms, "Space that ... has been lived in" (Bachelard, 1964, p. xxxii). It is space that seems near to hand and intimate.

Glassie urges historians to be alert to the vernacular meanings of space in everyday life, and to "remember … that time is but one axis in existence, and the other – space – might be its equal in experience and the construction of culture. Living at once in time and space, people use history to locate themselves in time, seeking a fortune in the temporal, and they use history to situate themselves in the wideness of space, seeking a home, a place of belonging" (Glassie, 1999, p. 35). Isaac recommends that these spatial inscriptions of social life and cultural belonging should be read by historians as "texts – both to understand the relations of production inscribed upon the land and to decipher as much as they can of the meanings that such relations assumed for those who were part of them" (Isaac, 1982, p. 19). Glassie's immersion in the vernacular landscapes of everyday life, and Isaac's interplay between relics and texts as tools for learning, have in common an ethnographic sensitivity to human space. In the pages that follow the associations between landscape, learning, and ethnography are considered in relation to the volatile essence of historical places.

***

A useful starting point is provided by three newspaper stories (or performances as they will be considered later in the chapter) about places in present-day Mumbai, a city of some 16.5 million inhabitants in India's Maharashtra State. Mumbai, the largest city in India, is a pastiche of neighbourhoods, the sum of diverse cultural practices brought to this booming metropolis by migrants from across the subcontinent. It is a spatial pot-pourri. In 2008 it was rocked by terrorist assaults that threatened to derail India and Pakistan's fragile detente. In 2009 it celebrated when the movie *Slumdog Millionaire* won eight Oscars and two child actors were thereby "plucked … from the slums of Mumbai … to Hollywood's glitziest party" (*The Hindu*, 2009, p. 1). A city such as Mumbai is simultaneously space and place, the multiple constructions of which (and intersections between) act as volatile drivers of human action.

The first story, from the *Guardian Weekly*, describes a particular place in Mumbai, the new 27-storey home of India's richest man. Mukesh Ambani's tower-block home, due for completion late in 2008, has been called the world's most expensive house. It will house him, his immediate family, and an estimated 600 staff. With a floor area greater than Versailles, it will include a helipad, a two-storey health club, guest accommodation, and six floors of car parking. The report concludes by noting that Ambani's one-billion dollar home has been damned by critics as highlighting the "new vulgarity" of the rich in India. A local journalist complained that "Mr Ambani is building an edifice to his own ego … It will not go down well with the public. There is growing anger about such absurd spending" (Ramesh, 2007, p. 8).

The second newspaper story is about anti-place: an alien space in the heart of Mumbai. It is presented as a footnote to the first story:

> The largest slum in Asia, a sprawling shantytown in the centre of Mumbai, will be demolished and replaced with free homes for the city's poor under a

$2.3bn scheme. The state government of Maharashtra placed advertisements last week inviting Indian and foreign developers to raze the tin shanties and maze of open drains that make up Dharavi slum and replace it with a new township (Ramesh, 2007, p. 8).

Dharavi has long been accorded "the dubious reputation of being 'Asia's largest slum'", and this latest scheme to obliterate it stems from the conventional assumption that slums – the antithesis of places like Ambani's home – "are breeding grounds for criminals and other 'antisocial' elements" (Sharma, 2000, pp. xvi, xvii). It seems common sense to replace such chaotic and dysfunctional spaces with proper homeplaces.

The third story concerns an alternative place. It humanises the alien space of Dharavi by focusing on particular places within this supposed slum. Originally written by Dan McDougall for the *Observer*, it was recirculated by the *Guardian Weekly* in March 2007. The report began by echoing conventional outside depictions of "Mumbai's labyrinthine Dharavi slum. A 175ha maze of dark alleys and corrugated shacks, Dharavi swarms with more than a million residents". But McDougall continued:

> if you have the patience to look closer, you will find here one of the most inspiring economic models in Asia. Dharavi may be one of the world's largest slums, but it is by far its most prosperous – a thriving business centre propelled by thousands of micro-entrepreneurs who have created an invaluable industry – turning around the discarded waste of [Greater] Mumbai's 19 million citizens. A new estimate by economists of the output of the slum is as impressive as it seems improbable: $1.4bn a year (McDougall, 2007, p. 29).

Such reassessments have been triggered by Kalpana Sharma's *Rediscovering Dharavi*. Sharma contends that "Too often places are known as geographical dots on a map; as historical landmarks or as politically significant areas. Dharavi is all these but above all it is an extraordinary mix of the most unusual people." Dharavi's inhabitants, she insists, are "people like us who can think out and plan their own future" (Sharma, 2000, pp. xvii, xii). However as a feature article in the *National Geographic* magazine highlighted during 2007, these plans and the intimate places in which they were hatched will be swept away if the state government's scheme to destroy the alien space of the slum proceeds (Jacobson & Bendiksen, 2007, pp. 68-93). McDougall explained:

> For Dharavi's detractors, mainly Mumbai's city fathers and real estate developers, keen to get their hands on the prime land, the shanty is an embarrassing boil to be lanced from the body of an ambitious city hoping to become the next Shanghai. But for a growing number of environmental campaigners Dharavi is becoming the green lung stopping Mumbai choking to death on its own waste (McDougall, 2007, p. 29).

In the wake of *Slumdog Millionaire*, which features Dharavi, the *Guardian Weekly* commented:

> The real-life Dharavi is a shock to the system, but not because it conforms to the stereotype, rather because it defies it. The reality for most of the inhabitants is a well-ordered community where most people have employment, children go to school and families try to make a better life for themselves by hard work (Chamberlain, 2009, p. 25).

One local activist quoted by McDougall in 2007 complained that the government's plan to bulldoze Dharavi is "inhumane because it ignores both the industry and hope of the slum. 'Why wreck the homes and lives of people who have built the city and lived in it for decades?' he said. 'Because from your luxury high-rise apartment you don't want the humiliation of India's poor in your line of vision as you make your money and succeed'" (McDougall, 2007, p. 29).

These three stories echo the three principles identified by Margaret Somerville in her introduction to this volume as providing the basis for a reconceptualised pedagogy of place: that our relationship to place is constituted in stories and other representations; that place learning is local and embodied; that identification with place occurs in a contact zone of contestation. Somerville's three principles complement the historical approach that Isaac applied in order "to inquire into the ways past peoples have understood or imagined the environments they have fashioned as habitats for themselves" (Isaac, 1992, p. 401). Glassie's landscape analysis likewise resonates with Somerville's first two propositions, as does Castells' with her second and third. Glassie argues that "Stories set in place bring history into the present"; his ethnographic study of Ballymenone contends that the idiomatic place-based history that is offered by rural Irish folklore

> makes the locality rich. Its names become cracks through which to peek into excitement. Its meadows and the fords of its little river become great tales. History is a consolation to the one who does not travel, a way to make the small place enormous, complete, inhabitable, worth defending ... Place is space rich enough to provide travel for the mind while the body sits still, space so full of the past that it forces people to become responsible for its future. History is the essence of the idea of place (Glassie, 1982, p. 664).

Castells' influential study of grassroots urban social movements argues that because space is "one of society's fundamental material dimensions" (Castells, 1983, p. 311), the ongoing structuring of spatial forms, meanings, functions, and relationships generates continuing interplays between, and reformulations of, dominant and subordinate social groups. This chapter focuses on two pedagogical challenges that are inherent in Somerville's framework and the Mumbai stories, and explores the opportunities that these friction points provide for nuanced analysis of historic places.

It is necessary to acknowledge, first, that places, like any other cultural construct, are not readily and universally transparent. It follows, secondly, that to understand these places requires translation. Scholars have traditionally ignored these issues, imposing their own constructs upon other people's places. A better approach is offered by the cultural relativist Clifford Geertz, who uses ethnography to translate the idioms of other places and thereby enter their local worlds. Language and landscape are intermeshed; both are "freighted with cultural meaning" (Bonyhady & Griffiths, 2002, p. 1). To accept that space is socially produced is to agree also that its forms are diverse, dynamic, and volatile. Understanding of the contours, meanings and associations of places that are intimately felt and widely shared by the "natives" who inhabit them are not readily transferable to "others" who live beyond their familiar boundaries. Places that are not our own are opaque. Place analysis therefore makes explicit the otherwise abstract division between the "experience-near" and the "experience-distant": in other words, the division between cultural affiliations and social practices which are immediate and comprehensible to us, and those which are culturally distant and thus foreign in their meanings (Geertz, 1983, p. 57). Place distinctiveness is part and parcel of the mental maps we employ in everyday living, but it poses a problem for pedagogues. Since "we" – teachers and students – can at best know intimately only a handful of places, we are necessarily "other" to most of the places which, as we apply the new conceptualisations of space, we strive to understand from "the native's point of view" (Geertz, 1983, pp. 55-70).

***

Historic landscapes are coded; their forms and meanings are not clear. Scholars are loath to make this admission. *Journeys into History*, a collection of essays by prominent Australian historians, confidently issues readers "an invitation to take a track winding back in time … into the Australian landscape", and the book's editor, Graeme Davison, likens "the present-day landscape [to] a visible history" (Davison, 1990, p. 15). The book depends upon the legibility of historic landscapes, but the views that historical landscapes provide are not clear-cut. Lefebvre cautions that the "illusion of transparency goes hand in hand with a view of space as innocent, as free of traps or secret places" (Lefebvre, 1991, p. 28). The essence of historic landscapes is ambiguity. Admitting as much is not to concede the impossibility of cross-cultural analysis; rather, it sweeps away the shallow interpretive frameworks that rest upon the supposed clarity of the present day's perspectives upon historic places. Once made, it liberates landscape pedagogy to delve into the entanglements of the past. It is an exciting but a difficult path to follow.

Historic landscapes are complicit with the actions of natives in the past, not of outsiders in the present. Their ambiguity results in part from the residual nature of place elements that survive as relics from the past (See Lowenthal, 1985, pp. 238-49). Isaac advocates reading historic landscapes as texts, but the surviving texts are incomplete. Like palimpsests – manuscripts in which earlier text has been over-written and partially effaced – human landscapes have accumulated layers over time, obscuring the inscriptions of earlier inhabitants. The analogy of the palimpsest is often used by historians to suggest that the accumulated layers of a social landscape can readily be peeled back in order to recover and repossess human space at any desired moment in time. This is an illusion. As archaeologists know from exploring the stratigraphy of excavated sites, the essence of a palimpsest is that its inscriptions are incomplete and disordered. If historic places can be likened to palimpsests, they necessarily come to us as fragments from past social worlds that have largely vanished, and have left little obvious presence in today's landscapes. If we are bold enough to set aside our preconceptions, there are no easy clues to guide us in reassembling the fragments and filling in the missing pieces. As Michel de Certeau puts it, only the "opaque and stubborn places remain" and the "legible discourses that formerly articulated them have disappeared, or left only fragments in language" (de Certeau, 1984, pp. 201, 202).

The ambiguity of past places is compounded because places are known and experienced differently by the miscellany of people who inhabit them at any point in time and across time. As Mumbai highlights, human spaces are pastiches of diverse and often contradictory places. Dharavi, for example, "is an amazing mosaic of villages and townships from all over India" (Sharma, 2000, p. xxii). Social space is a profoundly multi-dimensional and conflict-ridden medium. We attempt to cocoon ourselves from its dramas by fashioning borders of cross-cultural impermeability around the particular places we claim as our own. When I lived in Washington D.C. I was initially intimidated by the unfamiliarity of the city, and chose to live in an up-market apartment building on Pennsylvania Avenue. It was comfortable and conveniently located, but more importantly it seemed secure. It was my haven, my place of refuge. Such present-day living spaces have replaced the old alley communities that once occupied this district. As archaeologist Mary Beaudry remarks, for Pennsylvania Avenue's "present residents to be tied to these earlier folk would root Washington's elite to an unknown and unfamiliar space and time. To draw the link between the modern inhabitants, the Afro-American occupation of the nineteenth/twentieth century, and the even earlier Anglo-Americans living at poverty level, would be to link upwardly mobile city dwellers to poverty, instability, discontinuity, family upheaval, and exploitation" (Beaudry, 1988, p. 16).

In the hierarchies of public knowledge that endure, the knowledge systems of the subalterns invariably become hatched in shades of grey. The constructions, uses, and meanings of space by subordinate groups have been confined and overshadowed by powerful elites and majorities. This has been Dharavi's misfortune. These outcomes compound the ambiguities of historic space. As Beaudry points out, the past of the alley communities in Washington D.C. is largely unrecorded: "Family homes remembered and family homes forgotten are, in reality, two closely related elements in local historiography that tell of social structure and hierarchy within the community" (Beaudry, 1988, p. 15). Geographers such as David Ward and Jacinta Prunty have sought to recover the social dynamics of poor neighbourhoods in North American and European cities during the nineteenth and twentieth centuries, and to insert this knowledge into present-day debate about urban poverty abatement (Ward, 1989; Prunty, 1998). Social historians have begun to fill the gaps in our knowledge about how most people were housed in the cities of the nineteenth and early twentieth centuries (Daunton, 1983, p. 1). Historians have also joined with archaeologists to probe for traces of vanished inner-city neighbourhoods that – as will probably be the fate of Dharavi – have succumbed to the modernising imperatives of today's cities (Mayne & Murray 2001, p. 1).

A good example of the ambiguities, discontinuities, and the disconcerting silences experienced by present-day wanderers in historic places is afforded by the relic landscapes of European colonialism. One can feel it in Mumbai (still known as Bombay by outsiders and many locals) at places such as Chhatrapati Shivaji Maharaj Vastu Sangrahalaya (Prince of Wales Museum) and the World Heritage listed Chhatrapati Shivaji Terminus (Victoria) railway station. In a different post-colonial context, one can feel it in the relic landscapes of the Pacific Rim goldfields. Traditional histories of the gold rushes have bored generations of school students and undergraduates because they focused on a narrow range of historical activities and failed to connect even this selection to the places where they unfolded. By contrast, recent landscape analysis of gold rush sites in Canada, the United States, Australia, and New Zealand has sought "to evoke multiple voices, different angles of vision and diverse disciplinary frameworks" (McCalman, Cook & Reeves, 2001, p. 10). Such studies draw attention to the hidden histories of indigenous peoples, ethnic minorities, and women in these places. Gold rush sites are now listed on heritage registers because of their acknowledged historical significance, and they have become teaching spaces and magnets for tourists. But a nagging question confronts the visitor to, for example, the key Australian gold rush site of Hill End (now a heritage park administered by the New South Wales National Parks and Wildlife Service): Standing amidst the now-vacant township allotments of Hill End itself, or of the vanished township site of nearby Tambaroora, or clambering up to a rusting stamper battery that stands amid blackberry clogged mineshafts, one wonders "What precisely are we looking at here ... beyond empty spaces and silences?" There are few clear signatures from the past in this landscape, or in any of the other gold-rush landscapes around the Pacific Rim. We see relics in a vacuum (See Mayne, 2007, pp. 13-20).

Contemporary survey maps highlight the ambiguities of such places. The contour lines delineating hills and watercourses are mostly unnamed, and instead have superimposed across them bland generalisations such as "old gold workings", "ruins", or "Numerous Abandoned Mines". However historic maps of the same landscapes, made during the 1860s and 1870s, contain a dense miscellany of place names, rich in associations that have long since faded, for every hill, gully, flat, and human settlement. The newcomers took possession of such spaces not only by settling but by overlaying with new names the places of Aboriginal landholders: the newcomers "knew every detail of that district intimately, and could identify by name all the creeks, rivers, valleys and mountains. Many of these geographical features had been named after a local identity" (Goodwin, 1992, p. 17). Today, however, their taxonomies of landscape have also faded from public knowledge.

The cross-cultural ambiguities of such places are especially evident as one explores the landscapes of the Pine Creek goldfields in the Northern Territory, integrating fieldwork notes with archived letters that were scribbled as the goldfields boomed during the late nineteenth century. It is a remote place even now; back then it seemed an alien and intimidating space. Local police, quartered in a leaking tent reinforced with sheets of corrugated iron, bemoaned their lack of fire power to ward off Aboriginal attacks. In 1874 police chief Paul Foelsche urged that "the troopers here … should be armed with the best carbines that can be procured, for no one knows how soon their services may be called into requisition, it being a well known fact that the Natives about the goldfields are very hostile, and have already attacked several camps; and to send troopers in pursuit, into an unknown Country, merely armed with a revolver, would be making food for the natives" (Foelsche, 1874). Traditional Aboriginal landholders confronted the intruders upon their country not only by harassing European gold miners when the opportunity arose but by attacking the majority immigrant group, the Chinese.

The ambiguities of such places are often compounded by spatial discontinuity. For example, two widely separated places – Adelaide's West Terrace Cemetery and the Barrow Creek telegraph station heritage site in the Northern Territory – are connected to the same set of events that began with a double murder in 1873. The building of the Overland Telegraph Line between 1870 and 1872, with repeater stations along its path at new sites of European settlement such as Alice Springs, Barrow Creek, Tennant Creek, and Darwin, linked the Australian colonies with the world. Construction of the telegraph line led also to the Pine Creek gold discoveries, and telegraph communication along the new line subsequently facilitated the development of the goldfields. The staff of the Overland Telegraph saw themselves as the vanguard of European progress in the vastness of Outback Australia. Aboriginal landholders regarded them differently. In 1874 Barrow Creek became the flashpoint between these competing viewpoints.

A stone memorial in Adelaide's West Terrace Cemetery reads:

This Monument Is Erected By The Officers And Men On The Overland Telegraph Line In Memory Of Their Comrades Who Were Treacherously Murdered by The Blacks Whilst In The Discharge Of Their Duty.

An inscription on another face reads:

James Lorenzo Stapleton, Station Master, Barrow's Creek, Speared February, 22. 1874, Died February, 23. 1874, Aged 40.

John Frank, Speared At Barrow's Creek, 22. February, 1874, Died The Same Day.

It is a shrine to noble lives senselessly cut down. However the other side of the story – the viewpoints and grievances of the local Kaytetye people – has barely been told (Central Land Council, 2007).

South Australian Postmaster General Sir Charles Todd fumed upon hearing of the Barrow Creek spearings that "we should at once pursue the Blacks who have committed this fearful crime and teach them a lesson they will not forget. They have been treated with every kindness on the Telegraph". He added soon afterwards that "Our Stations are well able to protect themselves but they were caught unawares at Barrow Creek which is not likely to occur again. We must however teach [the] natives a severe lesson & I have written the Govt to that effect" (Todd, 1874; Todd, 1884). At the Barrow Creek Telegraph Station today, preserved as a heritage site, the graves of Stapleton and Frank are carefully tended. But there are no memorials there to the 90 Kaytetye people who were reputedly killed in 1874 during the European reprisals.

Amid these ambiguities and discontinuities one thing at least is clear: Isaac's invitation to read historic landscapes as texts is not a straightforward exercise. To do so requires translation.

***

Not only are we faced with fragments and silences as we explore historic landscapes; the relics we find belonged to strangers, to people whose cultural reference points were different from our own. How can one empathise today with Todd's blood lust? His values – the product of nineteenth-century British colonialism – do not endure in twenty-first century Australia. Historic places were created by people distant from us both in time and social custom. To understand them requires a translation exercise in cultural relativism: we have to crack open the beliefs and practices that shaped these past social worlds. Conventionally, historians sidestep this problem by superimposing their own commonsense assumptions in order to reduce the complexities of past social life into approximations that are comprehensible in the present. In doing so they depend upon the "miracle of empathy" in order to relate to people and places across time (Geertz, 1983, p. 56). They claim a spurious intimacy with the social horizons of people in the past, and Glassie has rightly mocked them for doing so, arguing that by disregarding as foreign and indecipherable what was idiomatic to the lives of people in the past, historians' constructions of the past "become but mirrors, infinitely reflecting back to us our own worn visages" (Glassie, 1982, p. 11). Empathy is an effect of good history; it can never be good historical method.

We must not project ourselves upon the past; we should instead strive to understand past times and places "from the native's point of view". To do this we need to develop a style of historical translation that, in Robert Darnton's words, "treats our own civilization in the same way that anthropologists study alien cultures. It is history in the ethnographic grain" (Darnton, 1985, p. 3). Darnton has applied this approach to the history of eighteenth-century France, noting that:

> one thing seems clear to everybody who returns from field work: other people are other. They do not think the way we do. And if we want to understand their way of thinking, we should set out with the idea of capturing otherness... [N]othing is easier than to slip into the comfortable assumption that Europeans thought and felt two centuries ago just as we do today – allowing for the wigs and wooden shoes. We constantly need to be shaken out of a false sense of familiarity with the past, to be administered doses of culture shock (Darnton, 1985, p. 4).

The ambiguities of historic landscapes certainly have that effect. But is its result, our complacency shattered, a realisation that we can achieve at best a detached appreciation of shadowy people upon an alien landscape?

Darnton clearly achieved much more than this. He translated the "experience-distant" into scripts that are comprehensible within the "experience-near". He did so, like Isaac, by applying to history the ethnographic approach that has been developed in cultural anthropology by Geertz. Impatient with the pretence of empathy as a rigorous method of cross-cultural analysis, Geertz cautioned that "We cannot live other people's lives ...[;] it is with expressions, representations, objectifications, discourses, performances ... that we traffic ... Whatever sense we have of how things stand with someone else's inner life, we gain it through their expressions, not through some magical intrusion into their consciousness" (Geertz, 1986, p. 373). Social space is one such expression, and the key to understanding it, as Geertz says, is to be "Found in translation" (Geertz, 1983, p. 50). Such translation is driven by ethnography, which allows us to edge closer to the hidden histories of past places. In historical ethnography we have both the tools and the conceptual framework to make comprehensible the local contexts and local knowledge systems of past social life. Part of the strength of this approach lies in the "thick description" and "the highly situated nature" of ethnographic analysis (Geertz 1973, p. 6. Geertz, 1988, p. 5). It zeroes in upon the things that are most puzzling in different times and places. The other strength of historical ethnography is its regular shift of gears, through different scales of analysis from the local to the general and back again. It thus provides traction when drilling down into the finer textures of particular places in the past, and also when building general arguments from them.

If we disregard the interpretative process of ethnographic translation we overlook the subtle traces in the landscape of grassroots expressions of social action and human agency. This is why the central theme of Sharma's *Rediscovering Dharavi* is the "many success stories" by the residents of this supposedly chaotic place – written against the grain of outside characterisations of the slum's inhabitants as powerless and dysfunctional – in translating aspiration into achievement despite adversity (Sharma, 2000, p. 189). As Sharma demonstrates, "poor people are survival artists. They are remarkable architects because within their restricted spaces, they have designed the use of space in ways that few trained architects could" (Sharma, 2000, pp. 200-201). Archaeologists and historians have recently demonstrated the same point in relation to the demonised – and consequently bulldozed – slum districts of nineteenth and twentieth century cities. This is the fate that Sharma seeks to avoid for Dharavi. Today's planners need to learn from the mistakes committed by their nineteenth-century equivalents, for example in New York, where they swept away the Five Points district, or by their twentieth-century Australian equivalents who destroyed Melbourne's Little Lon "slum"[1].

What these planners failed to recognise, and what Sharma has attempted to highlight, is that both form and plan exist idiomatically in places such as Dharavi, albeit obscured by others' judgements of them as chaotic and corrosive. In nineteenth-century Melbourne, Police Commissioner John Sadleir commented in 1874 that Little Lon 'always has been a low neighbourhood', and Senior Constable Patrick Drum noted in 1882 that its inhabitants were "a low rough lot of people" (Sadlier, 1874; Drum, 1882). But commonsense strategies sustained this rowdy and rule-breaking community. In 1905, for example, one local resident explained that she operated a brothel because of "having a large family to support and my Husband lying in a dying state in the Hospital" (Booth, 1905). Synthesising archaeological and historical research has pinpointed the sites of homes in Little Lon where, notwithstanding outside stereotypes of crushing poverty and behavioural abnormality, residents worked, saved, accumulated possessions, and bequeathed these assets to their next of kin. The Moloney household, which has been reconstructed from probate records, registers of births, deaths and marriages, municipal ratebooks, and some 2,500 domestic artefacts that were excavated from a former cesspit, is a wonderful example of subaltern adaptability and continuity within a supposed slum. Here was a family with minimal formal education and trade skills, and low wages, who nonetheless bought a small house, rebuilt it in brick, accumulated household ornaments and chinaware, and maintained their homeplace for over 50 years; their children secured careers in the skilled trades and the professions (See Mayne & Lawrence, 1999, pp. 325-48; Mayne, Murray & Lawrence, 2000, pp. 131-51; Mayne & Murray, pp. 89-105). Behind the slum stereotypes that cloud appreciation of neighbourhood resilience in the rapidly growing cities of the developing world today, and which similarly skewed public knowledge during the first urbanisation surge during the nineteenth and twentieth centuries, there persist the complex actualities and coping mechanisms of poor but energetic communities.

***

The social construction of space across time, and the translation of historical place elements into present-day understandings, both occur to a significant degree through the medium of cultural performance. The phrase has overlapping and complementary meanings: Greg Dening used it in a pedagogical sense to explain to his students and readers "the theatricality of history-making", and in doing so likened his historical narratives about the past to other forms of cultural performance such as art exhibitions, concerts and theatre (Dening, 1996, p. xv). Such formal performances simultaneously create as they explain human space, but cultural performance also includes the physical and imaginary construction of vernacular spaces through Victor Turner's "social drama" or Erving Goffman's characterisation of all social interaction as staged behaviour (See Turner, 1985). In this sense cultural performance includes all forms of social life that are premeditated and rehearsed. Social action that humanises space occurs as much through place-based performance as it does through material expressions of place. Place-based social action and performance are "fundamental to the establishment of personal and group identities" (Tilly, 1994, p. 18). The medium of cultural performance is in part an outcome of hegemonic constructs of social reality. Lefebvre points out that elite representations of space attempt to maintain the unevenness of existing social relations by concealing their visible spatial expressions "in symbolic fashion" (Lefebvre, 1991, p. 32). Representations of colonial landscapes and of slums are cases in point (See Truettner, 1991); Mayne, 1993). Performance is also an important element in parallel subaltern constructions of space and place (See for example Stewart & Praetzellis, 1997; Mayne, 2003; Rains, 2005; Reeves, 2005). Such performances are channelled in part through formal genres and rituals, but they also permeate the strategies that are played out informally in everyday social behaviour.

The slum is a potent example of the deceits of hegemonic representations of space. 'Slum' is a word invented in early nineteenth-century London; it is a trope of performance, not a neutral descriptor of poor places and people. When urbanisation transformed British and North American society during the nineteenth century, the resulting mis-match between wealth and poverty posed fundamental social and ethical dilemmas for the hierarchy of class groupings that benefited from the urban transformation of society. Sensational performances – in the mass circulation city newspapers, in theatre, novels, and illustration – created the slum as a universal caricature that reduced the complexities of urban inequality to a simple image of dysfunctionality and degeneracy. The slum was represented as an abhorrent and dysfunctional realm – as an anti-place – because the performances fashioned it as the antithesis of behavioural decency and spatial utility in the modern city. They sought to contain the social contradictions and tensions that cities highlighted, by mobilising public opinion around core principles about individual and collective behaviour which purported to identify and explain the causes and effects of urban poverty, and which offered straightforward solutions for these social ills. Dickens called this slum performance "the attraction of repulsion" (Wohl, 1991, p. 89). Tellingly, the word "slum" does not appear in the idiom of the nineteenth-century London poor, nor barely in the idiom of India's poor today. It persists, however, in the corridors of power; the slum performance continues. In Mumbai, Sharma deplores "the blindness that even the thought of a slum seems to induce in the middle class" (Sharma, 2000, p. 193).

Slum performances hinder appreciation of the actual social dynamics of contemporary places such as Dharavi in Mumbai, and past places such as London's East End, Melbourne's Little Lon, and New York's Five Points. They also obscure and contradict the subaltern performances that are played out in such spaces as elements in grassroots place making, neighbourliness and community building. Often these elements are evident in public and quasi-formal performances, for example through music, dance, and the visual arts. They are also evident in intimate spaces such as homeplaces. In historical analysis, ethnographic interpretation of the material culture of obscure, mundane and seemingly insignificant things and places has become a means of glimpsing these ongoing performances of homeliness and social identity. The elements of analysis might be the Staffordshire ornamental figurines uncovered from the Moloneys' cesspit in Little Lon, or the Staffordshire teaware (its interior border pattern showing a hive surrounded by busy bees and the legend "Temperance And Industry. Industry Pays Debts") excavated from the site of a tenement building in Five Points (See Yamin, 2000, p. B-35). They also include the collections of "moralising china", tableware, and ornaments excavated from home sites in the Rocks district in Sydney, which assist archaeologists and historians in probing the aspirations and practices of working class families during the nineteenth century (See Karskens, 1999).

Translating the idiom of local performances is contributing to a fuller understanding of a wide range of vernacular landscapes in the past. It can be seen in analysis of the rituals and etiquette of homeliness, neighbourliness and social status in the nineteenth-century Australian goldfields, and the local protocols for redress of rule-breaking and indiscretion. These performances are evident at Hill End – where they are recorded in oral histories and the Bernard Holtermann collection of over 600 photographs of local people and places during 1872 and 1873 – and largely revolve around domestic place-making in and around the town's small and roughly-built huts, each with a vegetable garden, orchard and ornamental garden beds, bounded by picket fences (see Mayne, 2003, especially chapter 6). Translating and performing the richly symbolic landscape of Hill End has stimulated a stream of later artists, beginning with Russell Drysdale and Donald Friend in 1947, to live at Hill End and interpret its varied place elements in paint (see Mayne, 2003, chapter 7; Wilson, 1995).

Art also connects more directly with indigenous performances of place. A good example can be found in the post-colonial landscapes of Borroloola, in the Northern Territory. Borroloola is located 1,000 kilometres south-east of Darwin, and comprises a township hub and 30 surrounding outstations where 600 Aboriginal people and 200 Europeans live. Borroloola is represented by outsiders as a remote and dysfunctional Aboriginal community: "it's as far as you can go in Australia without a passport" (Jose, 2002, p. 6). Local artists interpret it very differently. Some 40 Aboriginal artists are associated with the Waralungku art movement, which has developed in the district over the last half century. The name Waralungku is drawn from the creation legends that explain the forms of the nearby McArthur River, and Waralungku art celebrates the local landscape and its cultural storylines. Senior artist Gordon Landsen (Milindirri), a Gudanji elder, called this approach "telling about the country" (Landsen, 2006). Nancy McDinny (Yukuwal) uses local collective memory and historical imagination to depict the arrival of travellers and colonisers in this place: the Macassans since the late seventeenth century, and from the 1870s onwards European pastoralists from northern Queensland. Nancy, a Garrawa woman, paints the wagon trains and the shootings that disrupted these Aboriginal homelands (See Roberts, 2005). However she and her fellow artists mostly paint storylines about Aboriginal connectedness to land and culture rather than about dispossession and disintegration. They tap and perpetuate local knowledge systems, and the cosmology and seasonal rhythms of their country (See Baker, 1999).

Historical ethnographies of place not only recognise that the idioms of diverse local performances – whether artwork such as that at Borroloola, or the recorded memories and pictorial records of Hill End, or the material culture of vanished nineteenth-century city communities such as Five Points or Little Lon – are texts by which to read past landscapes; researchers such as Dening, Isaac, Darnton and Glassie are also experimenting themselves with cultural performance as a means of teaching about past places. Performance thus becomes a means by which to translate research findings into learning. Museums are now at the forefront of many of these innovations, using performance to communicate and to engage with present-day audiences. Since 1992, for example, over one million people have seen Ballarat's *Blood on the Southern Cross*, the Sovereign Hill Museums Association's theatrical extravaganza about the Eureka rebellion during the Australian gold rushes (See Sullivan, 2006, pp. 61-76). The National Museum of Australia's *Basin*

Bytes, an online digital photography outreach project that explores participants' sense of place and belonging in the sprawling Murray-Darling river basin, unfolded in communities across South Australia, Victoria, New South Wales and Queensland during the early to mid 2000s (See Wills 2007).

Storytelling is becoming the anchor point for pedagogical performances about place, belonging, and dispossession in the past. Peter Read used the technique effectively to underline the intensity of human associations with "a loved place" and the grief and trauma triggered when such places are lost or destroyed (Read, 1996, p. 196). Archaeologists have gone further, boldly using imaginative writing "to make dry material accessible to non-professionals" (Wilkie, 2003, p. xxiv). Some innovators use imaginative writing as a means of open-ended interpretation that invites response and amendment, rather than as an uncomplicated form of one-way communication that explains arcane archaeological evidence to general readers. This explicit use of imaginative writing as a technique that drives learning "implies a blurring of the absolute distinction between factual and fictional writing. The archaeological text becomes a literary form. Fact and the fictive form a continuous field" (Shanks & Hodder, 1995, p. 27). Carmel Schrire used imaginative reconstruction to explore the interplays between the Dutch East India Company and the Khoikhoi in seventeenth-century southern Africa: "Palpable though the documents and artifacts may be", she wrote, "in the end their deeper messages can only be read through acts of imagination". Echoing Glassie, she added mischievously that "a conversation set in a hunters' camp three hundred years ago may bear no written testimony, yet it might well have taken place" (Schrire, 1995, pp. 5, 10).

Storytelling is being used to puncture slum myths, giving voice to people past and present who inhabit these allegedly chaotic spaces. Sharma's *Rediscovering Dharavi* revolves around a series of first-person narratives from inhabitants of this maligned neighbourhood. Archaeologists have used fictional first-person narratives to embody the otherwise abstract badlands of nineteenth-century cities. Rebecca Yamin's experimentation with first-person vignettes to encapsulate the lived experiences of residents in Five Points exemplifies this harnessing of performance to learning. Speaking through Mary Callaghan, an actual resident of Five Points' Pearl Street from the mid 1850s until the 1870s, Yamin attempts "to weave together the documentary data, the stratigraphic analysis, and the artifact interpretation into narrative vignettes" which identify people in the past as active agents within their homes and neighbourhoods (Yamin, 2000, p. 91. See Yamin, 2001, pp. 163-165; Yamin, 1998, pp. 74-85).

***

This chapter has used Somerville's discussion of place studies in Australia as a starting point from which to delve into the strange entanglements by which human space encroaches upon historical analysis. Historians should inch their way into these confusing thickets rather than ignoring or attempting to cut back the entanglements. The best way to learn about the past is not by superimposing present-day roadmaps upon its unfamiliar landscapes, but by attempting to translate and comprehend the idiomatic content of past places. This approach can be described as an historical ethnography of place (Mayne & Lawrence, 1999). Historical ethnography constructs and continuously tests its conclusions by building interpretation outwards from the small and the local. In doing so ethnographers double-check the seemingly obvious, look for its subaltern counterpoints, dwell on elements that are strange and puzzling and unleash imagination to probe the clues and ambiguities and to weave together storylines that entertain and invite participation as they instruct. They recognise in relic landscapes the inscriptions that survive from active lives and unfolding happenings in the past. Translating those inscriptions is the surest path to understanding past places from "the native's point of view". The chapter has focused upon two especially remote and inaccessible historical spaces: city slums and frontier landscapes. Both are – in their ambiguities, perplexities, and polarities – crucibles for cultural imagination, mobilisation and social action. There is rich material in these ethnographically deciphered landscapes that can be used as a platform for learning: grounded in the idiom of local performance, layered by the uneven outcomes of social action and collective memory, and made public through the shared performance of exploring different places and cultures.

NOTES

[1] Nickname for a poor working-class neighbourhood defined by Little Lonsdale Street, occupying a sector on the north-east edge of early Melbourne's city centre. Little Lon was popularly notorious as a locale for crime and prostitution, particularly in the 19th and early 20th Centuries.

REFERENCES

Bachelard, G. (1964). *The poetics of space* (E. Gilson, Trans.). New York: Orion Press. (Original work published 1958).

Baker, R. (1999). *Land is life. From bush to town: The story of the Yanyuwa people*. St Leonards, NSW: Allen & Unwin.

Beaudry, M. (Ed.). (1988). *Documentary archaeology in the New World*. Cambridge, UK: Cambridge University Press.

Bonyhady, T., & Griffiths, T. (Eds.). (2002). *Words for country: Landscape and language in Australia*. Sydney, NSW: University of New South Wales Press.

Booth, E. letter, 30 March 1905, in Public Record Office Victoria, *Inward Correspondence to the Chief Commissioner of Police*. VPRS 807, Bundle 2, Unit 1198.

Castells, M. (1983). *The city and the grassroots*. London: Edward Arnold.

Central Land Council. *The land is always alive: Barrow Creek warriors*. Retrieved May 22, 2007, from http://www.clc.org.au/media/publications/landalive/barrow.asp.

Chamberlain, G. (2009, January 9). Mumbai's beating heart, *Guardian Weekly*, 25.

Darnton, R. (1985). *The great cat massacre and other episodes in French cultural history*. New York: Vintage Books.

Daunton, M. J. (1983). *House and home in the Victorian city: Working-class housing 1850-1914*. London: Edward Arnold.

Davison, G. (Ed.). (1990). *Journeys into history*. Willoughby, NSW: Weldon Russell.

De Certeau, M. (1984). *The practice of everyday life* (S. Rendall, Trans.). Berkeley, CA: University of California Press.

Dening, G. (1996). *Performances*. Melbourne, VIC: Melbourne University Press.

Dennis, R. (1984). *English industrial cities of the nineteenth century: A social geography*. Cambridge, UK: Cambridge University Press.

Drum, P. (1882, April 12). Police report. In Public Record Office Victoria, *Inward Correspondence to the Chief Commissioner of Police*. VPRS 937, Unit 306, Bundle 3.

Englander, D. (1983). *Landlord and tenant in urban Britain 1838-1918*. Oxford, UK: Clarendon Press.

Foelsche P. (1874, June 2). Letter to G.B. Scott (South Australian Government Resident in Darwin). In State Records of South Australia, *Letters Received in the Office of the Minister Controlling the Northern Territory*. GRS 1, Unit 5, Item 232/1874.

Geertz, C. (1973). *The interpretation of cultures*. New York: Basic Books.

Geertz, C. (1983). *Local knowledge: Further essays in interpretive anthropology*. New York: Basic Books.

Geertz, C. (1988). *Works and lives: The anthropologist as author*. Stanford, CA: Stanford University Press.

Geertz, C. (1986). Making experiences, authoring Selves. In V. Turner & E. Bruner (Eds.), *The anthropology of experience* (pp. 373–380). Urbana, IL: University of Illinois Press.

Glassie, H. (1999). *Material culture*. Bloomington, IN: Indiana University Press.

Glassie, H. (1982). *Passing the time in Ballymenone*. Bloomington, IN: Indiana University Press.

Goodwin, B. (1992). *Gold and people: Recollections of Hill End 1920s to 1960s*. Frenchs Forest, NSW: Bruce Goodwin.

The Hindu, (2009, February 23). p. 1.

Hoskins, W. G. (1955). *The making of the English landscape*. London: Hodder & Stoughton.

Isaac, R. (1982). *The transformation of Virginia 1740-1790*. Chapel Hill, NC: University of North Carolina Press.

Isaac, R. (1992). Imagination and material culture: The Enlightenment on a mid-18th-century Virginia plantation. In A. Yentsch & M. Beaudry (Eds.), *The art and mystery of historical archaeology* (pp. 400–423). Boca Raton, FL: CRC Press.

Jacobson M., & Bendiksen, J. (2007). Dharavi: Mumbai's shadow city. *National Geographic, 222*(5), 68–93.

Jose, N. (2002). *Black sheep: Journey to Borroloola*. South Yarra, VIC: Hardie Grant Books.

Karskens, G. (1999). *Inside the Rocks: The archaeology of a neighbourhood*. Alexandria, NSW: Hale & Iremonger.

Kern, S. (2003). *The culture of time and space 1880-1918*. Cambridge, MA: Harvard University Press.

Landsen, G. (2006, December 16). Recorded interview with Alan Mayne.

Lefebvre, H. (1991). *The production of space* (D. Nicholson-Smith, Trans.). Oxford, UK: Blackwell. (Original work published 1974).

Lowenthal, D. (1985). *The past is a foreign country*. Cambridge, UK: Cambridge University Press.

McCalman, I., Cook, A., & Reeves, A. (Eds.). (2001). *Gold: Forgotten histories and lost objects of Australia*. Cambridge, UK: Cambridge University Press.

McDougall, D. (2007, March 16–22). Success in a slum. *Guardian Weekly*, p. 29.

Mayne, A. (2007). Goldrush landscapes: An ethnography. In K. Reeves & D. Nichols (Eds.), *Deeper leads: New approaches to Victorian goldfields history* (pp. 13–20). Ballarat, VIC: BHS Publishing.

Mayne, A. (2003). *Hill End: An historic Australian goldfields landscape*. Carlton: Melbourne University Press.

Mayne, A. (1993). *The imagined slum: Newspaper representation in three cities, 1870-1914*. Leicester, UK: University of Leicester Press.

Mayne A., & Murray, T. (Eds). *The archaeology of urban landscapes: Explorations in slumland*. Cambridge, UK: Cambridge University Press.

Mayne, A., Murray, T., & Lawrence, S. (2000). Historic sites: Melbourne's 'Little Lon'. *Australian Historical Studies, 31*(113), 131–151.

Mayne A., & Lawrence, S. (1999). Ethnographies of place: A new urban history research agenda. *Urban History, 26*(3), 325–348.

Prunty, J. (1998). *Dublin slums 1800-1925: A study in urban geography.* Dublin, CO: Irish Academic Press.

Rains, K. (2005). *Intersections: The historical archaeology of the overseas Chinese social landscape of Cooktown, 1873-1935.* PhD Thesis, University of Queensland.

Ramesh, R. (2007, June 8). Indian tycoon builds tower block home. *Guardian Weekly,* p. 8.

Read, P. (1996). *Returning to nothing: The meaning of lost places.* Cambridge, UK: Cambridge University Press.

Reeves, K. (2005). *A hidden history: The Chinese on the Mount Alexander diggings, Central Victoria, 1851-1901.* PhD Thesis, University of Melbourne.

Roberts, T. (2005). *Frontier justice: A history of the Gulf Country to 1900.* St Lucia, QLD: University of Queensland Press.

Sadleir, J. (1874, August 19). *Memo.* In Public Record Office Victoria, *Inward Correspondence to the Chief Commissioner of Police.* VPRS 937, Unit 296, Bundle 1.

Schrire, C. (1995). *Digging through darkness: Chronicles of an archaeologist.* Charlottesville, VA: University Press of Virginia.

Shanks, M., & Hodder, I. (1995). Processual, postprocessual and interpretive archaeologies. In I. Hodder, M. Shanks, A. Alexandri, V. Buchli, J. Carman, J. Last, & G. Lucas (Eds.), *Interpreting archaeology: Finding meanings in the past* (pp. 3–29). London: Routledge.

Sharma, K. (2000). *Rediscovering Dharavi: Stories from Asia's largest slum.* New Delhi: Penguin Books.

Sharma, S. (1995). *Landscape and memory.* London: Fontana Press.

Sullivan, T. (2006). Sovereign Hill, *Blood on the Southern Cross* and telling the story of Eureka. In A. Mayne (Ed.), *Eureka: Reappraising an Australian legend* (pp. 61–76). Perth, WA: Network Books.

Stewart, S., & Praetzellis, M. (Eds.). (1997). *Sights and sounds: Essays in celebration of West Oakland.* Sonoma State University: Anthropological Studies Center.

Tilley, C. (1994). *A phenomenology of landscape: Places, paths and monuments.* Oxford, UK: Berg.

Todd, C. (1874, February 23, 24) Telegram to G.B. Scott. In *State Records of South Australia, GRS 14* (Incoming Telegrams, January to December 1874).

Todd, C. (1884). Report on the Post Office, Telegraph, and Observatory Departments. *South Australian Parliamentary Papers, 1884, 4*(191), 150.

Truettner, W. (Ed.). (1991). *The West as America: Reinterpreting images of the Frontier, 1820-1920.* Washington DC: Smithsonian Institution Press.

Turner, V. (1985). *On the edge of the bush: Anthropology as experience.* Tucson, AZ: University of Arizona Press.

Ward, D. (1989). *Poverty, ethnicity, and the American city, 1840-1925: Changing conceptions of the slum and the ghetto.* Cambridge, UK: Cambridge University Press.

Wilkie, L. A. (2003). *The archaeology of mothering: An African-American midwife's tale.* New York and London: Routledge.

Wills, J. (2007). *Museums, communities and participatory projects.* PhD Thesis, University of Tasmania.

Wilson, G. (1995). *The artists of Hill End.* Sydney, NSW: Beagle Press and Art Gallery of New South Wales.

Wohl, A. (1991). Social explorations among the London poor: Theatre or laboratory? *Revue Francaise de Civilisation Britannique, 6,* 76–97.

Yamin, R. (2001). Alternative narratives: Respectability at New York's Five Points. In A. Mayne & T. Murray (Eds.), *The archaeology of urban landscapes: Explorations in slumland* (pp. 163–165). Cambridge, UK: Cambridge University Press.

Yamin, R. (Ed.). (2000). *Tales of Five Points: Working-class life in nineteenth-century New York, vol. 1.* West Chester, PA: John Milner & Associates.

Yamin, R. (1998). Lurid tales and homely stories of New York's notorious Five Points. *Historical Archaeology, 32,* 74–85.

Yentsch, A. (1994). *A Chesapeake family and their slaves: A study in historical archaeology.* Cambridge, UK: Cambridge University Press.

Alan Mayne
University of South Australia

JANE KENWAY

12. BEYOND CONVENTIONAL CURRICULUM CARTOGRAPHY VIA A GLOBAL SENSE OF PLACE

As the development of a national curriculum in Australia continues and as economic globalisation continues to be invoked as a driving imperative for nationalising knowledge, it is important to ask 'Does place matter anymore?' Should school education have an intimate sense of place — not just of nation or state? I will argue that place has weighty implications for education. But I will also argue that conventional conceptions of place must be abandoned if we are to best comprehend place and change in globalising times. I offer to curriculum thought and practice a global sense of place with view to providing some conceptual resources for a consideration of a place-based global curriculum.

YOUNG PEOPLE IN THE NEXUS OF THE GLOBAL/LOCAL

In Coober Pedy, a remote desert town in South Australia, Aboriginal 'homeboys' adopt USA style hip-hop identities in opposition to local white racism. Certain white locals regard Aboriginal people as 'flies hanging around'; as rubbish making the place look untidy and putting off international tourists. Beach culture dominates youthful identities in the small town of Eden on the New South Wales coast. For the 'surf chicks' who live their lives at soap opera levels of high intensity, beach parties are weekend delights — fun, friends, boys, booze and casual sex. Greeks have become an important sector of the population in Renmark, a wine and fruit town on the Murray River in South Australia. Greek boys are at the top of the youthful pecking order and they compete with the 'ferals' doing laps of the town in their cars. Renmark is not a welcoming place for new arrivals, the Turks and the Vietnamese.

These stories draw from a major study of the implications of globalisation for places and people outside the major cities in Australia (Kenway, Kraack & Hickey-Moody 2006). For this, we conducted place-based global ethnographies[1] in Eden (NSW), Morwell (Victoria), Coober Pedy and Renmark (SA). Each place has vastly different economies and cultures. These young people can be thought of as place-based global youth whose lives and identities evolve at the complex intersections of the global/local nexus; many of which are only hinted at in the stories above.

But what do stories about kids like this, about the places in which they live, mean for national curriculum? In this paper, I draw on the book to offer some story snippets about place, and education in place, with a view to making the case for place-based global curriculum for school education.

M. Somerville, K. Power and P. de Carteret (eds.),
Landscapes and Learning: Place Studies for a Global World, 195–205

NATIONAL CURRICULUM CARTOGRAPHIES

How is educational geography represented by key national policy figures; how is it linked to curriculum? In other words, what are the most evident curriculum cartographies amongst Australia's national leaders? Below are selected quotations from senior policy makers at the national level.

> ... [p]eople have been talking about a national curriculum for many, many years .... Now it was cute politics for Labor to jump in and announce that they have got one too. That's fine but the point is that state Education Ministers have shown over many years, history shows, that unless they are actually forced to embrace change, they won't do it. They are complacent in their separate bureaucracies, and we need to take this on as a national issue, a national priority. And what they understand is tying this to funding, if it's a condition of funding, then the states will come to the table and talk about it sensibly. We have done it in the past with plain English report cards; a range of things, there's nothing to stop the states coming together now in developing a national curriculum (Julie Bishop, Liberal Party Minister for Education, 2007).

> What is required is the development of a common framework that sets out the major areas of knowledge and the most appropriate mix of skills and experience for students in all the years of schooling, but accommodates the different or specific needs of different parts of Australia. There is a need for regular assessment of the effectiveness and standards of our schools. A common curriculum framework should be complemented by a common national approach to assessment. We need to examine how schools can report to parents on their aims and achievements; how school systems can report to the nation on how well our schools are performing against established goals (John Dawkins, Labor Minister for Education, 1989).

> We have eight different educational jurisdictions, eight different commencement ages, eight different curricula. We would not be giving service to young Australians if we just accept that there are eight jurisdictions. I see it as our responsibility to prepare the next generation to be well-equipped as global citizens, to be proud and well-developed Australians as much as they are New South Welshmen or Queenslanders or Western Australians (Brendon Nelson, Liberal Minister for Education, 2006).

> Well let's go through it. Let's suppose there were real life differences ... between the different areas of Australia which require children to learn different things. Let's suppose for example, it was necessary to learn the different elements of weather patterns in South Australia as opposed to Northern Australia. I mean there is a legitimate difference and you would have room for geographical differences in the curriculum. But let's ask ourselves another question. Should the standard of history taught in Southern Australia be different to Northern Australia? Should the algebra be different, the language theory? I mean, plainly not, and so you don't actually need

separate boards to develop separate curricula in relation to issues like that. Plainly a lot of knowledge is universal and not a lot of knowledge is national, there will be a little bit which may vary according to geographic conditions, but you would think that you would be able to get some agreement nationally on things like history, English, mathematics, science – these are not just national issues by the way, these are international issues (Peter Costello, Liberal Treasurer, 2007).

What spatial units do these people employ to discuss school curriculum? Bishop's focus is the nation and the states with the nation as the primary geography. Dawkins is concerned with the "the different or specific needs of different parts of Australia" and how "school systems can report to the nation"; again the nation trumps the state. For them the binary geographical logics of state/national are unquestioned. Nelson mentions eight different educational jurisdictions as well as global citizens, proud and well developed Australians and New South Welshmen, Queenslanders, Western Australians. He does not too obviously privilege the national. For him there are two logics at work; national and state and national and global. Much more expansive and convoluted, Costello mentions the universal, international, national, states and different sorts of knowledge. Of course, these are all national figures and leading educators from state systems might provide differently inflected cartographies. But I simply offer these as examples of commonsense curriculum cartographies.

In the last few decades, debates about national and state curriculum between policy makers, curriculum developers and curriculum theorists have come and gone. Now, in the 21st century, they have come again. By and large these debates have not taken very seriously the links between place and curriculum. Place is often implicitly seen as the 'add in' space after other cartographies have framed the discussion. Sometimes it is left as the 'blank space' to be filled in by teachers with local colour; the space to be coloured in. But how best is it to be coloured in and is the space place is allocated in curriculum design big enough? Place also gets mixed up with the many other sub-national, sub-state or sub-city spatialities that constitute Australia's educational policy geography. These include the district, the region, the rural, the remote, the local, the suburb, the postcode and the neighbourhood. These spaces can also become either official or unofficial curriculum cartographies.

Despite all this boundary riding and eliding, it might be said that Australia's educational policy geography and its associated curriculum cartographies have not been sufficiently problematised or theorised. In this paper I trouble these spatialities.

When we mobilise such spatial terms — global, regional, national, state, local — we tend to treat them as obvious. Further, we tend to privilege certain spatialities over others. Currently the nation in the globe is also a privileged spatial relationship and has tended to attract the considerable conceptual concern from policy makers and curriculum policy analysts. A particular view of the nation state in the global world is evident here. So too is a particular view of globalisation. This can be described as globalisation from on high.

Globalisation from on high involves a top-down perspective, and the top is understood as peak multi-national corporations and multi- or supra-national political organisations. This common view from the top is often developed by those at the top or by those who adopt their standpoint. The master narrative is neo-liberal economics with its associated calls for structural adjustment in national economies and state promoted 'free' trade. The underlying logic is deterministic; economic globalisation that accords with the neo-liberal agenda is portrayed as unstoppable. The logic is often also advocatory: globalise (according to neo-liberal prescriptions) or perish.

However such views of globalisation and such conventional national/state cartographies in the statements above have some clear limitations. They offer a view of educational geography that is somewhat locked into global/nation state logics. These don't speak adequately to the complexity of globalisation. Nor do they speak to the complexity of place in a globalising world.

Within the discourse of national curriculum that draws on such 'globalisation from on high' thinking, place is constructed in a particular way. It is mostly an afterthought as I have noted; the space that we can all afford to leave behind. Or it is seen as a traditional space that lags behind: the space that must be brought up to date, up to speed. Either way, for many it has lost its lure as cartography for curriculum.

Clearly then, this view of globalisation is restricted and restricting and we require a richer perspective to inform curriculum development. So what other ideas about globalisation offer such perspectives? There are other ways to consider globalisation from on high. These certainly focus on the big picture and describe the major economic, cultural and political trends and patterns associated with globalisation. Yet each also suggests ways that we might develop a much more nuanced global sense of place.

THREE ANGLES ON GLOBALISATION'S GEOMETRY

Complex Connectivity

According to Tomlinson (1999, p. 2), "Globalisation refers to the rapidly developing and ever-densening network of interconnections and interdependences that characterise modern social life". He calls this "complex connectivity" and identifies the different modalities of "interconnection and interdependence" involved. Through the example of Eden, let us consider place from the perspective of global complex connectivity. Complex connectivity, says Tomlinson, "involves all sorts of contradictions, resistances, and counter veiling forces" (1999, p. 17). Eden is a fish and chips town that has experienced environmental globalisation and has been subjected to environmental reforms introduced by the commonwealth government to regulate the fishing and logging industries. This has led to local employment difficulties. In contrast, Eden's neighbouring town, Merimbula, has boomed due to tourism; a thriving global industry. Spatial tensions have arisen between Eden and Merimbula boys and these spill over into the school and sport. Eden's older generation don't see tourism as the best way forward for the town and some members particularly object to local boys being employed in what they see as feminine work in the tourist industry. Eden youth partake of global youth subculture of surfing; this is linked to many global brands, which include Billabong and Ripcurl, industries developed in Torquay, a coastal town in Victoria. The beach culture that so consumes the young is derided by school as anti-academic but the school has introduced marine studies to help get local boys and men on-side with both the school and the rising local tourist industry.

Global Scapes

Appadurai (1996) talks of global flows; he calls these scapes and they include media scapes (moving images), ideo scapes (moving political ideas), ethno scapes (moving people) and techno scapes. He argues that these often exist in awkward relationships with each other as they flow through space and place. Such global scapes are manifest in place in a range of combinations. Take the case of Coober Pedy's ethno scapes and its multi-ethnic population. In addition to the aboriginal people living in and around the town, there are over 45 different nationalities (Fairfax Digital Online 2005). Many such people have come to mine the local opal and have stayed either in the opal industry or jobs servicing the town. Opal buyers come from all over the world for the famous Coober Pedy opal. Various hostilities on the other side of the world re-emerge in Coober Pedy streets as the Bosnians fight the Serbs, and on the sports oval as the boys seek to out-perform each other in the name of their favourite global soccer team. Global media scapes flow through this remote small township not just with regard to politics and sport. Its unusual landscape has attracted the global film industry and hence images of this isolated desert town have been beamed around the globe in such major films as 'Mad Max', 'Red Planet' and 'Siam Sunset'. Other global media scapes and ethno scapes also flow through Coober Pedy. These are associated with the rise of the Indigenous tourist industry in Australia and its portrayal on various tourist websites. Aboriginal culture has become a highly marketable feature of the Australian tourist industry, particularly to those sorts of tourists whom Cohen and Kennedy (2000, p. 219) call "alternative tourists" (as opposed to mass tourists). They "are disposed to interact directly with locals and show interest in traditional culture". The local school always has to take into account, in one way or another, such global flows, to address their implications for identity and locality, to deal with any negative fallout from them and to see how they might be mobilised to the benefit of students' education. Thus, for instance, the school concentrates heavily on students' ICT skills and provides them with opportunities to connect with their overseas counterparts in their families' home countries. It also takes every opportunity offered by the tourist industry for students' work experience.

'Geographies of Centrality And Marginality'

Globalisation has its own "geographies of centrality and marginality" (Sassen 1998), its own integrating and fragmenting tendencies and clearly many power inequities are associated. This requires a sensitivity to globalisation's unevenness at regional, national, sub-national, sub-state levels and to how events in the global environment can effect a place's place in globalisation's power geometries (Massey, 1993). It requires attention to their implications for social stability, coherence and justice. Take Renmark with its family fruit blocks and viticulture. It increasingly experiences the constant ebb and flow of good fortune as its industries become more global. There is no certainty in global fruit or wine markets or in the weather. Renmark can link to global industries so long as it is able to irrigate from the Murray River. In the dry state of South Australia at the end of the Murray, Renmark is totally dependent on this water and thus on the national and state politics of water— a highly volatile politics that threatens to get worse as climate change intensifies. In this context, water becomes an equity issue. What would happen to Renmark if it runs out of water? Currently the young are encouraged to stay on the land and in the township. Courses at the local technical and further education (TAFE) college are conducted to help them to keep up with the changes in the industry and the school ensures the environmental awareness of its students. But the pull of elsewhere is strong and the local young are more attracted to the centres of globalisation, not so much its margins that run the risk of becoming more marginal as time goes on.

As all this implies, we cannot understand place(s) today, unless we have some knowledge of their complex global connectivity, their links to global scapes and how they are situated in globalisation's power geometry. These three angles on globalisation from on high invite national curriculum proponents and developers to take up much richer notions of globalisation. They invite them to consider different views of place from those they conventionally adopt. But also, they problematise other notions of place that have come into curriculum thought over the years. These are in contrast with those views that marginalise place in curriculum discourse.

PLACE PARABLES

When place is mobilised as central to curriculum it is often presented as the deeply embedded and embodied 'real', and juxtaposed against the dis-embedded, disembodied abstractions of curricula formations of the nation or state. Place-sensitive curriculum is offered as a counter to the remote control and distant engagements of the state or the nation curriculum. Place is framed as the genuine space of engagement; the space of community and identity formation and identification, of authentic relationships, of enclosed belongings and becomings. Place is seen as the space where curriculum can be up-close, personal and grounded. Within this view place may be romanticised, sanitised or even stigmatised but it is seen as the starting place for curriculum.

Such views have a certain resonance in an era that increasingly replaces the face to face with abstract and abstracted relationships. But they too run the risk of oversimplifying place, not to mention the problems associated with place prejudice. In my view, these understandings of place and therefore of curriculum are also inadequate. They fail to take into account not only globalisation, richly defined, but also richer views of place.

How then are we to understand place and globalising processes? Sassen (1998, p. xix) argues that "place is central to many of the circuits through which economic globalisation is constituted". Giddens (1990, p. 19) explains that "place becomes increasingly phantasmagoric" as it is more "thoroughly infiltrated by and shaped in terms of social influences quite distant" from it; it is "stretched out". Tomlinson (1999) talks of "dis-placement" (1999, p. 9) as global media images produce an increasing sense of worldwide "proximity". This is accompanied by connections that arise through economic, environmental and communicative links and through long-distance travel, tourism and migration. Equally, local events, practices and lifestyles are increasingly considered in terms of their global implications and consequences.

Clearly, place is not just an effect of globalisation, the nation or state. Neither is it simply a container of community processes. Place is not totally scripted from without or within, above or below. It is geography and geometry. It involves a complex range of connections, collections and scales in space and time. Massey calls this the "simultaneous multiplicity of space" and argues that spaces are crosscutting and intersecting, existing in relations of paradox and antagonism (Massey 1994, p. 120). Further, in her more recent book Massey talks of place as an "event", a "constellation of processes" and stresses, its "thrown togetherness" involving sets of negotiations between history and geography, humans and nonhumans including changing landscapes and climates" (Massey 2005, pp. 140-141).

A GLOBAL SENSE OF PLACE

We need to consider the implications of globalisation and of place, both richly defined, for curriculum thinking. I thus propose the idea of place-based global curriculum. What broad concepts might be invoked if we are to develop a global sense of place and thus a place-based global curriculum? I'd like to offer some starting points for this conceptual work and in the process offer a place study of Morwell, in the Gippsland region of Victoria, to help justify my claims that place-based global curriculum is necessary. If one adopts a global sense of place, place is understood as a mobile constellation achieved through negotiations between the following sorts of processes: temporal, spatial, ecological, political, imaginary and personal. Each process invites a particular angle of curriculum inquiry. Collectively these angles intersect to achieve a place-based global curriculum.

Temporal

In place histories, habits and memories intersect with the now and the future. Some histories dominate place, others are subordinate, emergent, and resistant. Morwell's dominant history is that it was once a potent power-town, established as the location of an industrial complex of state controlled coal mining and electricity generation. It was defined by men's work in the power industry and built in large part to house the men and their families. When the state controlled power industry was privatised and when the industry was then 'restructured and down sized' it was a serious blow to the economy and culture of Morwell. There was wide scale loss — loss of jobs, loss of people from the town and, for many, loss of heart and hope, as severe social and economic disadvantage became the norm. Places have different paces that derive from their history and in Morwell the pace of place slowed down. These changes had all sorts of educational implications. For instance, many sons used to follow their fathers into the power industry and their education was only seen as necessary to the extent that it supported this process. Technical education was most highly valued for boys; basic education for girls who largely went into local service industries. What was school education to do when Morwell had lost so much? Could it, should it, help the town to recover? How?

Spatial

Maybe it hardly needs saying, but places are spatial. They intersect with their beyond on different scales and in different ways. Morwell links to the rest of the state of Victoria, currently producing 85% of its power needs through coal fired electricity generation. It continues to live in fear that it will be "dug up for coal" (Fletcher 2002) as was the beautiful nearby town of Yallourn. In a sense, Yallourn was re-established at Churchill; off the main road, off the railway line in an out-of-the-way place. And it is in Churchill that the Gippsland Institute was set up and became a campus of Monash University. Place rivalries between local townships helped to prevent Monash being located in one of the other towns where ready access was available on the main Princes Highway and the railway line. An education precinct has been set up in Churchill including upper high school, TAFE and the University. It draws a global education discourse about the opportunities of ready transitions between education sectors and also about the importance of life-long learning for employment. The precinct was designed in part to speak to the new needs of local communities, but its location in Churchill also provoked local rivalries amongst parents, which delayed its establishment.

Ecological

Morwell has benefited from its location near rich deposits of brown coal to burn for power and near access to water for the industry's cooling ponds through the rivers and streams that feed the Gippsland lakes. Indeed, in public perceptions of the Gippsland area, the delicate beauty of the lakes tends to get overshadowed by the image of smoking power stacks. Morwell is now facing new pressures to adjust associated with climate change and the burning of fossil fuels. It is caught up in issues about the possibilities of clean coal, and a new power station has recently been announced that will try to develop clean coal technologies. In this context, what is the role of schools? At the very least they need to explore with students a host of climate change and water issues associated with the local industry (the links between water and power generation). But should they explore and promote alternative futures for Morwell as well as for the students? What might these be? Other educational politics are about how students might best address discourses of climate change given the locality's big investments in fossil fuel generation. Economy and ecology must come together much better in this place and schools can help students to at least consider the issue.

Political

"Places do not have single unique identities but are full of internal differences and conflict", as Massey (1994, p. 155) reminds us. These and their relationships to wider differences and conflicts can make places highly charged politically. Issues of ethics and justice are never far from the scene. When Morwell lost so many people through the restructuring of the power industry, local property lost its value and plenty of cheap houses came on the market. This led to the inflow of low-income people from the city for the cheap rental property. Subsequently, spaces of denigration arose as these people, especially single mothers on welfare support, clustered together in particular parts of town. One such place became known as the Bronx. There is considerable local resentment and hostility directed towards these not-really-local welfare poor. For instance, their school peers call the kids from the Bronx "the rats". The so-called "rats" are at the extreme end of the issue, for a number of their peers are also from families on welfare or who might be called the working poor. There are sensitive and pressing educational politics in Morwell around how schools best address intergenerational welfare, the creation of paths to work and alternative forms of livelihood.

Imaginary

Places are imaginary and as Appadurai (1996) argues the imagination has a social life. The face of place involves the stories that those in place tell themselves and others about their place and its relationships to other places. It also involves the stories others tell about that place over/out there. This means that place involves diverse and changing faces and may also involve saving face. At the time of the power industry's restructuring in Morwell, certain locals narrated themselves as either victims or brave survivors or both. They also narrated themselves as used and abused by the power-sapping city of Melbourne, which has had the gall to construct Morwell as an unrepentant polluting place. Morwell has also been narrated from outside as a hole, a place of no hope and no hopers. Some locals feel this way too, others are more optimistic as the town slowly rebuilds and new types of local work become more available. Students are caught up in the intersections of these narratives; pushed and pulled between staying and going, between the attractions of local loyalties and those of wider opportunities elsewhere. Schools are concerned about how to shape alternative stories about the possibilities that local education offers in the new local economy. An active and positive educational imagination is required.

Personal

"Place is latitudinal and longitudinal within the map of a person's life. It is temporal and spatial, personal and political". In a multi-centred world, there are many senses of place, says Lippard (1997, p. 7) in *The Lure of the Local*. People's experiences of place can be both patterned and unique, based on what they bring to their encounters with the temporal, spatial, ecological, political and imaginary. Some boys in Morwell have so internalised their father's distressing working experiences that they have developed quite melancholic masculinities. This has meant that they refuse to reinvent themselves around new educational or job opportunities. There is a sense that they feel unable to wound their already wounded fathers by taking up an identity that is too unlike the traditional power worker. Psychologically they are both in and out of place and time.

Teachers need to be provided with opportunities to develop a nuanced understanding of place and thus of the places that they are teaching in. It is vital that they are able to rise above place prejudice and to move beyond simplistic/romantic views of place. They need to be provided with opportunities to explore and develop the principles of place-based curriculum. They should have built into their work opportunities for them to explore with students and parents their understandings of their place. Also built-in should be opportunities for them to develop place-based curriculum for the places they are working in and the students and parents they are working with. This would be in dialogue with but not restricted to students' and parents' understandings of their place. They also need opportunities to share such curriculum development and practice amongst the profession and related bodies across a wide variety of places. Ultimately we know that in the end, curriculum only has meaning in the interaction of teachers and students in place.

CONCLUSION

This place study of Morwell and the story snippets about other places show that places connect somewhat differently to wider worlds; global, national and state. They have different faces, involve different paces. They are not unified, include different communities and involve very complicated matters of identity and intergenerational relations. I am suggesting that a focus on place allows us to see what 'globalisation' looks like from below; from the perspective of those on the ground, their everyday-every night experiences of the ways that globalisation links to what is in place and what flows through it. I have said that place involves a constellation of processes. Each process invites a particular angle of curriculum inquiry. Collectively these angles intersect and point to the necessity of a place-based global curriculum. I have also argued that place needs a bigger space in contemporary curriculum but that when it claims a space, teachers are expected to be able to colour it in. When they do however, there is a danger that they will adopt common-sense notions of place or that they will become unwittingly involved in place romanticisation, sanitisation or prejudice.

Curriculum does need to attend to a spatial paradox. It needs to have an intimate global sense of place. This involves challenging conventional curriculum cartography. Until we do, we will not be taking seriously the being and becoming of the home-boys, the surf chicks, the greeks, the ferals, the rats and all other young people who take up their identities and identification in and through a global sense of place.

NOTES

[1] These ethnographies consider youthful masculinities and gender relations in marginalised, stigmatised, romanticised and exoticised places beyond the metropolis. We call our approach "place-based global ethnography" (see Kenway, Kraack & Hickey-Moody 2006, pp. 35-59). This methodology links Appadurai's global scapes to Burawoy's (2000) notion of global ethnography and is concerned with flows through places. Our ethnographic fieldwork in each location involved in-depth semi structured interviews with 36 young people. For six weeks, 24 males were each interviewed weekly and 12 females were interviewed fortnightly. Loosely structured focus and affinity group discussions were held with mothers, fathers, community members, teachers and youth and welfare service providers. Informal conversations were held with a range of local people. All participants have been anonymised. Field research also involved time at a variety of community and youth-specific locales (e.g. the school, beach and main street) and events (e.g. sporting matches, discos, local carnivals). Bringing these localised texts together with global media and ideo scapes, we identified and analysed popular discourses in film, television, print media and internet media about places beyond the metropolis. I thank the Australian Research Council for funding this three-year study, and Anna Hickey-Moody and Anna Kraack for their contributions to this paper.

REFERENCES

Appadurai, A. (1996). *Modernity at large: Cultural dimensions of globalization.* Minneapolis, MN: University of Minnesota Press.

Burawoy, M. (2000). *Global Ethnography: Forces, connections and imaginations in a postmodern world.* Berkeley, CA: University of California Press.

Cohen, R., & Kennedy, P. (2005). *Global sociology.* New York: New York University Press.

Fairfax Digital Online. 2005

Fletcher, M. (2002). *Digging people up for coal: A history of Yallourn.* Melbourne, VIC: Melbourne University Press.

Giddens, A. (1990). *The consequences of modernity.* Cambridge, UK: Polity Press.

Kenway, J., Kraack, A., & Hickey-Moody, A. (2006). *Masculinity beyond the metropolis.* Hampshire and New York: Palgrave Macmillan.

Lippard, L. R. (1997). *The lure of the local: Sense of place in a multicentred society.* New York: New Press.

Massey, D. (1993). 'Power-Geometry' & a progressive sense of place. In J. Bird, B. Curtis, G. Robertson, & L. Tricker (Eds.), *Mapping the futures: Local culture, global change.* London: Routledge.

Massey, D. (2005). *For space.* London: SAGE.

Massey, D. (1994). *Space, place & gender.* Cambridge, UK: Polity Press.

Sassen, S. (1998). *Globalization & its discontents: Essays on the new mobility of people and money.* New York: The New Press.

Tomlinson, J. (1999). *Globalization & culture.* Cambridge, UK: Polity Press.

Jane Kenway
Monash University

MARGARET SOMERVILLE

13. TRANSFORMING PEDAGOGIES OF WATER

Biaime created the fish trap and that story relates to a lot of the communities, a lot of the different groups of people because Biaime not only created the fish traps in Brewarrina, he also created Mount Gundabooka, and he created a waterhole in Byrock where he did his carvings and stuff. So he moved around the area and then he went to Brewarrina and created the fish traps and the fish traps are like his stepping stones back into the heavens. At Mt Gundabooka there's pictures of the fish traps, a round sort of stone pebbles drawing and fish swimming into it. There's men with spears and a woman giving birth, there's animals and handprints. That's how I realised the connections between places; seein' that little fish trap painting on Mt Gundabooka was amazing (Lorina Barker, Muruwarri).

These stories are presented in layers of galleries of Aboriginal rock paintings on the walls of a cave at Mt Gundabooka National Park in western New South Wales. It is described by local Aboriginal knowledge holders as 'a teaching place' and shows how water places hundreds of kilometres apart are connected, and how people and places are interconnected through these stories. Narran Lake, Brewarrina, Mount Gundabooka and Byrock are all special water-story places that tell about significant events in the movements of the great ancestral beings as they travelled across the landscape creating the places and all living things. They are travelling water stories. Together they form a song cycle that connects special water-story places in a songline of travelling water stories. They are about the fundamental significance and sacred nature of water in a dry land.

The marks which signify the creator's presence in these places—footprints, drawings, landforms—continue to remind people of the events in the epic stories and their responsibility to these places. At each of these places we can see the giant footprint of the creator. Brad Steadman, Ngemba knowledge holder from Brewarrina, says that Biame's footprint at the fish traps in Brewarrina is "a sentence in the Aboriginal story". Such stories populate the waterways of the Murray-Darling Basin, the most endangered system of water in Australia. They are both traditional and very contemporary stories. They have been translated into English, use English place names, and are impacted by the histories of white settlement, but they speak urgently to the need for us to learn from the lessons of these places.

This chapter explores the application of the place pedagogies framework, outlined in the Introduction to this book, in a project about water in the drylands of the

M. Somerville, K. Power and P. de Carteret (eds.),
Landscapes and Learning: Place Studies for a Global World, 207–224

Murray-Darling Basin: *Bubbles on the Surface: a place pedagogy of the Narran Lake*. In this project we established a team of Indigenous and non-Indigenous researchers, including the Indigenous artists and cultural knowledge holders named in the acknowledgements as co-authors of this chapter. We asked: *How can places teach us about water?* and *How can we incorporate their pedagogical possibilities into educational processes to ensure the protection of people and ecosystems?*

LOCAL PLACES, GLOBAL EFFECTS

The dire situation of the waterways in the Murray-Darling Basin is complex and much has been written about it. It is clear that current practices of extracting water from the Basin to produce 40% of Australia's food and agricultural products are not sustainable. The drought which has impacted so severely on the region is believed to be the local effect of the global phenomena of climate change. It is a quintessential issue of place that links the local and the global. According to a panel of international experts: "The world is running out of water. It is the most serious ecological and human rights threat of our time" (Barlow, Dyer, Sinclair & Quiggin, 2008). The differential global impacts of climate change exacerbate the problem, with some parts of the world experiencing long term, severe drought. The problem of water scarcity, however, is not about whether there is enough water but how we use that water (Sinclair, 2008). As we pollute water, particularly in the global south, we are turning to ground water, wilderness water and river water, and extracting it faster than it can be replenished (Barlow et al, 2008).

Indigenous communities all over the world have harvested and managed water in sustainable ways throughout history (Shiva, 2006). During the first major wave of global colonisation, however, large dams and irrigation schemes were introduced by the colonisers (Schama, 1996). The acquisition of colonies was enabled by "a profound belief in the possibility of restructuring nature and re-ordering it to serve human needs and desires" (Adams & Mulligan, 2003, p. 23). These processes intensified during the latter half of the twentieth century because global population growth threatened food shortages (Pearce, 2006). New technologies and more productive crops were developed that further depended on harvesting water from most of the major rivers of the world. While these technologies have delivered increases in food production, they have failed in terms of ecological sustainability. Most of the major river systems are now in crisis (Pearce, 2006) and the water crisis is described as "the most pervasive, the most severe, and most invisible dimension of the ecological devastation of the earth" (Shiva, 2002, p. 1). In order to change the way we use water we need access to approaches to water that have been erased or made invisible by these technological interventions.

Australia is a particular example of the 'politics of water' as the driest inhabited continent on earth (Rose, 2007; Arthur, 2007), using more water per head of population than any other country in the world (Sinclair, 2008). The dire situation of water in the Murray-Darling Basin is well recognised internationally (Barlow et al, 2008) and it has entered the nation's imaginary as a system in distress. The

Murray-Darling Basin covers approximately one seventh (14%) of the total area of Australia, contains two thirds of the country's irrigated lands and produces 40% of the agricultural output in ways that are no longer sustainable. It includes most of inland south-eastern Australia, incorporating parts of the Australian Capital Territory, Queensland, New South Wales, Victoria and South Australia and is significant for the major metropolitan centres of Brisbane, Sydney, Canberra, Melbourne and Adelaide.

The Basin is watered by a series of rivers and networks of tributaries. These begin in the headwaters of the Balonne and Condamine Rivers in Queensland, flow down through the Narran, Culgoa and Bokhara Rivers to the Darling, eventually joining the Murray to flow into the sea at the Coorong in South Australia. In 1990 the Murray-Darling Basin Commission (MDBC) launched a strategy of 'integrated catchment management'; over ten years later it reported that "water quality and ecosystem health were continuing to decline" (MDBC, 2001, p. 2). The Commission emphasised the importance of people in the process of developing a shared vision and acting together to manage the natural resources of the catchment but research has continued to emphasise the physical rather than the social sciences (Ward, Reys, Davies & Roots, 2003).

Aboriginal people continue to inhabit all of the waterways of the Murray-Darling Basin but the stories and practices through which they have survived as the longest continuing culture inhabiting the world's driest continent are largely unacknowledged. A scoping study on Aboriginal involvement in the MDBC initiatives found a "chasm between the perception of the available opportunities for involvement and the reality experienced by Aboriginal people" (Ward et al, 2003). The study found that there is a strong case for involving Aboriginal people because of the "collective and holistic nature of Aboriginal people's concerns about the natural environment and their Country" (Ward et al, 2003, p. 29) and that "Aboriginal people are concerned and angry about the decline in health of the Murray-Darling Basin" (Ward et al, 2003, p. 21). The most significant barrier to Aboriginal involvement was identified as a "lack of respect and understanding of Aboriginal culture and its relevance to natural resource management" (Ward et al, 2003, p. 8). This barrier remains unaddressed: "The problems of the river have also been amplified by the persistent failure to recognise the importance of Indigenous custodians in deciding how the river should be managed" (Potter et al, 2007).

The issues of the relationship between Indigenous and non-Indigenous understandings of water and country, identified by the MDBC (2001), are echoed in the recent literature relating to Natural Resource Management (NRM). Suchet-Pearson and Howitt (2006, p. 118), for example, found that "the presence of Indigenous others in NRM debates shifts the terms of the debate to include issues of justice, history, identity and recognition" and concluded that "literacy in cultural landscapes is fundamental to reframing these relationships". However, similarly to the MDBC, they found that "key stakeholders have limited capacity and been unwilling and ill-prepared to take this on" (2006, p. 118). Others who have considered the implications of changing our approach to water through Indigenous knowledges have also posed problems rather than offering solutions. Allon and

Sofoulis (2006), for example, suggest there is a problem of cultural misalignment and that narratives of 'Big Water' must be re-imagined for patterns of consumption to change. Similarly Gibbs (2006, p. 79) has noted that while Natural Resource Management includes 'the triple bottom line', the reduction and simplification of meaning fails to capture the interrelatedness of environmental problems with economic and social issues.

Indigenous knowledge about water and water places is expressed in stories that have been translated into different forms since the first settlement of the Australian continent. These stories of 'care for Country' have survived as hidden and often inaccessible alternatives to the dominant storylines of domination and exploitation. It is important to recognise that these stories are deeply impacted by the histories of colonisation. Indigenous and non-Indigenous Australians are mutually entangled in issues of water, as one non-Indigenous writer articulates: "The story I am part of is one thread of a global web of stories about displacement and resettlement, dispossession and environmental degradation, and will be familiar to thousands of people in rural Australia" (Findlay, 2007, p. 311). The colonial history of Australia is a shared history in which we must learn to work together to care for this country, albeit from our fundamentally different perspectives and experiences. Changing our approach to water in the Murray-Darling Basin, and to Aboriginal cultural place knowledge and attachment, then, requires the development of fundamentally different and new approaches to how we understand the region, its people and communities.

A METHODOLOGY OF WATER

In order to provide the conceptual shift required to address the relationship between Indigenous and non-Indigenous approaches, our research has taken up the conceptual framework of 'Place studies'. Place has long been noted as an organising principle in Aboriginal ontologies and epistemologies and this relates to waterscapes as much as to land: "Aboriginal waterscapes are construed not only as physical domains but also as spiritual, social and jural spaces, according the same fundamental principles as our affiliations to places in the landscape" (Langton in Behrendt & Thompson, 2003, p. 1). Water is a fundamental *economic* resource for Indigenous cultures, embodied in the songlines of the great creation ancestors which mark water resources as sacred sites: "For Aboriginal people, issues of community health, economic development, care for Country and culture are all intertwined" (Rose in Ward et al, 2003). The concept of place enables a conversation about the complex social, cultural, spiritual, economic, ideological and political realities of Indigenous/non-Indigenous relationships to country.

Within the conceptual framework of place, *Bubbles on the Surface* is underpinned by the first element of a postcolonial place pedagogy: that our relationship to places is constructed in stories and other representations. The feminist poststructural concept of 'storylines' enables us to identify how stories shape our relationship to places: "A storyline is a condensed version of a naturalised and conventional cultural narrative, one that is often used as the explanatory framework of one's own and other's practices and sequences of action" (Sondergaard, 2002, p. 191). Stories, people and places are mutually constituted: "Landscape does not just shape language; the land itself is transformed by words" (Bonahady & Griffiths, 2002, p. 6). The concept of storylines enables the identification and analysis of dominant and alternative stories and how each of these positions us in relation to place and, in turn, shapes the places we inhabit. Changing our relationship to places means changing the stories we tell about places: "If human beings are responsible for place making, then we must become conscious of ourselves as place makers and participants in the sociopolitical process of place making" (Gruenewald, 2003, p. 627).

Dominant colonial storylines of place position us as separate from the places we live in, opening the possibilities for exploitation. Sinclair (2001), for example, describes stories about the Murray River as part of a "broader cultural and political narrative of technological and agricultural progress". Such stories of separation are shaped by "the vision of barren land being made productive; of a silent and timeless place being transformed and brought into history by the energy of an industrious and resourceful society" (Sinclair, 2001, p. 43). Pastoralists' dominant storylines about land in the study area have been described as "inescapably adversarial" Griffiths (2002, p. 240) because of the harsh dry conditions that European settlers found so confronting. These dominant storylines depend for their justification and legitimation on the suppression of alternative stories. Sinclair (2001, p. 42), for example, remarks on the "uncoupling of past from present Aborigines", even when there are signs of Aboriginal presence in the actual places. Pastoralists' emotional and aesthetic attachments to land are also suppressed "because it can appear to weaken their right of occupation" (Griffiths, 2002, p. 240).

We link the feminist poststructural concept of storylines methodologically with the Aboriginal concept of songlines, also known as storylines. Songlines are inextricably connected to country. A songline is a travelling route which joins the story places in the creation stories of the great ancestors. An Aboriginal story incorporates song, music, dance, body painting and performance, which intersect powerfully in a particular place (Somerville, 1999). Songlines, especially in dry country, follow water-story places. These special places are the sites of ceremony through which the place and all its creatures are sung into being. Contemporary Aboriginal art translates these stories and storylines into contemporary forms that are accessible cross-culturally as 'public pedagogies'. Public pedagogies enable particular meanings to be constructed within broader discourses and relations of power that allow, or prevent, resistance and change (Giroux, 2004). Indigenous art is a powerful public pedagogy because of its aesthetic appeal and universal acceptance as a genre of communication for transforming our understandings of place.

Narran Lake, in the northern drylands of the Murray-Darling Basin, was the beginning point of our project. The Narran Lake is a large inland lake located between the northern river catchments in southern Queensland and the Darling and Murray rivers to the south of the Basin. Because of its geographic location, its importance in Aboriginal stories, and its ecological significance, the Narran Lake is an iconic site in the Basin. It is a contact zone of Aboriginal and settler stories, of agricultural and environmental discourses, and a physical pulse of environmental wellbeing. In *Bubbles on the Surface,* Indigenous cultural knowledge holders from different language groups that belong to specific parts of the water places in the Murray-Darling Basin responded in artworks and stories to the research questions. These stories and artworks were presented in a series of art exhibitions, accompanied by extended catalogues documenting the research project.

TRANSFORMING STORYLINES

In the following we present a small selection of the alternative storylines that were generated in this project in order to understand how these alternative storylines transform our understanding of the Murray-Darling Basin. I[1] have artificially organised the categories of analysis sequentially and linked them loosely to the participating artist/researchers. This is to introduce the storytellers so that their individual biographies are not lost, but also in recognition of U'Alayi researcher Chrissiejoy Marshall's contribution to the methodology of this research and her unique connection to the Narran Lake as our beginning place. Each artist/researcher, however, embodied all of the following categories – Intimate attachment; Connections and flows; and Deep mapping – in their thinking through country.

Intimate Attachment

Chrissiejoy Marshall was in a unique position to tell the stories of Narran Lake, or *Terewah,* as she knew it. By the time she was born in the 1950s, the lake had long been locked away from its Aboriginal custodians. It was 'private property' according to white law. As the child of a white station owner and an Aboriginal woman, Chrissiejoy was protected by her white father. She grew up in a camp by the lake with her Noongunburrah grandfather and uncles. Noongunburrah, meaning water people, is a clan of the U'Alayi (Yuwalaraay) language group which inhabited the area in the immediate vicinity of the lake. The extended family group continued to live a semi-traditional lifestyle by and with the lake.

I don't remember a time
without the lake.
There were times
when it dried back
but they were quite rare
it was always full
and in season
there'd be thousands and thousands
of birds
so you'd wake up
in the morning
to birds getting a fright

and taking off
and making a terrible clatter.
And then going to sleep
of a night time
listening to all the birds
that lulled chatter
that you hear
of an evening.

Chrissiejoy's senses were formed by the lake — its smells, sounds, the feel of its air, its dryness and wetness, its tastes; eating from the lake. The seasons and cycles of the lake were the rhythms of her waking and sleeping. Before knowing, in a formative primal sense, to be a subject was to be present with the lake. For Chrissiejoy, to be in the world was to be in the world of the lake; to know the world was to know through the lake's stories.[2] Stories integrated the sensory experiences of the physical presence of the lake, the intimate knowledge of the cycles and seasons of the lake, and a cosmology or spirituality that taught Chrissiejoy what it means to know the world in this way.

The first stories
are almost beyond my memory.
I grew up knowing the stories
so I'm guessing I was told
as a very, very small child.
They talk about Biaime
who is the creator.
He was here on earth
and he sent his two wives
to go and dig yams
while he went to
gather honey or something and they
were to meet at
this waterhole.
He got to the waterhole
and the wives were missing,
so he figured out what had happened
and tracked them.

It was Guria, the giant lizard,
Guria had swallowed his two wives.
So he waited in ambush
and killed Guria
slit open his belly
and got his wives out
put them on an ants' nest
and brought them back to life and
everyone lived happily ever after.
But while he was killing Guria,
Guria swished his tail around
and knocked the big hole
in the ground
that then became the lake.
Biaime said in honour of Guria
it would fill up with water
and there would always be water
and many birds and things there.

Chrissiejoy was emphatic that these stories could not be reduced to Western concepts of 'myths and legends' as they have been by non-Aboriginal recorders in the past. To her they contain deep truths, including scientific truths, about the distant past. The stories had different levels of meaning. The simplest, public level was told to children as a cautionary tale: "kept the kids away from the waterholes because, you know, 'look out, Guriya'll get you', it was a story to keep you safe". As she got older, the layers got deeper: "they sort of change from men turning into birds or birds turning into men or whatever, something that's quite extraordinary, yeah". The deeper layers embodied the rituals to make things grow and flourish, knowledge of the co-presence of spirit and human worlds. The interconnections of all life forms in and around the lake is partially captured in her story of *terewah*, the black swan. The Noongunburrah name for the lake, *terewah* is also the name of the black swan and the black swan is the main *yerti*, or totemic being for Chrissiejoy's family group.

Black swans	and the lake was part of them
were always there	they owned the land
even before the lake	to us we belong to it
it was always *terewah*	they have more right to it than we
home of the black swan	did
they were part of the lake	because they were there first.

When I asked Chrissiejoy about her mother's *yerti*, she said simply, "she was swan". This understanding of the complex interrelationship and connections between *terewah* the lake, *terewah* the swan, and *terewah* her mother, reveals something of the complexity involved in the creation of her sense of self by the lake. It is more than a sense of individual identity because it derives from a different ontology, epistemology and cosmology, in which self, place, time and the meaning of life are differently conceived. Identity is understood as being as much about the material body of things and beings as it is about their spiritual presence. It is deeply connected to the place of the lake and its creatures.

Telling the stories of the lake makes knowledge. Country creates connections between people and between people and Country. Even at this simple level of the story, the ancestral being is present, manifest in the lake and in the story. The creator leaves his marks at the story places. There are indentations where Biaime sat down and made 'bum prints' in the sand, there's a footprint and handprint and the tracks of Biaime's dog at the lake. These marks in the landscape become code for the special places in a storyline, places of intimate intensity in the flow of creation, highly energised and libidinous sites in the relationships between people and places. They also evoke powerful and important connections between one story place and another.

Connections and Flows

Our geographic and metaphysical imaginary flowed with the waterways in Badger Bates' stories and images of the Darling River. Badger, a Paakantji knowledge holder, said "we call the river *Paaka*, the Darling, that's how the Paakantji got their name, the River People". We sat with a conventional road map between us to record his stories. The Darling River begins at the fish traps at Brewarrina, a hundred kilometres south of the Narran Lake, and Badger lives a further 200 kilometres south at Wilcannia. Badger traced with his finger the length of the Darling River from the Menindee Lakes to Bourke, describing this vast stretch of country as the place of his most intimate attachments, his "really sentimental particular place":

> In all of that from down there where I went to Menindee right up to Bourke, that's where my really sentimental particular place is. Also over here on the Paroo, Lake Peery, and back on the Warrego is really sentimental to me, this area, because this is where I lived most of my life, right up to Brindingyabba, but it's sentimental where, more or less the triangle what I done from Wilcannia up to Bourke, across to Cobar, Lake Cargelligo, back to Ivanhoe and back home.

In our first interview we mapped two great sweeps of country—the map of the creation stories of the *ngatyis*, the rainbow serpents, in their travels throughout the region, and the map of Badger's movements to 'dodge the Welfare'. In traditional times Paakantji people moved through this dry country from one water-story place to another, following the trails of the ancient songlines. By the time Badger was born much of this traditional movement had stopped. However, as a child born to a white father and an Aboriginal mother, Badger was in danger of being removed from his family by the Aboriginal Protection Board. He was moved vast distances to avoid 'the Welfare', learning stories from his relatives as he travelled from place to place:

> [I learned those stories] off my grandmother and off old people when I used to dodge the Welfare ... we started from Wilcannia, up to Tilpa, Louth, Bourke, only went to Bre once in my welfare movements, I had to go up there for one of our relations had a car accident there, and then down here, down to Cobar and then there, Lake Cargellico, Murrun Bridge Mission, and then out to Willara Creek with my old uncle for a while, back to here on the train, when you come to there, we'd come on a mail truck or people would come across and pick up in old cart, old horse and cart, to there. But when I was real small at a place I's reared up, Gran and them used to work on the Dog Fence, Uncle Ted and them, always around Brindingyabba, Yantabulla.

These travels are a mixture of (post) colonisation – travelling for work, avoiding the Welfare, mail trucks and car accidents, and traditional storytelling. At each place where Badger stopped with his relatives, he learned more of the places and stories of the songlines that criss-cross vast areas of the landscape. We began our mapping work with an extensive road map of western New South Wales, spreading over the borders into Queensland, South Australia, and Victoria. We marked the water places where the brolgas fly to because, for Paakantji people, brolga and humans are the same:

> ['C]ause they depend on the same things nearly that we do, they depend on the water, and the brolga they mate for life, they'll get out and they'll all get around in a circle and have their dances and if something happened the other one'll come and just put its wings over 'em and cries.

Badger is intimately connected to the brolga and its places. Like the waters, the brolgas move from place to place and Badger's finger roves over the map marking the places where he has seen the brolgas in his travels through this country:

> Now I'm here doin' a brolga, right, and I'll say if you look on your map the brolga gonna relate to number ten, Brindingyabba, right, and I'll say also it'll relate to Narran Lake and Wilcannia on the Darling. Yeah, so I can say, that with this brolga this is where it's relatin' to, cause Narran Lake, I seen about twenty or twenty-five there and then at Brindingyabba, number ten, I see

hundreds, but then you go down to Wilcannia and you only see one or two, they come and visit and they go. They'll come down as far as Menindee or between Wilcannia and Menindee and then they go back home.

Badger's travelling stories of the brolgas connect his places on the Darling River to Chrissiejoy's stories of the Narran Lake through their migrations. We number each of these places where Badger will focus his art-making. The map becomes a tool of communication between us, and for my learning. It is another 'bubble on the surface', another means of "tracing out the creative ways people have tried to make sense out of their relationships with their environment" (Goodall, 2002, p. 37). Each story place is numbered on the map so that when Badger returns to Broken Hill to do his art work and record his stories, I can follow where he is from the numbers on the map. Mapping becomes story, translation, communication, physical grounding, and a place to make visual images.

We marked a place just over the border in South Australia where the rainbow serpent emerged from the underground waterways to travel over the surface of the land, making wavy parallel lines with his movements. The marks made by the rainbow serpent's body in the sand create the characteristic patterns of sandhills in that place: "This one where Ngatyi went through and created and went back in the ground here. He came out here crawling along the ground and formed all the sandhills". We also marked many other special water-story places where other characters and events in the great creation epic stories took place:

Gulawarra, another person from the Dreaming, came through, caught a giant kangaroo near White Cliff and went to Mount Poole then up into Queensland a bit then he turned and came back to Peery Lake where his sister and her husband was. The people fed him a lizard and he thought they tried to poison him. So he took his sister and family, turned the other people into stone, clogged the mound springs up and he came up somewhere towards Bourke and Louth where he met the kingfisher from the Dreaming. He had to pull a tree root out of the ground. When the root was coming out he was singing the tree root and the tree root was all wriggly. When he was pulling it out, he was singing, and making the depression where he was pulling the root out go bigger and sink down, and then he poured the water he got from Mount Poole and Peery Lake and the mound spring, so he poured the water from there into where he made the tree root depression, and he made the river, the Darling River. That's why the Darling River got a lot of bends in it, it's like a tree root.

Water-story places across an area bigger than Belgium are connected in these songlines. The material terrain and waterways come into being as intricately connected parts in a dynamic story of events and movement. For the non-Aboriginal listener, these mapping conversations are confusing, opening us to the profound reorientation required to enter a different way of seeing the world. Reading these maps requires a process of unlearning and relearning. They are acts of translation, of moving across. They are an opening to a vision of how a map of the story places in these songlines is also a map for understanding our relationship to water in a dry land differently.

Deep Mapping through Contemporary Artworks

In the original version of deep mapping developed with Gumbaynggirr people on the mid north coast of New South Wales (Somerville & Perkins, in press) we used a similar process with conventional road maps. Special story places were marked on the map as we recorded the stories. The roads and towns were then removed using Photoshop, and story text and photos were inserted in a symbolic reversal of the processes of colonisation. These maps were then printed as a series of posters to be used as educational resources for a postcolonial pedagogy of place. In this way special place stories that have been erased, or rendered invisible, are reconnected to place.

With Badger a different process of mapping through artwork evolved. Many of the special places that Badger talked about in his stories can only be identified on very local maps that show very small sections of the country that Badger's knowledge spans. Other story places are too personal and local to be identified on any map, and the process through which meaning extends to include vast networks of connections cannot be made visible. Badger is primarily a print maker. His lino prints, made by carving lino with the marks and stories of the landscape, continue the process he learned from his grandmother of carving emu eggs. Emu egg carving itself was a (post)colonial invention through which the best Indigenous artists could achieve symbolic motifs in sixteen shades of blue-grey to tell their stories of country.

The continuity with traditional mark making and landscape meanings was evident in Badger's detailed explanation of the rock engravings at Peery Lake. When we visited Peery Lake it appeared as an extraordinary body of water stretching from horizon to horizon in this otherwise parched landscape. Here Badger showed us the symbolic tracks made in the hard rock surfaces on the edge of the lake that point to the mound springs in the middle of the water. When the lake is full, as it was at this time, the tracks disappear into the waters of the lake, and the mound springs appear as little green islands of trees and shrubs. When the lake is empty the mound springs are an oasis that continues to supply the water that is essential for survival in these dry lands. The lake with its mound springs is highly significant in the water creation stories, as told by Badger above. The translation of this mark making and story telling into lino prints is a means of making visible the meanings of water. These meanings are not immediately evident, nor are they meant to be. They embody pedagogical processes of teaching and learning through which non-indigenous peoples can begin to become knowledgeable in these alternative stories.

In the linoprint that Badger made of 'Iron Pole Bend, Darling River Wilcannia', for example, the connections between places of intense intimate attachments and the vast networks of other story places is made evident.

217

Figure 1. Iron Pole Bend, Darling River Wilcannia. Badger Bates, linocut print.

The text that goes with this lino print is minimal but contains a great deal of codified information that is further made visible in the work:

> The Iron Pole Bend on the Darling River is where Granny used to sit down to fish and she saw the water dog or Ngatyi there. We lived near this bend in a tin hut when I was a kid. In the print you can see the dead fish in the dried-up Lake Wytucka on the left hand side, this hasn't had water in for long time. The two Ngatyi are in the river with fish, mussels and shrimps. In the sky you can see Bytucka the moon, the Seven Sisters, and the emu in the Milky Way.

We are looking down on the landscape in this print, at a place where different waterways come together. We know from the title and the text that the place is marked by a sign of the colonisation of the River, the iron pole, but the iron pole itself does not appear in the work. It is only a place marker for another set of stories. The print is structured around the Ngatyi, or rainbow serpents, who play a central part in the great creation stories, particularly in relation to water. Badger says the Ngatyi are his signature symbol. In this print the Ngatyi are almost indiscernible, immersed deep in the radiating lines of force that represent the energy of the waters. From their mouths the flow of waters bursts forth; their bodies create the shape of the rivers. The waters of the river are alive with the river's creatures – cod, catfish, shrimp, yabby and mussels.

The story text tells the viewer that the image is replete with stories that incorporate the contemporary with the distant past. It is a story of the every day – of the place where Badger's Granny caught fish for their daily food, near where Badger grew up in a tin hut on the banks of the Darling River. It is a place where

Granny, and later Badger himself, saw the 'water dog', the spirit creature of the waterways that warns of a special place. It tells us about the current environmental state of Lake Wytucka that has been dry for a long time, so the fish are represented in skeletal form. Around the edges of the water we can see the mythical creatures whose movement and storylines link to other places, the Kangaroo with the hump of Koonenberry Mountain, the Goanna from its story place, and the Brolga, flying in from elsewhere. We know they are spirit creatures because we can see their internal structures.

At the top of the print, in a hybrid combination of a bird's eye view and a more typical western vertical view where the sky is at the top, we can see the moon, and the emu in the Milky Way. From other stories we know that the position of the black shape of the emu within the stars of the Milky Way tells people about the cycles of feasting and ceremony. Daphne said that her mother calls her when the emu's head is in the right position for collecting eggs. She will then make the thousand kilometre trip to join her family in Lightning Ridge. They pile into the back of a truck and the fastest runner has to collect the eggs from the nest when the emu leaves it to find food. The rest of the mob laughs from the truck as he runs in fear of the fierce father emu returning to the nest to attack him. They collect the eggs, always leaving one or two to hatch. One egg made an omelette big enough to feed their family of seven children. In traditional times, the time for collecting emu eggs, signalled by the position of the emu in the Milky Way, was the time for feasting and ceremony. Earth country, water country and sky country are interconnected in this print that opens the intimate attachments of the everyday and home to the rhythms of water, earth, moon and stars.

The representational processes in this print are an example of Deep Mapping. In deep mapping, the deep time and knowledge of story places is represented as a time that exists beyond personal or intergenerational memory. It is also, importantly, a time that is connected to the present in cyclical rather than linear time. Space, and the way the artwork delineates the spaces and places of these stories, is conceived differently. The frame of the print does not foreclose meanings within its square boundaries because the meanings are both allusive and elusive. The edges of the print point always to connections elsewhere in the flow of the waters and the storylines. The waters flow in from somewhere else and travel to elsewhere. The mythical creatures travel into the frame of the print but are not bounded by it. The meanings of the storylines are *elusive* too, in the sense that no-one can know all the layers and complexity of any story, or know all of the stories.

As viewers we are positioned as unknowing learners; the meanings of the artworks can only be glimpsed in their collective connections with other works, stories and places. These connections are made through processes of contemporary artistic and cultural translation in the process of deep mapping. The stories and images are made through deep intergenerational processes that are both individual (the place where I was born) and fundamentally collective (of traditional songlines). As viewers we are drawn into these collective processes of what we have called in our project the always unfinished business of singing the country.

ART EXHIBITIONS AS PUBLIC PEDAGOGY

In each year of the three year project the relationships between members of the team grew and the stories and artwork deepened through conversations and exchange, and through the hard work of the contact zone. In the following I trace just one thread of these collective conversations to show how they were materialised in the collective space of the exhibition. This thread begins towards the end of the second year when we met at a remote station near the Narran Lake to visit the lake through one of the private properties. Chrissiejoy had not been at the lake for thirty years and because she had heard stories about how it was empty much of the time now, she was fearful of what she might see.

I've got a vision	because it is
in my head	completely different
of how it was	after an autopsy
when I was a child	or something like that
and I know	it's almost turned
it's not that way	completely back to front
anymore	where the lake
it's like when people	would stay full
are in grief	for five to seven years
do they want to see	it's dry now
the body	for that length of time.
after someone has died	

It was a very long way to travel out to the lake. Chrissiejoy had sustained a spinal injury in a car accident and had been ill since the project began. She drove herself there, such was her determination, and while there her stature changed from stooped and ill to her full height as a leader in her country. It was difficult to get access through private property, and then to find our way through barren paddocks, threadbare from years of drought. When we got there it was a quiet and sobering experience as we tried to imagine the bare red earth of the empty lake as it might have been when full of water, stretching from horizon to horizon. The air shimmered with heat and the sound of bush flies as we walked a little and then ate our lunch on an old dead log in the middle of the barren expanse.

We stopped at one point on our drive around what must have been the edges of the lake where Chrissiejoy once camped. She called us to get out and look at the lignum. It's a high woody weed that used to grow prolifically across the lake. Once the place where migratory birds nested, holding the fabric of earth, sky and land in its embrace, it was now a mass of woody stalks. In the place where we stopped you could see traces of a creek that must have brought flows of water into the lake. Chrissiejoy examined the green shoots coming on the bare woody stalks. Just that, no more. It was not until we met again three months later that she told us that she had realised the lake was not dead, it was dormant. She said it was the responsibility of our work together "to sing it back to life". Badger's response was to make a large lino print of the lake bursting with life as he had imagined it when he heard Chrissiejoy's stories of her childhood memories. One of many gifts of stories and artworks exchanged during this project, he made it for Chrissiejoy to heal her body and spirit.

We called our final exhibition of this three year project the *Always Unfinished Business: of singing the country* and gathered together all of the artworks and stories that spoke to Chrissiejoy's injunction. Instead of telling the world about the dreadful state of the Murray-Darling Basin, our story was about our responsibility to sing it back to life, together, all of us. In the catalogue, we focussed not on finished works but on the process of place-making through which singing the country takes form. The catalogue showed works-in-process and stories recorded in team conversations during the precious times when we could get together from thousands of kilometres apart.

Working on these conversations and artworks-in-progress, constructing them into text for the catalogue was an interesting business in itself. It became clear that even when individual voices could be discerned, the stories were becoming collective. The experience of our work together over three years was now part of the new storylines of place. Sometimes it was not possible to identify individual voices at all. Yorta artist Treahna Hamm from the Murray River and Badger from the Darling, joined up the Darling and the Murray rivers in their conversations that traversed vast areas of country and waterways, threading new stories into old songlines of connection.

Connecting the river
everyone's got different
creation stories
right along
like just past Bourke,
it changes
from the Paakantji story
to the Muruwarri
to the Ngemba story
theirs is Biaime
and his two dogs
as the dogs go off
that's all the tributaries.

Badger Bates

Even the name
for the Murray River
is different
all the way down.
Milawa up in Albury –
we call it *Dunghala*
in Yorta Yorta
and *Indiyi*
up Mildura way
there's different names
for the river
all the way along
and different stories.

Treahna Hamm

The exhibition space of the gallery became the place where these conversations were materialised for the viewing audience. We chose a selection of artworks and stories around the theme of singing the country. These included such works as the Binem Binem butterfly story about transformation; a baby possum skin cloak inscribed with identity in Country; and the Iron Pole print of the birth of the waters. The artists were present to talk about their place-making in their country. The opening of each of the exhibitions was timed as the culmination of a place symposium so the possibility of further conversations in relation to the intellectual work of the symposium was opened up. The conversations grew as visitors came from all over the world – from the Vygotsky Institute in Russia; from the north east of England; and a party of First Nations visitors from Canada. Each of these visitors took artworks and their stories back to their countries. The artworks function as a form of transitional objects, bridging different cultures and meanings. There is now an invitation, based on Badger's print that is hanging in an office in the University of Newcastle-on-Tyne, for an artist-in-residence program where the Indigenous artists from this project will work with secondary school children in a project about the endangered Bay of Seals, a wetlands where migratory water birds and seals breed amongst chemical factories and oil refineries in Hartlepool, in north east England.

The way we weave
we tell stories
through our weaving
every time we sit down
together
we're talking
if we're in a group
like we were in the car,
those words
and those sentences
and those stories
get woven into the work

Making links
and connections
that's the beauty
of working
in groups and communities
you get inspired
it's a dialogue
between people
to reach out
right through country
cross over boundaries
cross over cultures.

ACKNOWLEDGEMENT

This paper is drawn from material produced in *Bubbles on the Surface*, a project funded by the Australian Research Council and collaboratively designed by Chrissiejoy Marshall. It represents the work and collective ideas of a team of researchers including Badger Bates, Lorina Barker, Phoenix de Carteret, Treahna Hamm, Daphne Wallace and Sarah Martin. The Indigenous artist/researchers whose story quotes appear in the paper are acknowledged as co-authors. The stories and art works generated in this project are available for use by the project members for research purposes but remain the intellectual property of the individual Indigenous storytellers and artists.

NOTES

[1] As author of this written chapter I take responsibility for the structure of the ideas and the analysis presented in this paper so occasionally it seems appropriate to use the first person pronoun 'I'. Generally, however, these ideas were generated collectively from mutual conversations, either one on one in recorded storytelling sessions or in recorded group conversations, often in situ.

[2] The scanned lines about the lake are constructed from three interviews that I recorded with Chrissiejoy Marshall and which have been reproduced in full in the catalogue of the first exhibition from the project, *Bubbles on the Surface: more than a catalogue.*

REFERENCES

Adams, W., & Mulligan, M. (Eds.). (2003). *Decolonizing nature: Strategies for conservation in a post-colonial era.* London: Earthscan Publications Ltd.

Allon, F., & Sofoulis, Z. (2006). Everyday water: Cultures in transition. *Australian Geographer, 37*(1), 45–55.

Arthur, J. (2007). Tracking water through the National Archives of Australia. In E. Potter, A. Mackinnon, S. McKenzie, & J. McKay (Eds.), *Fresh water: New perspectives on water in Australia* (pp. 59–72). Carlton, VIC: Melbourne University Press.

Barlow, M., Dyer, G., Sinclair, P., & Quiggin, J. (2008, November 21). Parched: The politics of water. In J. Panichi (Producer), *The National Interest – on ABC Radio National.* Podcast retrieved from <http://www.abc.net.au/rn/nationalinterest/stories/2008/2426405.htm>

Behrendt, J., & Thompson, P. (2003). *The recognition and protection of Aboriginal interests in NSW rivers.* Sydney, NSW: Healthy Rivers Commission.

Bonahady, T., & Griffiths, T. (Eds.). (2002). *Words for country: Landscape and language in Australia.* Sydney, NSW: UNSW Press.

Findlay, M. (2007). River stories. *Futures, 39,* 306–323.

Gibbs, L. (2006). Valuing water: Variability and the Lake Eyre Basin, Central Australia. *Australian Geographer, 37*(1), 73–85.

Giroux, H. (2004). Cultural studies, public pedagogy and the responsibility of intellectuals. *Communication and Critical/Cultural Studies, 1*(1), 59–79.

Goodall, H. (2002). The river runs backwards. In T. Bonahady & T. Griffiths (Eds.), *Words for country: Landscape and language in Australia* (pp. 30-51). Sydney, NSW: UNSW Press.

Griffiths, T. (2002). The outside country. In T. Bonahady & T. Griffiths (Eds.), *Words for country: Landscape and language in Australia* (pp. 222-244). Sydney, NSW: UNSW Press.

Gruenewald, D. (2003). Foundations of place: A multidisciplinary framework for place-conscious education. *American Educational Research Journal, 40*(3), 619–654.

Murray-Darling Basin Ministerial Council. (2001). *Integrated catchment management in the Murray-Darling Basin 2001-2010: Delivering a sustainable future.* Canberra, ACT: Murray-Darling Basin Commission.

Pearce, F. (2006). *When the rivers run dry: What happens when our water runs out?* London: Eden Project Books.

Potter, E., Mackinnon, A., McKenzie, S., & McKay, J. (Eds.). (2007). *Fresh water: New perspectives on water in Australia.* Carlton, VIC: Melbourne University Press.

Rose, D. B. (2004). The ecological humanities in action: An invitation. *Australian Humanities Review.* Retrieved September 18, 2009, from http://www.lib.latrobe.edu.au/AHR/archive/Issue-April-2004?rose.html

Rose, D. B. (2007). Justice and longing. In E. Potter, A. Mackinnon, S. McKenzie, & J. McKay (Eds.), *Fresh water: New perspectives on water in Australia* (pp. 8–20). Carlton, VIC: Melbourne University Press.

Schama, S. (1996). *Landscape and memory.* London: Fontana Press.

Shiva, V. (2002). *Water wars: Privatization, pollution and profit.* London: Pluto Press.

Shiva, V. (2006). *Earth democracy: Justice, sustainability, and peace.* United Kingdom: Zed Books.

Sinclair, P. (2001). *The Murray: A river and its people.* Carlton, VIC: Melbourne University Press.

Sinclair, P. (2008). *Parched: The politics of water.* In J. Panichi (Producer), *The National Interest – on ABC Radio National.* Podcast retrieved from http://www.abc.net.au/rn/nationalinterest/stories/2008/2426405.htm

Somerville, M., & Perkins, T. (in press). *Singing the coast .* Canberra, ACT: Aboriginal Studies Press.

Somerville, M., & de Carteret, P. (Eds.). (2008). *Always unfinished business: of singing the country.* Churchill, VIC: Margaret Somerville.

Somerville, M. (2008). A place pedagogy for 'global contemporaneity'. *Educational Philosophy and Theory* (Online Early). Retrieved January 21, 2008, from www.blackwell-synergy.com/doi/pdf/ 10.1111/j.1469-5812.2008.00423.x

Somerville, M., & de Carteret, P. (Eds.). (2006). *Bubbles on the surface:... more than a catalogue.* Churchill, VIC: Margaret Somerville.

Somerville, M. (1999). *Body/landscape journals.* Melbourne, VIC: Spinifex Press.

Sondergaard, D. M. (2002). Poststructural approaches to empirical analysis. *Qualitative Studies in Education, 15*(2), 187–204.

Suchet-Pearson, S., & Howitt, R. (2006). On teaching and learning resource and environmental management: Reframing capacity building in multicultural settings. *Australian Geographer. 37*(1), 117–128.

Ward, N., Reys, S., Davies, J., & Roots, J. (2003). *Scoping study on Aboriginal involvement in natural resource management decision making and the integration of Aboriginal cultural heritage considerations into relevant Murray-Darling Commission programs.* Canberra, ACT: Murray-Darling Basin Commission.

Margaret Somerville
Monash University

CONTRIBUTORS

Roslyn Appleby is a Senior Lecturer in language and literacy at the University of Technology, Sydney. Her research interests include gender and pedagogy, the cultural politics of English as an international language, and the role of English language teaching in international development.

Laura Brearley is an Associate Professor in the Faculty of Education at Monash University, Victoria. Laura specialises in creative approaches to research and culturally inclusive teaching, learning and research practices. Laura has worked closely with members of the Indigenous community in Australia and has developed strategies of working in the space between Indigenous and non-Indigenous knowledge systems. Laura is the founding Editor an electronic journal called 'Creative Approaches to Research'. She is co-author with Elizabeth Grierson of *Creative arts research: Narratives of methodologies and practices*, published by Sense as part of their Educational Futures Series.

Paul Carter is Creative Director of Material Thinking, a creative research and design studio that specialises in placemaking. He is well-known internationally for such books as *Parrot* (2006), *Material thinking* (2004), *Repressed spaces* (2002), *The lie of the land* (1996), and *The road to Botany Bay* (1987). His latest book, *Dark writing* (2009), explores the nexus between spatial history, and placemaking theory and practice. He collaborates with graphic artists, performers, architects and landscape designers and has received many national and state awards.

Phoenix de Carteret is a Research Fellow in the Faculty of Education at Monash University where she teaches in Sustainable Community Development. Her interest in place as a conceptual framework further expands her PhD research concerned with women's classed and gendered subjectivities. She has worked closely with Aboriginal co-researchers/artists and community groups on place-based research projects. Phoenix has published in the areas of qualitative methodologies, adult and informal learning, narrative inquiry, and collective biography.

Barbara Comber is a key researcher in the Centre for Studies in Literacy, Policy and Learning Cultures in the Hawke Research Institute at the University of South Australia. Her particular interests include literacy education and social justice, teachers' work and identities, place and space, and practitioner inquiry. She has worked collaboratively with teachers in high poverty locations focussing on innovative and critical curriculum and pedagogies which address contemporary social challenges. She has recently co-edited two books *Literacies in place: Teaching environmental communication* (Comber, Nixon & Reid, 2007) and *Turnaround pedagogies: Literacy interventions for at-risk students* (Comber & Kamler, 2005).

Noel Gough is Foundation Professor of Outdoor and Environmental Education and Director (Learning, Teaching and International) in the Faculty of Education at La Trobe University, Victoria. His current research focuses on the diverse implications of globalisation, internationalisation and multiculturalism for education, and on refining poststructuralist research methodologies in education, with particular reference to curriculum inquiry, environmental education, and science education.

Debra Hayes is an Associate Professor at the University of Sydney. Her research interests primarily relate to achieving more equitable outcomes from schooling for young people who benefit the least from education, by working with school-based educators to understand and improve how schools function as sites of learning for teachers and students.

Anna Hickey-Moody is a Lecturer in the Department of Gender and Cultural Studies at the University of Sydney. She is interested in exploring ways of re-framing questions of social justice; her research intersects across cultural studies of youth, disability and gender. Drawing on philosophy and the arts, Anna is interested in how bodies marked as somehow being 'disadvantaged' might be thought in new ways. She is co-author of *Masculinity beyond the metropolis* (Palgrave, 2006), co-editor of *Deleuzian encounters* (Palgrave, 2007) and author of *Unimaginable bodies* (Sense, 2009).

Jane Kenway is a Professor in the Faculty of Education, Monash University. She has a strong interest in educational reform, curriculum and issues of justice. Her research expertise is in socio-cultural studies of education in the context of wider social and cultural change. Publications include *Masculinity Beyond the Metropolis* (Palgrave, 2006), *Haunting the knowledge economy* (Routledge, 2006) and *Consuming children: Education—Advertising—Entertainment* (Open University Press, 2001).

Alan Mayne holds a Research Chair at the University of South Australia, where he is Professor of Social History and Social Policy. He is also a Visiting Professor in New Delhi. His core interests revolve around issues of social sustainability and social justice. His major publications include *The archaeology of urban landscapes* (with Tim Murray, Cambridge University Press, 2001), *Hill End: An historic Australian goldfields landscape* (Melbourne University Press, 2003), and *Beyond the Black Stump: Histories of outback Australia* (Wakefield, 2008),

Helen Nixon is a key researcher in the Centre for Studies in Literacy, Policy and Learning Cultures in the Hawke Research Institute at the University of South Australia. Her research interests and collaborative school-based projects include literacy education and social justice, and literacy, identity and place. She has recently co-edited *Literacies in place: Teaching environmental communication* (Comber, Nixon & Reid, 2007).

Doris Paton has worked in Indigenous education in a range of capacities for over 30 years. She has worked across all the levels of the education spectrum. Over this time she has completed Bachelor, Graduate Diploma and Masters qualifications and is currently completing her PhD. She is actively involved in Indigenous education and is currently the Team Leader in the Koorie Unit at GippsTAFE in Gippsland, Victoria.

Emily Potter is a Research Fellow in the Institute for Citizenship and Globalisation, Deakin University, Victoria. She works across the fields of creative research, cultural theory and environmental politics. She is the co-editor of *Fresh Water: New Perspectives on Water in Australia* (MUP, 2007), and her academic articles have appeared in both Australian and international journals including *Antipodes*, *Media International Australia*, *Cultural Studies Review*, and *Continuum*.

Kerith Power is a Senior Lecturer at Monash University where she teaches in undergraduate and postgraduate programs in teacher education. Her significant research contributions are in the fields of collaborative cross-cultural research in early childhood education, early literacy, and situated and subjugated knowledges. She is currently managing editor of the *Journal of Australian Research in Early Childhood Education*. Prior to working in higher education she worked in preschools and child care centres in rural and remote New South Wales for many years.

Jennifer Rennie is a Senior Lecturer at Monash University where she teaches in undergraduate and postgraduate programs in teacher education. Her significant research contributions are in the fields of reading instruction, Primary English education and Indigenous literacies. She is currently managing editor of the *Australian Journal of Language and Literacy*. Prior to working in higher education she worked in both primary and secondary schools in the north of Australia for a period of twelve years.

Katrina Schlunke is a Senior Lecturer in Writing and Cultural Studies at the University of Technology, Sydney. An enduring interest in her research has been in the significance of narratives of Captain Cook to cultural studies researchers. This has led to a method of analysis of contemporary cultural forms in Australia as they link to various local, European, and Indigenous histories and sites. She is the author of *Bluff Rock: Autobiography of a Massacre*, Curtin University Books and *Cultural Theory in Everyday Practice*, Oxford University Press, (with N. Anderson).

Margaret Somerville is Professor of Education (Learning & Development) and Research Director of the Institute for Regional Studies at Monash University. She is a leading researcher in postcolonial place studies with sole authored and collaborative publications with Indigenous communities. Her latest publication, *Singing the Coast* (Somerville and Perkins, in press) explores how we can care for country differently. She leads the 'Space, Place, Body' research group in developing new theories of bodies and spatiality for educational research to engage with the big questions of our time.

Breinigsville, PA USA
28 March 2010
235068BV00002B/7/P